The science of
Formula 1
Design
Third Edition

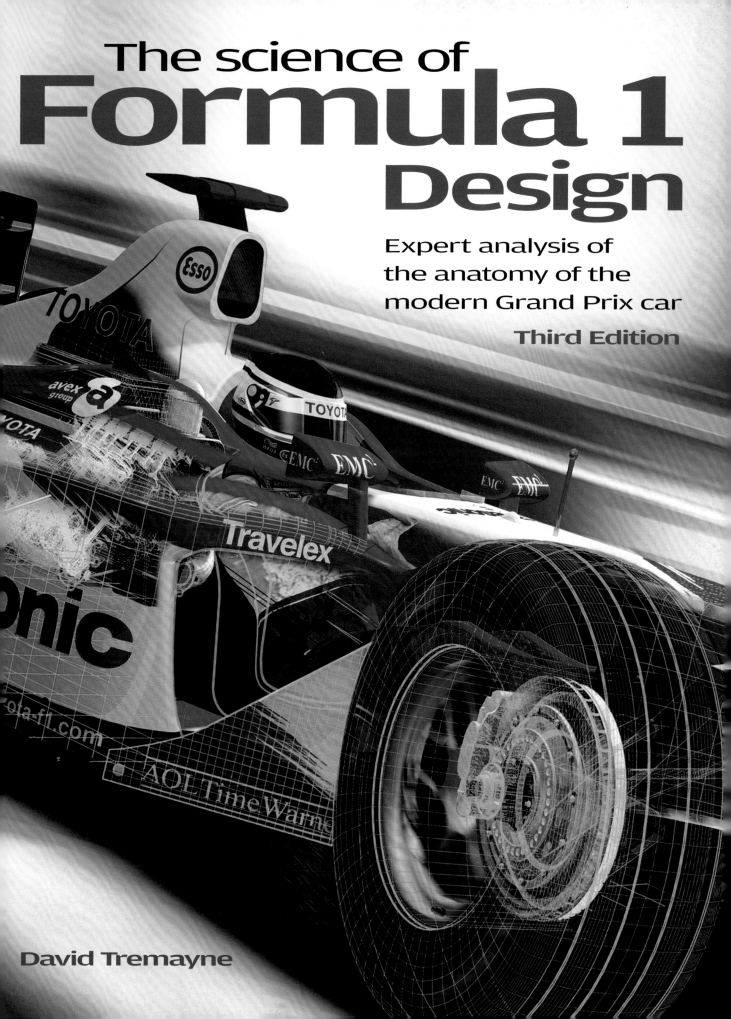

The science of
Formula 1
Design

Expert analysis of
the anatomy of the
modern Grand Prix car

Third Edition

David Tremayne

First published in 2004
Reprinted in 2005 and 2006
Second edition published September 2006
Third edition published October 2009

A catalogue record for this book is available from the British Library

ISBN 978 1 84425 718 8

Library of Congress control no. 2009927975

Published by Haynes Publishing, Sparkford, Yeovil, Somerset BA22 7JJ, UK
Tel: 01963 442030 Fax: 01963 440001
Int. tel: +44 1963 442030
Int. fax: +44 1963 440001
E-mail: sales@haynes.co.uk
Website: www.haynes.co.uk

Haynes North America Inc.
861 Lawrence Drive, Newbury Park,
California 91320, USA

Printed and bound in the UK

Contents

Introduction

What is a Formula 1 car? By 21st-century definition, it might be described as a combination of the most updated technologies. A confection of the most state-of-the-art techniques and research created within a timescale that is inevitably too short, to be sent into white-hot competition from which there is no respite during 'the season', which is a euphemism for the vehicle's lifespan. In days gone by teams might roll a model over into a new season, perhaps even three or four. In the distant past Lotus's 49 was introduced in 1967 and still won a race in 1970; its successor, the 72, won in 1970 and was still winning in 1974. Likewise McLaren's M23 had a successful life from 1973 to 1977. However, such is the pace of technological development these days that it was unusual for McLaren's MP4-17 to win in 2002 and still prove itself capable of doing likewise and challenging for the World Championship in the following season. Today a Formula 1 car's life is usually no longer than 17 or 18 races. This is due not just to the pace of development, but also to the continual need to repackage a car's layout to optimise its performance.

In the past a designer would complete his work during the winter 'off-season', the fruits of his labours would be built in time for the first European races, usually around March, and he would not seriously begin designing a replacement – assuming one was needed – until the following winter.

Not any more. That is too close to standing still. As former Ferrari technical director Ross Brawn, who became the owner of Brawn GP at the start of 2009, says, 'If you do that, you go backwards.'

So now the development of the Formula 1 car is a continuous process. There are rules from the Fédération International de l'Automobile which not only govern, very strictly, what is and what isn't permissible in design terms, but also what constitutes a new car. It's fair to say that McLaren's D specification development of its MP4-17 in 2003 amounted almost to a new car, but since the chassis was essentially the same it retained the 17 nomenclature, to satisfy not just McLaren's records but also the FIA's. But you get the picture: even before the design has been signed off and the team is preparing to build the components and then assemble them, the design team is already working on updated ideas to incorporate into the car before it races.

McLaren's MP4-18 appeared in 2003 but did not race due to a number of problems. It paved the way, however, for the evolutionary MP4-19 which appeared in December 2004 well in advance of the March kick-off to the 2004 FIA Formula 1 World Championship. McLaren managing director Martin Whitmarsh explained why the MP4-18 had failed, and his remarks were an illuminating insight into just how Formula 1 machines evolve in the modern era.

'Three-quarters of the way through 2002 we reviewed our development programmes, what we perceived to be the performance deficit to Ferrari, and we took the decision at that point that we needed a big step forward to compete. So we took a decision to take quite a lot of risk in the design of the engine and the chassis. Both were completely new. We really said are we on course to overhaul Ferrari, and we took the view at that time no, we needed to be doing more. So inevitably when you are trying to take a bigger jump, there is inherent risk. We threw everything into it. In my 14, 15 years with the company, MP4-18 was the biggest incremental change; everything was changed on that car. We didn't go into that blindly. In order to manage the risk we embarked upon a development programme for MP4-17 and for the old FM engine. The 17D programme was very substantial, and that of course meant two parallel programmes. With hindsight we overestimated the task. I think everyone in 2002 thought that Ferrari were uncatchable. And we actually had a competitive package in 17D, a car that had been unfit to compete in 2002.

Opposite: This head-on shot of Jenson Button on his way to winning the Spanish GP shows off the characteristics of the 2009 F1 car: wide front wing, small rear, and scalloped sidepods. (LAT)

'Having set ourselves up as a front-running team we set ourselves up to be kicked if we don't achieve our objectives. And with MP4-18 we set ourselves up very well. People estimated the figures squandered on MP4-18, but people misunderstood the process. The reality is that we have a very substantial engineering team at McLaren, and at Mercedes-Benz in Brixworth and in Stuttgart, and a whole range of development programmes: suspension, the engine, the chassis, aerodynamics. And traditionally it is easier for people to visualise that progression of technology by vehicle designation. Here is vehicle one, vehicle two, vehicle 17 or vehicle 18. The reality is that we never race the same vehicle twice. Every single race we modify the vehicle and that changes because it is a relatively immature concept and we work on the reliability, and we adapt and optimise that vehicle for each circuit. And then we are also still developing it. The people who are working on, say, the development of steering systems are continuously improving them. So the engineering team leaders have to say, as we get an incremental improvement, do we change that for the next race or wait and collect up a series of modifications and bring that out as an upgrade package of the steering and front suspension? Or do we group them altogether and put it on to the next car? So 17D captured quite a lot

Arguably two of the greatest Formula One engineers and strategists of recent history; Ross Brawn and Adrian Newey, seen here in 2003. (Mark Thompson/Getty Images)

of the aerodynamics and structural thinking of the 18 early on and moved on, and then the upgrade packages at Monza at the end of the year were also pulled off the 18. In a development programme we embody the positive findings in our car at various stages. It's not as if we set a team to design the 18, and if we don't use it we have wasted all that effort. If it was positive on the 18, you can be sure we were going to exploit it, either early or later on the 17. Or it was incorporated into the 19.'

The latter naturally bore a very close family resemblance to the 18, and because much of the process had been completed it was the first 2004 contender to be unveiled. There were frank exchanges on this timing between Whitmarsh and technical director Adrian Newey, because naturally the latter would always like as long as possible before 'finalising' the design. Whitmarsh argued that in this particular instance, given the fate of the MP4-18, it was wiser to start testing the new car sooner rather than later so that they could properly understand and hone it, and that they could still bring further modifications and updates on stream well before the 2004 season started in Melbourne the following March. Whitmarsh admitted in December 2003 that he thought McLaren had now created a car that would be competitive, but asked: 'Have we done enough? You never know. During the season you are able to gauge where your competitors are. But they are off the radar at the moment. But we know that we have a stable and competitive car, with tremendous development potential. We can say we are in good shape, we have all these resources, and we have enough time now until the end of February to go through substantial changes and improvements to the car. I believe the car is competitive now, and I believe we are going to make it a quicker car before we go to Australia.'

Was it ever thus.

His comment about 'managing the risk' summarised one hidden aspect of Formula 1. Today, managing a design project is a major undertaking that requires the man in charge to juggle a very complex schedule. It is yet one more factor in which the sport mirrors the aerospace industry.

Naturally, all of the myriad components must be conceived and designed (or sourced) at the right time and must then fit together to create a unique product. The result must not only be the best-performing car, but the most reliable. To achieve this, several groups must work harmoniously and efficiently:

Research & Development

Aerodynamic

Electronics

Design Office

Structural Analysis

Vehicle Dynamics

Metallurgy

Production Departments

Suppliers

Quality Control

Car Assembly

All of the departments answer ultimately to the technical director, which gives you some idea why such men are the highest paid people in Formula 1 outside the drivers and team principals. They tend to be very intelligent, very resourceful men, with an enduring ability to withstand pressure and to manage and motivate.

Each team, to a greater or lesser extent, depending

on their budget, has a strategic planning group whose task is to manage the activities of all these departments, keep everyone informed of progress, and everyone on schedule. This is a group largely unseen by the outside world, yet whose contribution to a project's success can be highly significant.

The project management aims to optimise and focus the resources within the project, locate any critical areas or problems, and generate solutions. It thus enables the technical director to make the strategic decisions. The three variables they must all juggle are:

Time

Quality

Cost

Time is perhaps the greatest restraint (certainly for the big teams), but the project must be completed within the defined targets of quality (performance/ reliability) and within the defined cost (the budget).

Project management first defines the contents of the project. What will the new car incorporate? First, have there been any significant rule changes? These inevitably have serious knock-on effects because each area of the car is so highly optimised for a given function and within a given framework, and impact on all the others. As an example, for 2004 teams had to use only one engine per race weekend, and were limited to rear wings with only two elements, rather than the multi-elements they had previously been allowed.

Then there is the question of any new technical or aerodynamic solutions that are to be applied, having previously been identified by the R&D department. Performance enhancements are usually expressed in terms of potential lap time improvement.

Once brainstorming sessions have been held between the technical director, the chief designer, the head of aerodynamics, and the design office, R&D, structural analysis and vehicle dynamics managers, the strategic planning begins. The group in charge then defines the project in terms of time, quality and cost as it evolves into three distinct sections:

Concept development

Design

Production

Each of these can give different results depending on the timescales imposed. For example, the longer concept development goes on the bigger the step forward that will be achieved in terms of performance, but that will leave less time for design and production (particularly if it affects long lead time components such as crankshafts or transmissions). Therefore the quality may also suffer and that can impact upon reliability, which in turn might negate the performance advantage achieved. Strategic planning must therefore impose that most derided of Formula 1 words: compromise. In the hyperbole of the sport people like to think compromise does not exist, but of course all of the technical packages on the grid are defined by it.

Much of the process of making a Formula 1 car occurs concurrently, not in sequence, which of course saves time. But that is why crucial decisions, such as engine configuration and packaging, need to be decided early on so that they do not hold up the project later. That is one reason why a change of engine manufacturers can often cause technical departments nightmares. Equally, the basic aerodynamic definition is usually arrived at early, though fine-tuning never subsequently stops.

Once these areas have been addressed, planning is defined for the individual components groups:

Engine

Electronics

Chassis

Aerodynamics (nose shape and wings)

Transmission

Systems (fuel, hydraulics, cooling)

Suspension, steering and wheels

Brakes

Driver comfort

In parallel with all this it is also necessary to cater for the FIA's mandatory and stringent crash tests. If a car fails to pass these, it will not be homologated by the FIA to race.

Once the main milestones have been defined, such as the aerodynamic concept definition and the general arrangement (the physical layout of the car and its components), the main aerodynamic definition dates are set:

Chassis aero definition

Crash structures aero definitions

Suspension aero definition

Wing aero definitions

Bodywork aero definitions

Opposite: The main components of BMW-Sauber's 2007 F1.07. (BMW AG)

1 *Tyre/rim*
2 *Wheel nut*
3 *Brake pads*
4 *Brake disc*
5 *Brake calliper*
6 *Upright*
7 *Brake duct*
8 *Front lower wishbone*
9 *Front upper wishbone*
10 *Front pushrod*
11 *Front track rod*
12 *Side damper*
13 *Fairing*
14 *Front wing endplate*
15 *Front wing mainplane*
16 *Front wing flap*
17 *Nose cone*
18 *Steering housing*
19 *Front 3rd element*
20 *Headrest*
21 *Steering wheel*
22 *Bullwinkle*
23 *Main turning vane*
24 *Forward turning vane*
25 *Seat*
26 *Pedals*
27 *Airbox*
28 *Radiator*

29 *Radiator duct*
30 *Engine heat shield*
31 *Engine*
32 *Wheel nut*
33 *Brake pads*
34 *Brake disc*
35 *Brake duct*
36 *Brake calliper*
37 *Driveshaft*
38 *Rear lower wishbone*
39 *Rear upper wishbone*
40 *Rear pushrod*
41 *Rear toe link*
42 *Gearbox*
43 *Rear crash structure*
44 *Rain light*
45 *Rear lower mainplane*
46 *Rear upper wing*
47 *Rear wing endplate*
48 *Sidepod*
49 *Mirror*
50 *Monocoque*
51 *Engine cover*
52 *Scallop*
53 *Earwing*
54 *Top exit*
55 *Undertray*
56 *Diffuser*

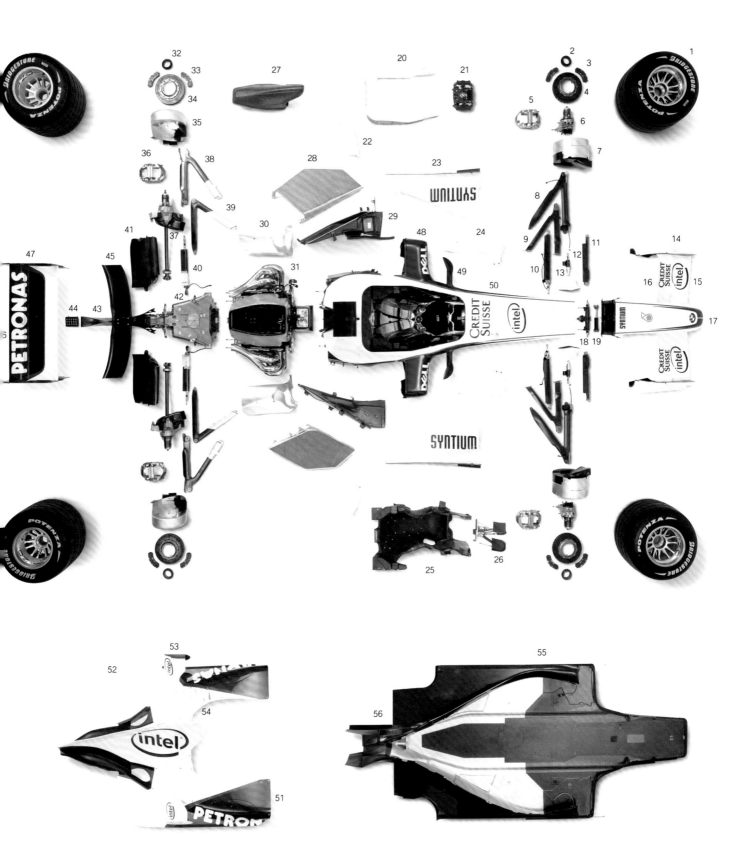

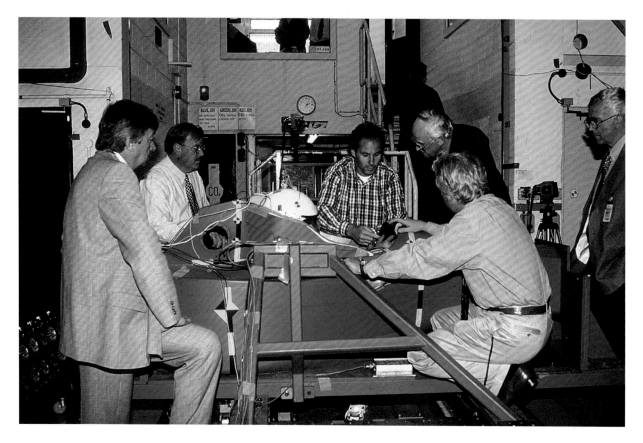

Then the timing for the main components such as chassis, bodywork, suspension and transmission are set. The third step is to define the production timing for all of these components, together with quality checks and tests. The last part of the planning is assembly.

Now that a project plan has been defined and the path to the final product has been mapped out, it is broken down into the detailed activities that will be followed and implemented during its execution. Charts of the project plan allow the team to follow the critical path and the critical activities and thus to highlight potential problems before they arise and find solutions early on. By creating this plan the engineers can develop the necessary overview of the entire programme, while also going into the minutest detail when necessary. Along the way there will be a design review and progress is analysed closely. If necessary, changes are implemented to keep everything on target. The strategic planners also keep everyone with an interest updated at all times, so that everyone is fully aware of the status of the undertaking. That not only facilitates collaboration, but enhances harmony and generates team spirit, all vital factors in any race team but even more critical when a company grows to 400 or 500 employees, and thus moves beyond the point where the team principal or even the technical

Crash testing has always been stringent since it was introduced, and gets tougher each year. It is a major factor in the development process. (John Townsend)

director can be said to know everyone personally.

As far as timescale is concerned, the transmission is defined in May, assessment of the internals allowing the main casing design to be finalised as soon as possible. For instance, will the designer want a longitudinal or transverse gearbox? Will the casing be aluminium, titanium or composite? The choices affect weight distribution, general arrangement and structure, since the casing is part of the FIA rear-end crash test. It also has a very significant influence on the all-important design of the rear-end aerodynamics. The other main aerodynamic definitions are made in July and August, as the current car is still being developed. The design process begins.

The suspension is aerodynamically defined by September, and during October and November the final systems definitions are made. Crash testing can begin as early as August, but usually doesn't end until February. McLaren achieved a company first by getting all of the MP4-19's crash testing out of the way before the car first ran in December 2003, but that is unusual.

While all of this is going on the engine department has already been hard at work for many months on the next evolution power unit that will go into the new car. Generally, developing a car takes nine months, but developing an all-new engine takes around twice that and manufacturers often run two separate design teams, one leapfrogging the other.

Electronics and systems design goes on at the same time as the aforementioned processes, while chassis manufacture may start as early as September. Production of other components also begins at the same time and continues through until at least March. This is a lengthy process, of course, because the top teams will not only produce up to ten chassis a season but also need all of the associated spares to service them. The manufacturing departments for suspension and wings are always particularly busy, since these are the most easily damaged parts once the testing and racing gets under way.

By January all of the components have been delivered, and go through quality control before final assembly begins. The car is then checked over minutely, not least to make sure that it complies with the FIA's critical rules governing its dimensions. The final stage is the first fire up, and then the rollout. The first car is usually launched to the world in January or early February. In the economic climate of the early 21st century few teams opt for the 'bells and whistles' launches seen in the mid '90s and prefer instead to unveil their car to the media as part of a test session at a circuit. By this time the strategic planners have already turned their attention to the next season's new project.

Just to complicate all this, teams do not always decide to debut a new car at the beginning of the new season. McLaren planned to run its MP4-18 in May in 2003. In 2002 and 2003, Ferrari opted to run its previous year's cars for the first few races, and to bring their new challenger on stream once the European leg of the championship got under way in April. This is Ferrari's case study:

The team made an analysis of the positive and negative aspects of introducing its new car later rather than sooner. On the positive side, rules stability would allow it to run the previous year's car without having to make major modifications. Since the car was strongly competitive at the end of the previous season, and

Early testing of the 2003 Ferrari F2003-GA indicated the need for further development. The team responded ably to the challenge, and the car went on to win both the drivers' and constructors' titles. (Clive Mason/Getty Images)

had been developed further over the winter, it should maintain its advantages over newer but less well sorted competitors. The older car was also highly reliable, whereas the new car, which was ready for testing, had not yet quite been 'bullet-proofed'. Furthermore, the newer car would have been at an early stage of its development, and the engineers and drivers would thus be less familiar with its inner workings than they were with the older car, which might compromise setting it up. Finally, there would be more time in which to develop the new car, so that it could be debuted when testing had shown it to have reached its targeted levels of performance and reliability.

As far as negatives were concerned, the older car would face stronger competitors with newer cars which had taken bigger steps forward in terms of performance (though on the plus side they might not be as reliable). The team would have to double its commitment in order to work on two separate types of car, which would be potentially decisive and onerous. It would also impact strongly on the budget, especially early in the season. There was also an associated risk of mistakes in doubling up, to both the internal groups and to suppliers.

The data supplied by the strategic planning department at Ferrari, such as activities charts, time, resources and expenditure, provided the technical department with the necessary input to make its decision. In 2002 the plan worked superbly, with the F2001 holding the fort until the F2002 proceeded to wipe the floor with its opposition. A bad start to 2003 with the F2002 almost jeopardised things, but as President Luca di Montezemolo summarised, 'We made a terrible start to the season through mistakes, we had a good second quarter, winning in Imola, Austria and Canada, then a month of panic in August before we got back on the road in the final quarter and won a record sixth drivers' title for Michael [Schumacher] and a record fifth consecutive constructors' championship.'

The foregoing perhaps gives an indication of just why Formula 1 is such a pressure cooker, and why individuals and organisations can only stand the heat for so long. It also places into sharper perspective those who can keep it up year after year, why Ferrari has done such an incredible job since the late '90s, and why Williams and McLaren are to be applauded for their utter refusal to concede defeat and their relentless determination to win.

'If nothing else,' says Ross Brawn, 'all of this is the answer to those people who inevitably come sidling up to you when a season is over to ask the question: "What on earth do you do when you aren't racing!"'

And it was Brawn who illustrated so graphically at the start of the 2009 season just how intense F1 development has become. In 2008 Ferrari and McLaren threw everything they had into their battle for the World Championship, as did outsider BMW-Sauber. McLaren won the Drivers' title with Lewis Hamilton, Ferrari the Constructors'. While they were doing so much of the winning, Honda languished at the back of the grid, and at the end of the season, to everyone's huge surprise, it succumbed to the growing world economic recession and withdrew from F1. At the 11th hour technical director Ross Brawn and former team principal Nick Fry completed a management buyout. In their renamed Brawn BGP001, now powered by one of Mercedes-Benz's V8 engines, they won six of the opening seven grands prix with Jenson Button at the wheel. As these words were written, the Englishman led the Drivers' World Championship,

and the team did like likewise in the Constructors'. McLaren, Ferrari and BMW-Sauber were nowhere... It took the red team four races before it scored points.

The Brawn had been under development since 2007, and while still in charge of Honda Brawn had taken the decision to write off 2008 and focus on the raft of new regulations that the FIA had imposed for 2009: dramatic aerodynamic changes; the introduction of kinetic energy recovery systems (KERS) and a return to slick tyres. The extra development time reaped a huge dividend.

'They were in a nightmare situation where neither could give up their fight for the title,' Brawn said of McLaren and Ferrari, 'but they were doing that at a time when the regulations were going to change for 2009, so all the development they were still doing right to the end of the season took time and could not be rolled into a new car. Everything they did at the

Testing is often referred to as the 'Winter World Championship', but it is only the 'summer' series that counts. Here in Australia in 2009, Brawn GP proved the testing form of its BGP001 was no fluke, with a 1–2 in qualifying and the race. (LAT)

end just had to be thrown into the bin. Now we have new regulations and more difficult constraints, such as a restriction on testing.

'In the future, it is quite possible that a team will have to accept that it might be able to fight for the World Championship one year but not in the following season because of this.'

That was serious food for thought as, in August 2009, teams finally signed up to a new Concorde Agreement which, while outlawing refuelling and imposing a cost restriction closer to Nineties budgets, would take them through to the end of 2012.

Chapter 1

Aerodynamics
Tunnel vision

In the world of Formula 1, the aerodynamicist is king. And the man who can figure out how his team can generate more downforce for less drag than any of his rivals, is going to be worth in real terms more than the $30m plus that Ferrari pays Kimi Raikkonen.

Those are the simple facts of Formula 1 design. Once, aerodynamics was a black art. Teams made pencil-slim little cars and trimmed them at times with the odd tab here or there to negate lift. It wasn't until 1968 that Formula 1 designers really cottoned on, the way that sports car design ace Jim Hall had, that using inverted wings to generate downforce was what real speed was all about. The first wings were precariously mounted on stilts, which in turn were mounted directly on the car's uprights. Soon these proved so ludicrously fragile that they were banned in favour of bodywork-mounted wings which were part of the car's sprung mass. Nevertheless, they continued to push the tyres into contract with the road, and therefore to develop downforce which made the car corner faster.

So how does a wing work? On an aeroplane it works thus. A wing uses an aerofoil, teardrop shape. As air flows over the upper and lower sides, the air on the bottom has less distance to go because the lower surface of the wing is flat. Meanwhile, air flowing over the curved top has a further distance to travel. This is where the theory expressed long ago by scientist Daniele Bernoulli comes into effect. He suggested that when air's flow is restricted the air will speed up and its pressure will drop. The air flowing on the underside of the aeroplane wing is flowing at its normal rate; the air clamouring to get over the curved upper side is speeding up, and its pressure is thus falling. This means that there is more pressure acting on the underside and less on the upper side, so the wing lifts. That, in a nutshell, is the theory of flight.

Now, apply the wing to a racing car and what happens? For a start, the wing is inverted. Now the straighter side is the upper, and the curved arc is on the bottom of the wing. Thus the low pressure area occurs below the wing, and the greater pressure is being exerted downwards. In the early days this was described in aeroplane parlance as negative lift; today it is simply known as downforce, and it is the single most important thing in Formula 1.

An additional complication arose in the '70s when Lotus chief Colin Chapman and his designers, Peter Wright, Tony Rudd and Ralph Bellamy, all worked towards harnessing the air flowing beneath the car, again using principles figured out on the remarkable Chaparral 2J CanAm car by Jim Hall.

Again, Bernoulli's venturi theory applied. This time the air was being restricted as it passed through a venturi created by the ground and the underside of the car. As it was restricted, the air's flow sped up and the whole underside of the car became a low pressure area and the vehicle was sucked down to the track. Ground effect had arrived.

Opposite: The scale wind-tunnel models are held in place by an overhead 'sting', through which all the forces acting on the model are measured. (BMW AG)

Today Formula 1 cars must use flat-bottomed chassis (as they have had to since 1983), but they have a diffuser at the rear which curves upwards and helps to generate a degree of ground effect. The downforce created here is complemented by that from the wings and carefully shaped bodywork.

Overall, the aerodynamicist is looking for a stable car with a good ratio of lift over drag, in other words one which has plenty of downforce and not much drag. He also wants one on which the sensitivity to pitch – the up and down movement – is minimal. This is the key to good handling. On a car that has low pitch sensitivity the aerodynamic balance doesn't shift around as the car pitches up and down over bumps, or tends to shift its centre of gravity under acceleration or deceleration. Pitch sensitivity tends to be more influential on a car's overall behaviour than either yaw or roll stability.

The modern Formula 1 car is highly sophisticated aerodynamically, and can generate close to 2,000kg of downforce at speeds of 300kph. If you put it on

a suitably curved piece of road it could, in theory, generate enough grip to stick itself to the ceiling should it be suddenly inverted...

When a designer begins to create a new car, he first defines the aerodynamic performance profile that he is seeking. In order to do this, models must be tested so that different shapes and configurations can be assessed. The designer uses two main tools here: the wind tunnel, and a computer modelling technique known as computational fluid dynamics, or CFD.

The wind tunnel is the primary tool, and all of the top teams have significantly increased their investments in this field. In 2003, for example, WilliamsF1 invested in a second tunnel that came on stream in 2004. At that time the most state-of-the-art tunnel belonged to Peter Sauber's team in Hinwil. The quiet Swiss team owner grasped a $50 million nettle in 2000, and the new tunnel became operational at the end of 2003. 'Given the importance of aerodynamics, it was a logical decision for me to build a wind tunnel that sets

Stilt-mounted rear wings first appeared in Formula One in 1968. By Monza, where Ron Dennis watches over Jack Brabham's eponymous BT26, they were fitted at the front too. Drivers hated them, and after two serious accidents on the Gold Leaf Lotus 49Bs in the 1969 Spanish TP (Graham Hill's car is seen here in South Africa), they were banned overnight at Monaco. (sutton-images.com)

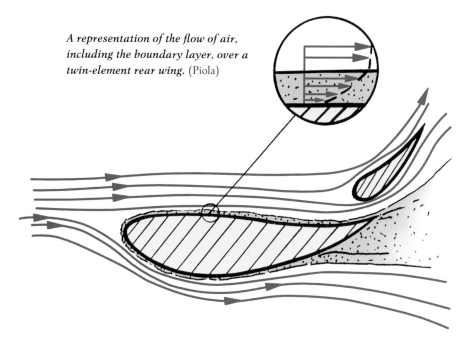

A representation of the flow of air, including the boundary layer, over a twin-element rear wing. (Piola)

new benchmarks,' Sauber explained. 'The interesting thing is that had we invested less in the wind tunnel, the risk would have been higher. At an early stage the tunnel was planned to be smaller, but then the consideration was that you don't know what is going to happen to Formula 1, so we wanted to have a working tool that you can also use outside of Formula 1. It was important to look as far into the future as possible.'

After several seasons in which body-mounted wings provided all of a car's downforce, Lotus chief Colin Chapman experimented with under-car ground effect in 1977. A year later his elegant Lotus 79 (seen here at Zandvoort with World Champion-elect Mario Andretti leading Ronnie Peterson) dominated the sport. Ground effect is still a major contributor to downforce today. (sutton-images.com)

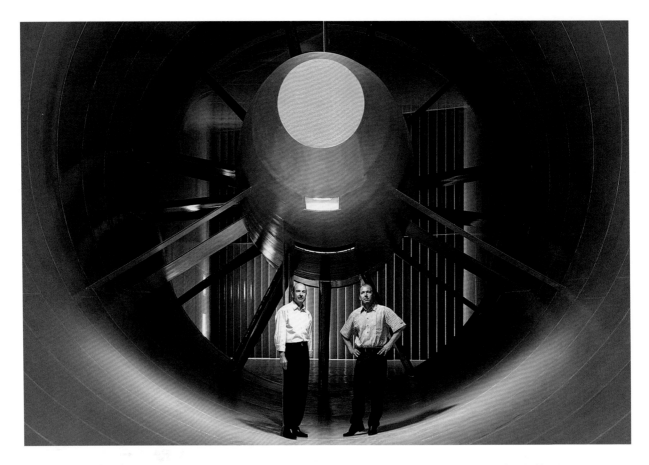

The better-financed teams have their own tunnels. In 2004 arguably the most advanced was Sauber's in Hinwil, built at a cost of more than 50 million dollars. Here team principal Peter Sauber and technical director Willy Rampf pose with their new baby. (sutton-images.com)

The tunnel was so modern that it attracted the attention of Sauber's then operating partner, Ferrari. Now it is the property of BMW, following its takeover of the team for 2006. The basic facility comprises two buildings under one roof, with the accent on aesthetics and functionality. Normally tunnels are located at ground level, but part of the reason why architect Atelier WW in Zurich won the contract was its design for a structure that is eight metres from the ground, enabling visitors to walk beneath it even while it is operational. Everything is visible except the data acquisition section, which is embedded in a concrete construction. The overall building is 65m long, 50m wide and 17m high, with a volume of 63,000m³. Its glass facade manages to combine its industrial purpose with its joint function as a museum. The two separate sections are separated by a glass wall which also damps out noise. There is also a facility to enable Sauber teams

to work on different projects for different customers with complete secrecy and confidentiality.

The tunnel uses the most advanced technology Sauber could source and was developed in conjunction with specialist firms Turbo Lufttechnik GmbH (TLT) and MTS Systems Corporation, in Germany and the United States respectively, and Sauber's aerodynamic engineers.

MTS supplied the 'Flat-Trac' rolling road system, which simulates the relative motion between car and road and comprises a steel belt which was chosen in preference to the more common polyester belts. The steel belt is the largest ever developed for a wind tunnel. It is less than a millimetre thick and runs on an air bearing. It runs faster and with less distortion than a conventional polyester belt, and because it generates less friction it not only lasts longer but is also more accurate because there is less surface heat. MTS also supplied the 'Model Motion System' which handles suspension and control of the test model. Data acquisition is by UK-based RHS Harntec.

In common with other Formula 1 tunnels, BMW-Sauber's is of closed-circuit design. Its tubular steel air circuit is 62m long and 28m wide, with a maximum diameter of 9.4m. Dirk de Beer, the head of Sauber's aerodynamic group, was particularly pleased with the corners that turn the air through 90° and link each section of the tunnel. 'A circular tunnel would be ideal, but if you tried to build one it just wouldn't work, and there would be an enormous space requirement. As it is, these corners are very efficient.'

Power comes from a single-stage axial fan with carbon rotor blades, which supplies the system's 3,000kW demand when operating under full load. At maximum output it can generate wind speeds of up to 80m per second (which de Beer claims is faster than Ferrari's tunnel) or close to 300kph within the test section. This is very close to the air speed over a full-scale car in action on the track, again enhancing data accuracy.

The test section is the heart of any tunnel, and at 15m² Sauber's is unusually large and has a longer rolling section than any other Formula 1 facility. There is a strong correlation between the size of the moving ground plane and the degree of realism of the test results. Though Sauber continued to test primarily with 60% scale models, the tunnel can accept full-scale cars and BMW may elect to pursue this option in the future. Its primary aim in 2006 was to treble the tunnel's work rate by initiating 24-hour usage with three eight-hour shifts, something that Sauber could not afford to do. Because of its unusual length it can also accommodate two of them, in tandem, so that the aerodynamicists can explore the interaction of cars running close together at very high speeds. This could prove particularly useful in the design of front wings and diffusers.

'Due to their highly efficient aerodynamics, modern Formula 1 cars are particularly vulnerable to changes in airflow,' explains technical director Willy Rampf.

Wind tunnels are absolutely de rigueur in Formula One today. Scale models are placed on a moving ground plane so airflow can be simulated as accurately as possible. BMW-Sauber's tunnel, which can accept full-scale cars, uses a very sophisticated steel band for its rolling road for maximum accuracy (BMW AG and IPA)

Left and below: Williams has two wind tunnels at its impressive Grove facility, one of which, seen here in 2004, can accommodate a full-size car. (BMW AG)

'For the first time this test configuration now enables us systematically to measure these influences and to take appropriate corrective action. Moreover, given the additional possibility of testing full-size Formula 1 racing cars, we can precisely measure such factors as the cooling, or the airflow around the driver's helmet.'

When very large objects such as full-scale vans are under test, the test section can be converted from closed-wall configuration into a slotted-wall configuration to avoid blockage of the airflow which would distort test results.

Another innovation is the facility to rotate the test section turntable. Formula 1 cars don't usually get more than 5° out of line before they use up their steering lock and spin, but the turntable allows cars to be tested at a yaw angle of up to 10°.

The upper floor of the wind tunnel control room houses the entire computer system, which includes the high-performance computer for BMW-Sauber's CFD department. The ability to test scale models and full-scale cars allows engineers to cross-check data, and CFD provides a third avenue of research to cross-check further. But at present CFD still has some way to go in Formula 1 before it will match the wind tunnel as a research tool.

'At the moment we are increasing our CFD effort quite considerably,' said de Beer in 2004. 'It's probably 15 to 20% of our personnel that are involved with CFD, and it's something we are putting more and more effort into. It's an area where you can get very significant gains. But it is still one in which everybody in Formula 1 is finding out exactly what you can do. The resources that you need to do CFD effectively are quite huge. You need very large computers, obviously, to run accurate simulations. We are certainly putting a lot of effort into it, but it's not a short-term thing. I think essentially the view of the team is that we intend to be in Formula 1 for a long time and are investing a lot of resources in stuff like building this facility and increasing our capacity with CFD, all with the aim of being there for the long run.'

Rampf and his team had very high hopes for the new facility when it opened. 'We're expecting the new wind tunnel to enhance the quality of our tests, improve the correlation between our wind tunnel measurements and the results obtained on the racetrack, as well as improved repeatability of the various tests we perform,' he said. 'All of these factors combined will enable us to build an even faster car.'

Peter Sauber accepted the huge investment with equanimity, and said: 'If you want to survive in Formula 1 and be successful, and particularly if you want to be attractive to a potential manufacturer, then you have to have these things. It is an investment in our future that was not undertaken with cost-saving as its primary goal. With the new facility we will have a great deal more confidence that what works for us during tests in the wind tunnel will also work for us on the racetrack.'

Ultimately his investment turned out to be very shrewd, as BMW bought a controlling interest in his team in 2005 when it split from Williams.

The aerodynamics of the car dictate its shape, and also the type of engine that will be used. In the days when all Formula 1 engines were V10s, the angle of the vee could be altered if the aerodynamicist sought a particularly narrow rear-end package. That was one reason why the traditional 90° angle gradually decreased as low as 72° in some instances. The fact that aerodynamics can have such influence gives you a clear idea of just how much importance is attached to this area of design. In the past a team would get its engine, make a chassis into which to fit it, and then worry about the bodywork last of all. For a while the process worked the other way round. The aerodynamicists would come up with the outer shape of the package that would make the fastest and most efficient car, and the other engineering departments had to make their components fit into that profile. That is still primarily the case after the introduction of 2.4-litre V8 engines for 2006, but the FIA made life a little more difficult for the aerodynamicists by insisting that the vee angle be 90°.

Several dimensions on the chassis are also fixed by the FIA, but beyond that the aerodynamics dictate the chassis' design. Usually it is a matter of the slimmer the better, but aerodynamics can even influence whether the car has a short or a long wheelbase.

Controversy arose at the start of the 2006 season when, after the Bahrain Grand Prix, some teams complained to the FIA that they believed others were running flexible wings. Now all such structures, front and rear, must have a degree of flexibility. If they were mounted rigidly they might easily be fractured by a car's inherent vibrations, so a degree of compliance is necessary. Watch the wings when the onboard cameras capture a car in a corner, and you see some of that. But what the complainants referred to was wings whose fundamental geometry and/or orientation moved at very high speed. They alleged that, for example, a rear wing would bend back or that the space between upper elements might close up, all to the benefit of the drag coefficient.

Formula 1 being what it is today, such things can be very difficult to measure physically. FIA technical delegate Jo Bauer and race director Charlie Whiting investigated the wings on the Ferraris in Malaysia following increasingly vehement comment from the team's rivals, but could find nothing wrong. The complainants argued that this is because you would need a whole raft of hydraulic actuators, such as you might get in aircraft manufacturing plants to measure bending loads across a wing, to measure compliance with any true degree of accuracy. And they argued that they could prove their case in a different way, by looking at straightline speed measurements, and recording the engine notes of relevant cars and using the audio data to compare them with a base model. A popular comparison was between Ferrari and Red Bull Racing (formerly Jaguar), as each used identical Ferrari V8 engines. According to the gathered data, the Ferrari appeared able to 'bend' the laws of physics by gaining top-end speed just at the point where all the various drag-inducing factors came together to put a brake on further acceleration from the Red Bull RB2.

A clarification of sorts was issued, and after Ferrari performed relatively poorly in Australia everyone relaxed. Then Michael Schumacher won the San Marino and European Grands Prix in his Ferrari F248, and the whole can of worms was opened again until Renault's R26 gave the red car a thrashing at Spain's Circuit de Catalunya, a track deemed to be the ultimate test of a car's myriad characteristics and the best guide to seasonal form. Confusion reigned.

Flexible surfaces were not a new phenomenon in racing. Back in Mexico 1986 Lotus ran into a lot of trouble with the Ayrton Senna-driven 86T when rivals alleged that its floor was sufficiently flexible that it got sucked down closer to the road surface at high speed and therefore generated superior downforce. Ferrari had a problem for a while with flexible barge boards in Malaysia in 1999, when it was alleged that its boards sank as much as 10mm on their mounts, thus significantly closing the mandatory 150mm gap to the road and enhancing downforce. Eventually a visit to Maranello from the FIA's Peter Wright sorted the matter out in Ferrari's favour. Now, thanks to the use of CFD modelling in conjunction with finite element analysis (FEA), it is possible for designers to do this with a much greater degree of accuracy and predictability while remaining safely within the elasticity of the materials used. There had been no examples of wings failing because of excessive flexibility.

The way a 'flexible' rear wing works is that it effectively rotates backwards on its central mount at very high speed on a straight – 250kph plus – thus decreasing its angle of attack. This reduces drag and

enhances top speed further, but as the car slows for the next corner the flexibility in the structure pops the wing back up, increasing downforce again. It is a means of reproducing the sort of concept that Ferrari used back in 1968, before movable aerodynamic aids were outlawed, when its centrally mounted overhead wing could be feathered along the straights, albeit now using carefully calculated structural materials instead of hydraulic actuation. That early Ferrari system was itself a development of the 'flipper' style of wing used previously on Jim Hall's CanAm and world sports car racing Chaparrals.

The other method of gaining an advantage from the flexibility of structural components is to have upper rear wing elements that can flex together at very high speed. In 2006 teams were allowed two upper elements in their rear wings, above the main plane. Usually these upper elements have small separators mounted in the middle, to ensure that they stay apart and that flow through what is called the 'slot-gap' is maintained. Rivals maintained that Ferrari's refusal to use separators was because at speed the two upper elements bent together, thus closing the slot gap and reducing the associated drag, thereby boosting top speed. At Imola, competitors pointed out, the Ferraris were 7kph quicker down the straight than their rivals.

In Malaysia, Honda technical director Geoffrey Willis attempted to explain a difficult situation in layman's terms. 'The issue about the flexibility of rear wings is a difficult one because clearly all engineering structures do deflect. The question is whether you are allowed to make performance benefit from that, and the FIA – Charlie Whiting – has clarified on several occasions that you are not. The difficulty is what sort of test you come up with that is safe to perform in *parc fermé* conditions because the rear wings do have very significant loads on them that you probably wouldn't want to place on the car in *parc fermé* in case they fell off and hurt somebody. The designs of the wings that people have used in the past certainly have allowed what we call the slot gap – the gap between the first element and the second element of the wing – to either close up or to open up and by doing so change the drag and the lift on the car, and you can see that in the past a number of teams have gained extra top speed from that. That's been tightened up a certain amount by regulation changes in the last year or so or more stringent application of certain stiffness tests.

'I think we probably still need to see a change in the regulation there to ensure that that geometry has to remain constant all the way across the speed, and one way to do that is to make sure that the physical

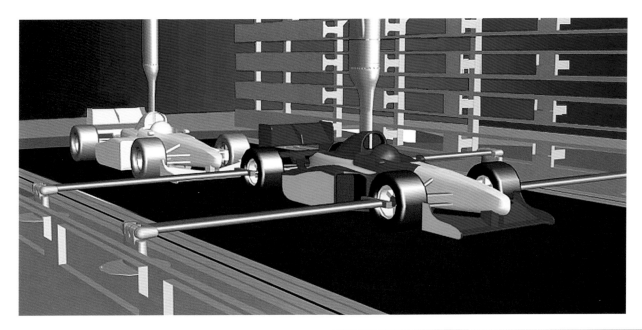

Above: Besides the ability to skew the rolling road turntable to a yaw angle of up to 10 degrees, BMW-Sauber's tunnel also allows scale models to be tested in tandem. Ultimately this could be of significant assistance in facilitating the design of a car that can run in a rival's turbulent air without losing its downforce. (IPA)

arrangement of what the rear wing is like is consistent with not being able to change that gap.'

Watched at a press conference by Ferrari technical director Ross Brawn, who had said it was time for wing technology to be opened up the way traction control technology had been because of the difficulty of policing it, and that it was time to end 'a culture of innuendo', Willis had another go at the Nürburgring in May. 'The whole issue of flexible wings has come and gone quite a lot over the last two or three years. It's an area which a lot of the teams often talk about to Charlie Whiting, the race director, seeking clarifications, asking what we can do, and it's a subject which we discuss in the Technical Working Group from time to time, so I'm not quite sure why this issue became quite so heated this week. It is the case that people have been playing around with wings quite a lot. There are two main ways. People either try and get the whole wing to bend off… to twist off, to reduce the drag at high speed, or play around with mechanisms that close or open the slot gap, and I have to say that what we've discovered over the last year or so is quite impressive, the amount of innovation out there. We've seen wings that bend in one way, flaps that bend in another way, wings that aren't bonded together. I think we've even seen an inflatable wing, which I must say I was very

Above: Computational fluid dynamics (CFD) is a vital part of aerodynamic research today. This screen image shows the airflow over the 2008 BMW-Sauber F1.08. (BMW AG)

impressed with. But it's something where, if we hear something or we have an idea, then it's all part of the regular business of making technical inquiries to Charlie Whiting, asking whether we can do it. It's a little bit of a game generally with technical advances in Formula 1, when you have a clever idea, or you think somebody else has got a clever idea, you either try and do it yourself or, if you think it's close enough to a grey area, you ask the right sort of question of the FIA, so it either gets stopped for everybody or permitted for everybody.'

The aerodynamic components exert the following influences:

Front wing

The front wing plays an important role. At a maximum speed of over 300kph, for example, it will generate around 560kg of downforce. That means that eight full-grown men could step on it without causing any visible deflection. The front wing is mounted beneath the nose on two vertical stalks, and probably accounts for 25% of overall downforce. This is an area of great experimentation. One 'tweak' that appeared in 2003 was the distinctive rippled w-shaped wing on the McLaren MP4-18 which was carried over to the 2004 MP4-19. Subsequently, the 2007 MP4-22 introduced the 'bridge' wing, which spanned the nose of the car.

Though never raced in 2003, McLaren's MP4-18 paved the way for the evolutionary MP4-19 in 2004. The latter retained this very complex front wing. (Piola)

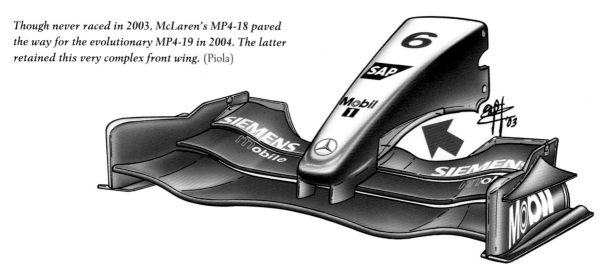

Ferrari's controversial 2006 front wing was thought by rivals to possess an element of flexibility to enhance performance. (LAT)

2007 Toyota TF107 front wing. (Toyota)

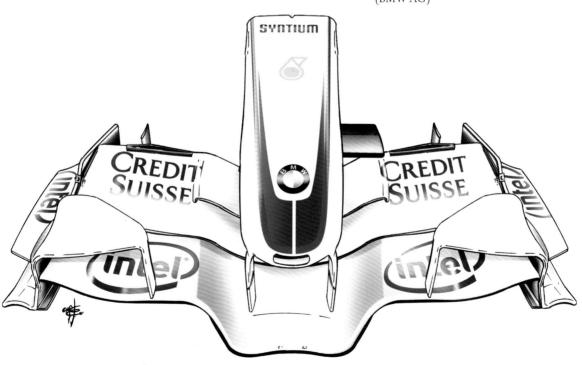

BMW-Sauber F1.07 Monaco front wing. (BMW AG)

The 2007 McLaren MP4-22 introduced the 'bridge' wing concept, the upper wing element spanning the nose of the car. (sutton-images.com)

BMW-Sauber F1.08 Monaco front wing. (BMW AG)

Above: BMW-Sauber F1.09 front wing. Spanish GP 2009. (sutton-images.com)

Left: Brawn BGP001 front wing. Testing, Barcelona March 2009. (sutton-images.com)

Front wing endplates

The front wing endplates are the vertical fences that primarily stop air spilling over the side of the wing, as that would compromise its efficiency. They help to draw air over the front wing to maximise its effectiveness, but they also play a significant role in smoothing the airflow towards the back of the car. They are thus instrumental in sending the best possible airflow back towards the undertray and then to the diffuser to make both of those components work to their optimum. The aerodynamicists are always aiming to get the maximum out of every component. Interestingly, adding frontal downforce levies a minimal drag penalty; it is the rear end of the car that can do that, so the aerodynamicists do whatever they can to make the rear work better. When you achieve that you can run with less rear wing, which means less drag and a more efficient car.

Right: BMW-Sauber F1.09 front wing endplates. Monaco 2009. (sutton-images.com)

Above: Ferrari F2009 front wing endplates. Monaco 2009. (sutton-images.com)

Right: Toyota TF109 front wing endplates. Monaco 2009. (sutton-images.com)

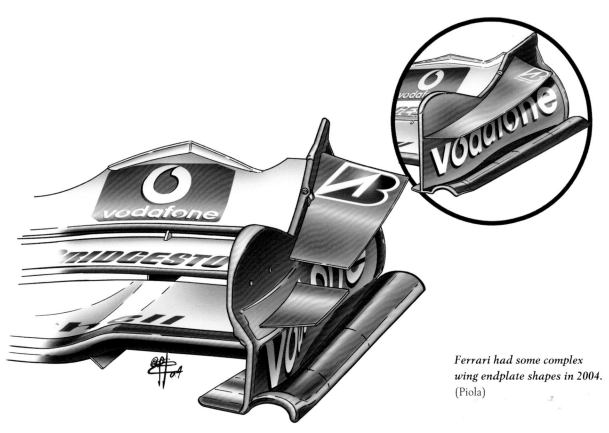

Ferrari had some complex wing endplate shapes in 2004. (Piola)

The endplates are one area in which the sport's rule makers are continually imposing restrictions, in an effort to curb rising cornering speeds.

Nose

High noses were almost universal by the late '90s, having been introduced by Tyrrell's Dr Harvey Postlethwaite and Jean-Claude Migeot in 1990, but now they are tending to droop a little once again, even though wings remain underslung. This design concept helps to channel air round the front wing and direct it efficiently back towards the undertray and diffuser. Again, McLaren introduced some subtle changes on the 2003 MP4-18 by using a very narrow drooping nose, and since then there has generally been a trend back to that configuration.

'Crocodile' snout on McLaren's 2006 MP4-21. (LAT)

The distinctive 'walrus' nose of the early-season 2004 Williams FW26 broke new ground in the search for greater aerodynamic efficiency, but the team later reverted to a conventional design. (Piola)

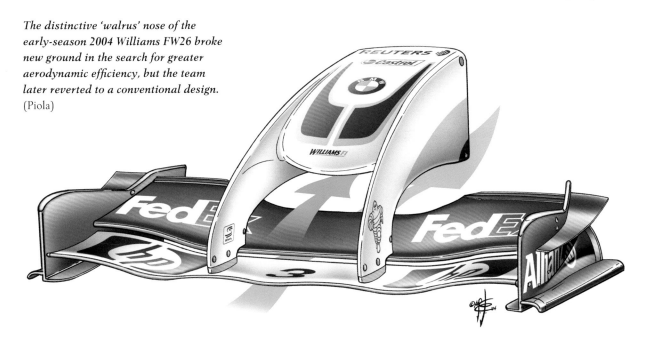

Red Bull RB5 nose. Launch, Feb 2009.
(sutton-images.com)

Renault R29 nose. Testing, Jerez March 2009.
(sutton-images.com)

Suspension

Until 2001, the suspension's contribution to aerodynamic efficiency was confined to using aerofoil-section wishbones and steering arms to help minimise drag. That season, however, Argentinean designer Sergio Rinland introduced the first true twin-keeled chassis on his Sauber C20. Normally the lower suspension arms would pick up at a point in the middle of the underside of the chassis. Reasoning that this created a blockage to smooth airflow, however, Rinland moved the lower front suspension mountings further outwards, creating two distinctive pick-up points, or keels. The large gap between them permitted a much

Differing philosophies: In 2002 (inset) Jaguar opted for the twin-keel chassis design on the R3, but reverted to single-keel for the 2004 R4 (main picture). (Piola)

Twin-keel arrangement on stripped-down 2002 McLaren MP4-17. (sutton-images.com)

smoother flow of air, and was deemed to be one reason why that year's Sauber Petronas was such an excellent car; but the jury is still out on the concept. McLaren embraced it and took it a step further on its extremely elegant but expensive-to-make MP4-17 chassis. Since 2005, however, most teams have reverted to the single central mount, albeit at the bottom of a shallow and hollow vee structure attached to the base of the monocoque.

Barge boards/guide vanes

The vertical plates mounted within the front suspension or just behind it, which are often referred to as turning vanes or barge boards, are similar in function to the front wing endplates and first appeared when the latter were reduced in size in 1993. They may be horizontal or, more usually, vertical, and their job is to influence the wake of the air flowing over the front wing and to tidy it up before it gets to the back of the car. As an indication of their importance, the barge boards on Ferrari's 1997 F310B, with their

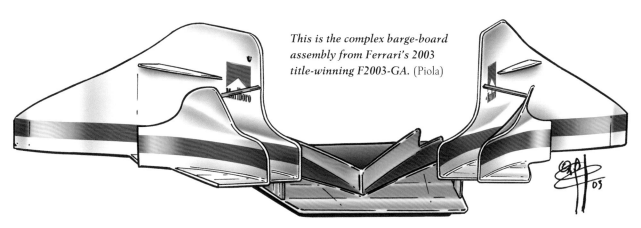

This is the complex barge-board assembly from Ferrari's 2003 title-winning F2003-GA. (Piola)

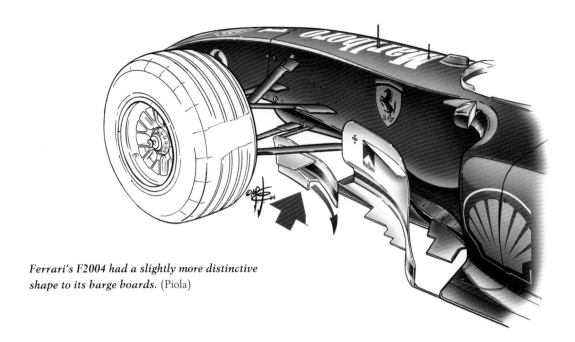

Ferrari's F2004 had a slightly more distinctive shape to its barge boards. (Piola)

distinctive curved top lip, were instrumental in cutting down the serious understeer which plagued the car's handling during its initial test sessions. When Michael Schumacher damaged those on his Ferrari F2002 after an off-course moment in the 2003 Australian Grand Prix, he lost the race. At the same time, the argument within Williams over whether to have barge boards behind the suspension or guide vanes within it materially influenced the FW25's concept, and it was some time before the team got on top of setting the car up as a result.

Right: 2007 BMW-Sauber F1.07 barge boards for Monaco. (BMW AG)

Above: Ferrari F60 barge board. Jerez test, March 2009. (sutton-images.com)

Above: Brawn BGP001 barge board. Jerez test, March 2009. (sutton-images.com)

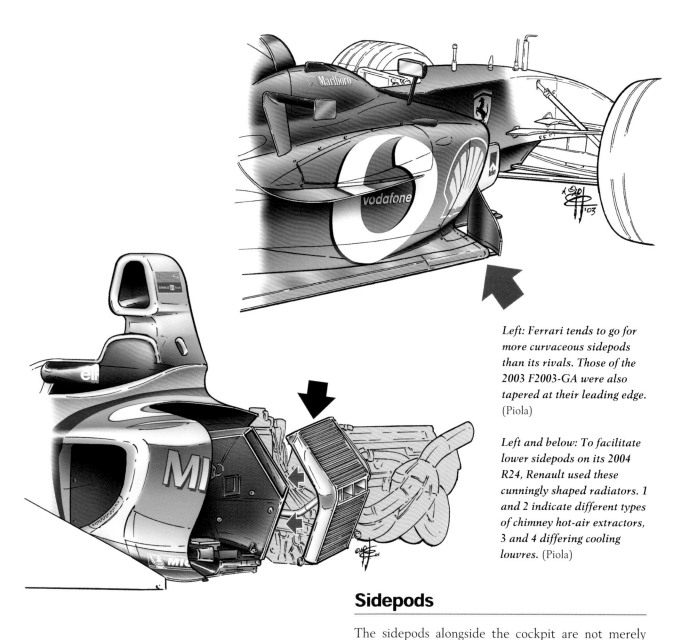

Left: Ferrari tends to go for more curvaceous sidepods than its rivals. Those of the 2003 F2003-GA were also tapered at their leading edge. (Piola)

Left and below: To facilitate lower sidepods on its 2004 R24, Renault used these cunningly shaped radiators. 1 and 2 indicate different types of chimney hot-air extractors, 3 and 4 differing cooling louvres. (Piola)

Sidepods

The sidepods alongside the cockpit are not merely there as a cosmetic means of housing the water and oil radiators. Their internal shaping is crucial to the way in which the car's cooling system operates, and they also play a safety role by providing deformable structure on the side of the car.

Above: 2009 McLaren MP4-24 sidepod detail.
(sutton-images.com)

Above: 2009 Renault R29 sidepod detail.
(sutton-images.com)

Undertray

The floor of the car, or the undertray, is an extremely important component. There is, of course, a separate floor to the chassis itself, while the undertray is a full-length carbon-fibre moulding that presents a smooth and flat bottom to the road and influences undercar airflow into the kinked area ahead of and between the rear wheels. It thus plays a crucial role even before its trailing end flicks up to form the diffuser that creates so much ground effect downforce at the rear of the car.

The flow of air beneath a Formula One car is nicely illustrated in this artwork of the 1999 Ferrari F399. (Piola)

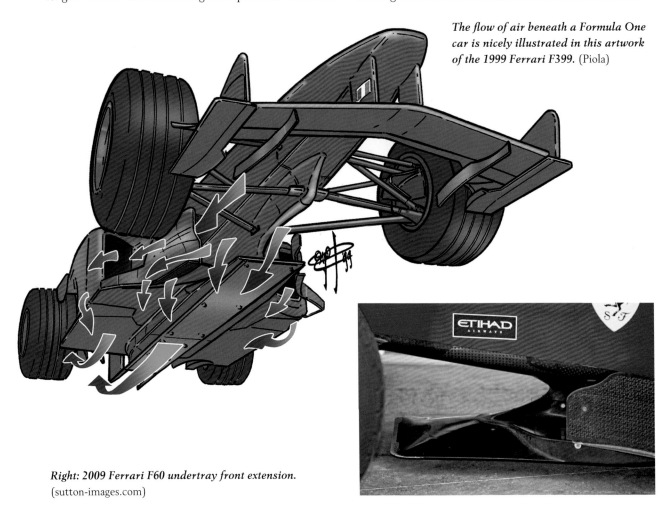

Right: 2009 Ferrari F60 undertray front extension.
(sutton-images.com)

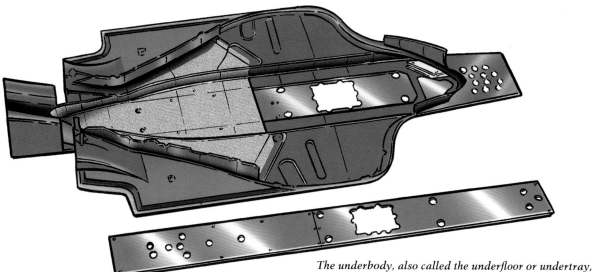

Safety cockpits

The need to provide a high-sided safety cockpit around the driver's head and neck initially caused problems with aerodynamic efficiency when the FIA made them mandatory for the 1996 season, as their bulky shapes increased drag. Now, however, all of the teams have found graceful and efficient ways in which to incorporate them, although they do still hurt rear downforce a little as the airflow around them is not quite as good as it was before they were introduced.

The underbody, also called the underfloor or undertray, generates a considerable degree of downforce. The one-piece moulding can be removed quickly in the event of damage after running over a kerb. In the centre of the underside of the undertray, all cars must carry a Jabroc wooden plank. (Piola)

After the near miss between David Coulthard and Alex Wurz in Australia in 2007, in which the Austrian's Williams slithered over the scuttle of the Scot's Red Bull, cockpit sides were raised further.

In comparison with Felipe Massa in the 2009 Ferrari F60 (bottom), Gerhard Berger has markedly less head protection in the 1995 412T2 (top). (LAT)

Airboxes

The airbox collects cold air and feeds it into the engine. The faster the car goes, the greater the so-called ram effect as air is forced into the intake. Its design is therefore a crucial element in both aerodynamic efficiency and engine performance.

Right: 2009 McLaren MP4-24 airbox. (sutton-images.com)

Below: 2009 Red Bull RB5 airbox. (sutton-images.com)

Winglets

These are mounted towards the rear of the sidepods, in an area of the strict regulations that is still open to such devices, and they are employed on circuits such as Monte Carlo or the Hungaroring where higher downforce is required.

For 2009, the FIA sought, via the OWG, to clean up the body furniture along the sidepods, but Ferrari was one team that was quick to exploit a loophole that allowed upright winglets at the leading edge. Other teams would soon follow.

Above right: 2007 Renault R27 rear sidepod-mounted winglet. (sutton-images.com)

Right: 2007 Toyota TF107 rear sidepod-mounted winglet. (sutton-images.com)

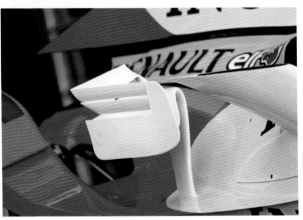

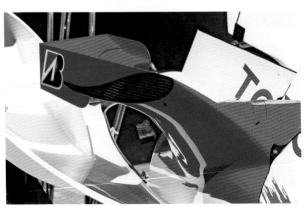

Above: 2009 Renault R29 front sidepod-mounted vane. (sutton-images.com)

Left: 2009 Ferrari F60 front sidepod/undertray-mounted mirror mounting/vane. (sutton-images.com)

Below: Renault's 2006 R26 made full use of its low sidepods and sweeping scallops to clean up the airflow around the rear tyres. (sutton-images.com)

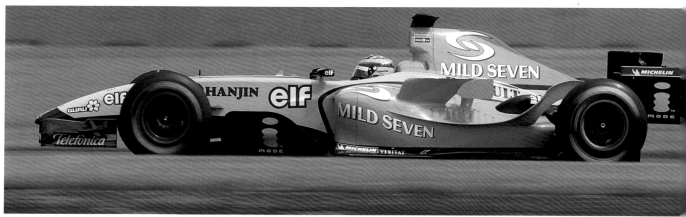

Rear wheel scallops

These are the shaped sections ahead of the rear tyres, where the 'Coke bottle' effect begins as the bodywork sweeps in. Their purpose is to help clean up the airflow and to influence it around the rear tyres to maximise the efficiency of the diffuser.

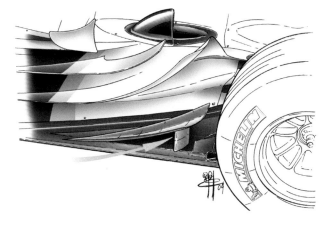

Williams adopted a series of rear wheel scallops on the 2004 FW26. The lower scallop was added to increase the speed of the air ahead of the rear tyres. (Piola)

2009 Ferrari F60 diffuser. Spanish GP. (sutton-images.com)

2009 Brawn BGP001 diffuser. Turkish GP. (sutton-images.com)

Diffuser

This is the upcurved section of the undertray that allows the restricted air beneath the car to open and spill out at the rear. The regulations do not permit the diffuser to extend beyond the rear axle line, as it used to in the early '90s, but it still accounts for almost 50% of the car's total downforce and is a key element, as it affects the whole pressure distribution beneath the car.

Rear wing

Prior to 2004 the rear wing generated some 33% of a Formula 1 car's downforce. This could be as much as 1,000kg, meaning that a car could carry another 16 unwanted passengers there too, assuming they could all fit on... However, for 2004 the FIA banned multi-element rear wings and instead mandated only two-element wings. This means a main plane, with a smaller plane to help generate more downforce without the drag penalty a larger single main plane might create.

McLaren introduced an unusual droop shape to its rear wing in Austria in 2003; inset is detail of the front wing endplate. (Piola)

Below left: Ferrari was alleged to be running flexible or 'inflatable' rear wing components at the start of the 2006 season on its controversial F248 which Michael Schumacher used to win at San Marino and Nürburgring. The Ferrari and BMW rear wings attracted great attention from rival designers, but were initially deemed kosher by the FIA. The gap between the upper elements allegedly closed up under load. (LAT)

Below: The rear wing on Toyota's 2006 TF106 has a separator mounted between the upper and lower elements to prevent the gap between them from closing up. (Toyota)

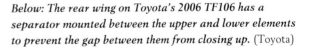

Below: 2007 BMW-Sauber F1.07 Monaco rear wing details. (BMW AG)

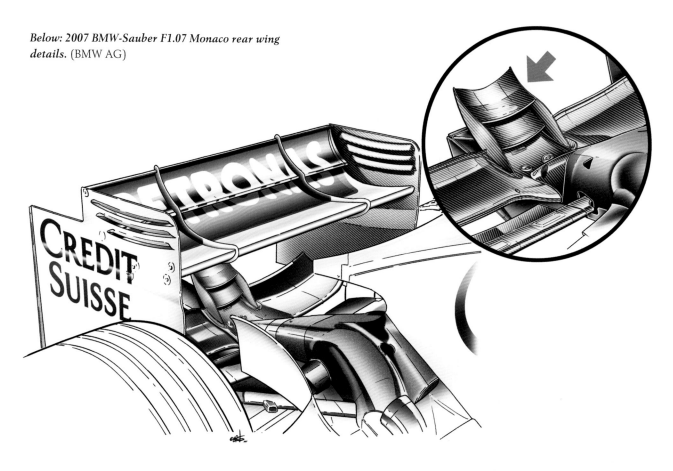

Right: 2009 BMW-Sauber F1.09 Turkish GP rear wing details. (sutton-images.com)

Right: 2009 McLaren MP4-24 Australian GP rear wing details. (sutton-images.com)

Gurney flaps

The Gurney flap is a small and very simple device that can have a major effect. Named after legendary American Formula 1 pilot Dan Gurney, after he and driver Bobby Unser developed it for the Gurney Eagles that raced at Indianapolis in the '70s, it comprises a simple strip of metal with a 90° angle. This is fitted to the trailing edge of a wing, front or rear, and forms an extra flick-up which can generate significant additional downforce on circuits where plenty is required.

Wheels

The wheels on a Formula 1 car have always created a drag problem. They account for more than a third of the car's total drag. There is, though, nothing anyone can do about that as enclosed bodywork is not permitted in Formula 1.

This arrangement of wing elements shows high and low pressure areas, and the Gurney flap, which is the lip on the trailing edge of the second element. (Piola)

2009 McLaren MP4-24 front wheel spinner detail.
(sutton-images.com)

Chapter 2

Aerodynamics II
Wind of change

Formula 1 is an insular, self-protective society in which teams will never agree with one another and nobody works for the good of the sport. Right? Well, not quite. At a time of further controversy involving the rule-makers, the story of how the regulation proposals were generated for 2009's new breed of overtaking cars is a heartening tale of engineering commonsense and mutual effort leading the sport to an exciting new horizon.

It all began with a meeting of the Technical Working Group in the autumn of 2006, to which all teams sent along their technical directors, a senior engineer and an aerodynamicist. There were thus 25 opinions to be heard (Prodrive was at this stage still intent on joining in for 2008 and Super Aguri was still running), and the meeting took two hours and, not surprisingly, made little significant progress. One party wanted changes made to the diffuser to slow cars down, another to the barge boards. Or the tyres. Or the front wing. Everyone had a different point.

Then chairman Charlie Whiting came up with a stroke of genius, and decided instead that they would cut straight to the chase by calling for a representative apiece from the top three teams of that moment: Ferrari, Renault and McLaren. Each could nominate its representative, and thus Pat Symonds from Renault, Rory Byrne from Ferrari and Paddy Lowe from McLaren, all of them highly experienced and respected operators, were selected to outline the key areas for investigation. They would operate as a sub-committee known as the Overtaking Working Group.

One observation was that, while overtaking wasn't particularly worse than it had ever been over the last 20 years – despite poor races in places such as Monaco and Hungaroring – circuit design was a bigger factor in the lack of it than car design. Yet the onus was always on the teams to change their cars, which manifestly was unfair.

'Valencia,' OWG member Rory Byrne pointed out, 'was a brand new circuit, yet where was the overtaking there?'

The strongest feeling, however, was that overtaking should not be easy. Nobody wanted the sort of syndrome that can spoil basketball, where goals every few seconds tend to dilute the overall impact of a game.

'Great overtaking,' Lowe suggested, 'is appreciated most where the guy has really worked for it. My personal favourite – ever – was when Mika Häkkinen caught and passed Michael Schumacher at Spa in 2000 as both of them overtook on either side of Ricardo Zonta going up the hill to Les Combes.'

The OWG had something to investigate already, after Max Mosley had hired former Simtek and Renault engineer Nick Wirth to come up with a proposal for an F1 design in which the aerodynamic turbulence in its slipstream was lowered dramatically, thus in theory facilitating more overtaking. The result was the CDG wing of 2005, created in conjunction with AMD's computational fluid dynamics program. That was intended to be incorporated into the rules for 2008.

Opposite: The 2009 season ushered in new-look cars – in this instance Nico Rosberg's Williams, Robert Kubica's BMW and Fernando Alonso's Renault – with much wider front wings and much smaller rears. (Getty Images)

The teams, however, had serious misgivings about the benefits claimed for the CDG wing, and lacked confidence in the research that had gone into it. The TWG had already been exploring, via what was then the Grand Prix Manufacturers' Association (GPMA, now FOTA), other avenues of research when the OWG was formed. This work had been carried out by the Italian company Fondtech, an offshoot of Fondmetal Technologies run by former Tyrrell aerodynamicist Jean-Claude Migeot. That had shown that CDG was flawed, and that other possible changes offered better opportunities.

This was a necessarily short programme, but the team principals met in September 2006 to confirm the basic approach for the 2008 rules. It would be a case of the CDG wing, or whatever set of proposals the GPMA came up with…

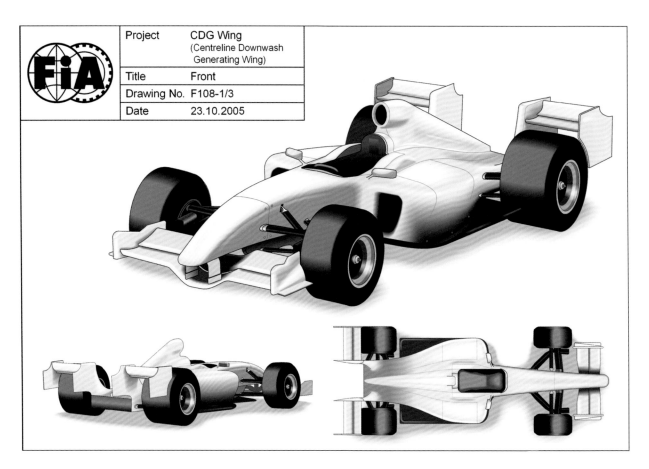

	Project	CDG Wing (Centreline Downwash Generating Wing)
FiA	Title	Front
	Drawing No.	F108-1/3
	Date	23.10.2005

The FIA's proposed CDG rear wing concept, first mooted in the summer of 2005 and originally proposed for introduction in 2008. (FIA)

Since the lack of confidence in CDG was so widespread, it was agreed with the FIA to defer introduction of the new aerodynamic rules until 2009 and that research should be accelerated significantly.

The first meeting of the OWG was in January 2007 in Nice, with subsequent meetings in Oxford and at Fondtech's base in Palosco, Italy.

A basic research budget of half a million euros had been created after Symonds persuaded each of the 12 team principals to kick in a share, starting with Flavio Briatore at Renault. It was also agreed to continue with Fondtech.

The first step was to define two essential elements of the research: the downforce targets; and the character of aerodynamics that was required to improve overtaking.

That required the three teams to adopt blind data; each provided relevant data to Whiting, who then averaged it out to provide the OWG and Fondtech with the targets they needed. The plan at this stage was to make the current cars (2006 vintage) five seconds

per lap slower. That had to factor in technological progress in the intervening years and slick tyres, which were due to make their comeback in 2009 and would increase mechanical grip by between 1.5 and 2 seconds a lap. This meant slowing the cars down significantly via changes to their aerodynamics.

Once this preliminary number-crunching had been done, the aim became to reduce downforce by 50% while retaining similar drag coefficients to the 2006 car. Lowe, Byrne and Symonds wanted the same 2006 free-stream drag (*ie* normal car not in wake) for base lap time performance.

One of the crucial factors at this time was the availability of McLaren's highly advanced simulator, which was used to baseline aerodynamic performance parameters with Pedro de la Rosa driving the 'test' car. The key element here was to determine what aerodynamic characteristics were required.

The Spaniard drove various sets of laps of the old Barcelona layout as experimental changes were compared to baseline laps, and when these were all overlaid it was determined that in order to be able to overtake the 'other' car going into Turn One, which was deemed to be the easiest place to do it, he would need to be two seconds a lap quicker. Halving the downforce brought that advantage requirement down to 1.5s.

The next step was to seek and apply to this 'model' the means of maintaining the balance of the following car and halving its loss of balance in the preceding car's wake. That resulted in the 'overtaking advantage' being reduced to a second. Symonds, Lowe and Byrne agreed that was a reasonable point to reach.

All three also realised that they could not solve the overtaking problem overnight, and agreed that the 'overtaking advantage' target was not zero. It was the basketball thing all over again.

Prior to 2009, when one car got within a few lengths of another it immediately began to lose around 40% of its frontal downforce in the dirty air, which resulted in crippling understeer that frustrated overtaking attempts. Now that figure had been reduced to 20% as the 'overtaking advantage' figure fell to one second. While investigating the 'drag effect in wake' factor, Byrne, Lowe and Symonds found that drag reduction in the wake (such as historically has been considered vital for overtaking) was not a significant factor in helping Pedro to overtake. The two crucial aspects were: reduce the amount of lost downforce (*ie* halve the loss from 40% to 20% when 1.5 car lengths behind), and secondly, maintain the balance in the wake (rather than generating gross understeer). As an interesting aside, they found that oversteer in the wake was disastrous.

Much attention was paid to de la Rosa's subjective view after his laps in the simulator. He would try a configuration, and report: 'Yes, with the car this way I can stay with the one in front and attack. I don't have the classic problem through the last corner on to the main straight, and if the guy ahead makes a mistake I am in a better position to take advantage.'

Once this basic data had been accumulated, the next stage was to ask Fondtech to devise means by which the desired changes might be achieved. Ferrari provided baseline data for the two models that Fondtech ran in tandem in its 25% moving ground wind tunnel. They in turn had drawn on an experiment by Ferrari at Monza in 2004, when it ran two cars in tandem round the *autodromo*. This full-scale Ferrari data was used to validate the twin model behaviour in the tunnel, and in turn to validate the entire experimental technique. This was a very important step that justified the use of the wind tunnel rather than CFD.

Byrne did a lot of hands-on work at this point in a series of sessions between March and August 2007, and given the limitations on time, technology and budget it was felt that the OWG did a thorough job, as all sorts of ideas were investigated.

The final configuration pretty much hit its targets though baseline drag fell by 10%.

The next step was to feed the actual data back into McLaren's simulator and to compare it with the original baseline model. De la Rosa was immediately able to confirm the benefits in terms of improved chances to overtake.

The OWG presented its proposals to the TWG early in October 2007, and all of the teams agreed to them.

'It was expected that they would,' Lowe says, 'but teams are naturally suspicious about things they have not directly been involved in, especially when their competitors have been dealing with them.'

The other teams had been kept up to speed with developments, but while they were invited to comment via email they were not invited to meetings. Whiting's rule of keep it tight, which had been responsible for so much progress being made in such a short timescale, remained sacrosanct.

The result was an intensive scientific quantification of the inherent aero problems that frustrate overtaking, invested with precise numbers. It was not the usual suck-it-and-see process that, in the past decade, had generally resulted in regulation changes that had precisely the opposite effect to that which was intended. 'Almost all of the attempts to reduce downforce in the recent past have been retrograde in terms of overtaking possibilities and wake behaviour,' Lowe observed. 'If we had wanted to make overtaking chances worse, that's what we would have come up with…'

One of the key factors to emerge from the OWG's empirical research was that the reliance placed by Max Mosley and Wirth on CFD as a tool for research was flawed. The group agreed early on that while CFD was very interesting it was not yet ready for this kind of work, hence the faith it placed in the wind tunnel. It was not possible to use CFD to study unstable behaviour of the air behind a car, hence the reliance on tried and trusted methods. Having used McLaren's state-of-the-art simulator, the OWG and Fondtech were able to optimise their wind tunnel investigations. The whole secret to the new regulations was to study that airflow behind the car.

Other past studies of aerodynamic behaviour, notably by the FIA's Peter Wright in conjunction with Tony Purnell, were intended to look at what characteristics would help overtaking by answering questions such as: is drag reduction in the wake useful? The OWG used the McLaren simulator to test and answer such questions. That proved a far more flexible tool that represented some 30 man/years of development, used a real driver (Pedro), and hence provided, without any disrespect being intended, answers that were far superior to any simulation run on a laptop.

And there was a critical imperative over and above the intention to improve overtaking, and therefore the spectacle of the sport: Mosley had retained CDG as part of the 2009 rule proposals, just to make sure he had the necessary leverage to ensure that a viable alternative was created. Small wonder that the OWG's ideas were accepted with only minor grumbling.

Once the proposals made by Byrne, Lowe and Symonds had been accepted by all of the teams, and put forward to the FIA, things began to move and the 2009 F1 car finally took shape.

'We were able to show that we had been completely objective,' Lowe said. 'Getting the three top teams to work so closely together was a real first.'

The fundamental concern was the wake behind a car travelling at speed. How was it created, and how did a following car behave in it?

One aspect of the proposal was to remove what Lowe described as 'all the rubbish' from the cars. The barge boards, the radiator air extraction chimneys,

A CFD illustration comparing the airflow over a 'standard' rear wing (above) with that over the proposed CDG wing (below). (FIA)

the little flick-ups, McLaren's airbox-mounted Viking horns, and all of the different types of appendages atop the nose or scuttle: Honda's elephant ears and gull wings, Toyota's fins, McLaren's and BMW's nose horns, strakes atop the sidepods... While these were undoubtedly of interest, the idea was to make the 2009 cars smooth between the axles, with fewer drag-inducing appendages.

One of the OWG's most significant findings was that the rear wing is a very important device in characterising the wake that a car generates.

'You think that upwash from the rear wing is bad,' Lowe said. 'But actually the front wing endplates generate very strong vortexes. The upwash is strong, but the inwash at ground level is driven by these swells from the front wing. That inwash brings new high-energy air in at ground level. If you took the rear wing off altogether you would lose that effect but it would be worse.'

Nick Wirth's CFD-generated CDG rear wing eliminated the central section altogether, effectively comprising instead two separate rear wings, to eliminate that upwash, but the OWG argues that is why it simply didn't work. The upwash is not necessarily a bad thing, so long as the new-energy air refreshes the wake and eliminates some of its effects.

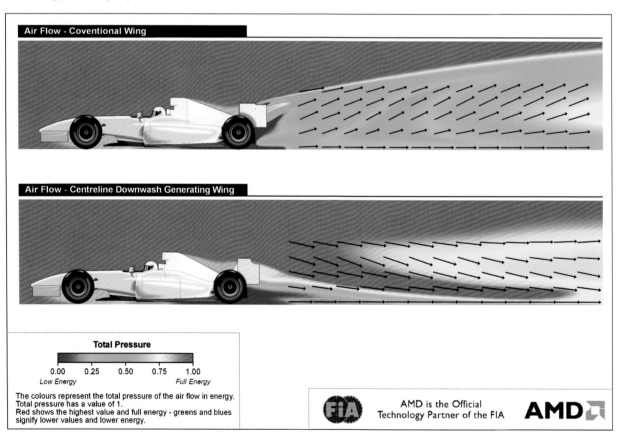

Air Flow - Coventional Wing

Air Flow - Centreline Downwash Generating Wing

Total Pressure

| 0.00 | 0.25 | 0.50 | 0.75 | 1.00 |

Low Energy   Full Energy

The colours represent the total pressure of the air flow in energy.
Total pressure has a value of 1.
Red shows the highest value and full energy - greens and blues signify lower values and lower energy.

AMD is the Official
Technology Partner of the FIA

Right and below: Detail of the adjustable front wing on the 2009 Brawn BGP001, with the covers in place (below), and with the covers removed to show the actuator and linkage (right). (sutton-images.com)

Changes to the underfloor height also exerted a key influence as part of the rear wing package that would generate the level of downforce required. Lots of different floor shapes were tried, and the OWG selected the one that helped to generate the best wake pattern. The diffuser section was also mounted further back to see the benefit of the inwash.

Above: Close racing at the 2009 Monaco GP between Lewis Hamilton's McLaren and Nick Heidfeld's BMW-Sauber demonstrates the changes devised by the OWG. (LAT)

2009 Red Bull RB5 diffuser. Bahrain GP.
(sutton-images.com)

The front wing was mounted lower and, at 1,800mm, was 400mm wider than 2008's. The key here was that the aerodynamic profile of the central section was now fixed so that it remained neutral and would not generate downforce. Lowering the wing's mounting position was good for generating that upwash-influencing ground-level inwash, and making the wing wider meant that it was now the part of the car that got the good air first. The middle section was the last bit to see the upwash from the car in front and the wider edges and disabled centre section helped to maintain the downforce and thus to manage the following car's balance better while it was running in a wake from the car in front.

Another crucial development of the front wing, however, was to allow the front flap to be adjustable while the car was in motion, albeit only to plus or minus 3°.

'The problem comes if the car oversteers in another's wake,' Lowe explained. 'That would be a complete disaster. The driver of that car is going to fall off! We were worried that we were not going to

be able to control that, so we went for the adjustable front flap.'

'To be honest,' Felipe Massa said in Bahrain in 2009, 'I don't think the adjustable wings do anything for overtaking. I use mine for setting up the car. Increasing the angle while following another car increases the downforce, but then you run into the other car's turbulent wake and that can give you big oversteer. It's actually much easier to lose the rear end of the car now.'

The drivers are only allowed to change the angle twice a lap, if necessary to reduce frontal downforce to prevent oversteer in the wake, or else to trim out any remaining understeer if that's how the car behaves.

This is all controlled by the standard electronic control unit (ECU), so nobody will be able to adjust their front wing more than twice each lap. Effectively that will also oblige the driver to choose his overtaking opportunity carefully on any given lap, and is in keeping with the OWG's desire that overtaking should not become too easy.

When the new rules came into force, the so-called two-tier or double-decker diffusers on the Brawn, Toyota and Williams cars immediately caused a furore, not least when the FIA International Court of Appeal

2009 Brawn BGP001 diffuser. Bahrain GP.
(sutton-images.com)

ruled them legal and obliged the other seven teams to adopt similar configurations.

The difference of interpretation revolved around whether the surfaces of the step in the diffuser and the reference planes should be considered as one (which was what protesters Ferrari, Renault, Red Bull and BMW-Sauber believed), or separately (as Brawn, Williams and Toyota believed). The latter's 'clever' interpretation was that an outlet or hole in the diffuser, which increased the speed of the airflow and enhanced efficiency, was simply a gap between two individual surfaces, thus making it legal. That was the view that the FIA's Charlie Whiting took all along, and which the Court of Appeal ratified in April 2009.

Red Bull team principal Christian Horner echoed most sentiments when he said in China, the first race after the hearing: 'It's no coincidence that seven teams didn't go down the double diffuser route. A lot of work was done in the Overtaking Working Group and within the regulations there is a spirit or essence of what the regulations are set to achieve. Certainly the precedent of holes in the floor, from our perspective, was deemed to be illegal, so that's why we chose the route that we did to protect the cars. We feel that we had a fair appeal hearing, where the facts were presented from either side and I think the bottom line is that there was a lot of ambiguity within the regulations and you can call it a clever interpretation, if you like, that the three teams took.

'We had no choice but to develop our own solution which is time and money and a big development channel that becomes open, because the underbody of the car is the most powerful aerodynamic device on the car.'

The last word should belong to Brawn team owner Ross Brawn. It is well documented that at a teams' meeting back in March 2008 he had suggested that downforce targets for 2009 should be reined in, as it was likely they would be exceeded if the diffuser design his engineers envisaged (but which, naturally, he did not reveal) was permitted; and that Renault's Pat Symonds was among those who accused him of scaremongering. In any case, the diffuser was not the single secret of the Brawn's speed.

'When we came up with the concept, we didn't think it was radical,' Brawn said in his quiet, owlish manner. 'We thought it was clever, but it wasn't a *Eureka!* moment. It was no surprise to us that other teams had it at the beginning of the season. In fact, the surprise was that there were not more.'

Chapter 3

Chassis
Fine bridgework

If the engine is the heart of a car, the chassis is the body. Traditionally it is the part that gives the car its name. In the case of Eddie Jordan's cars, for example, which in their time used Ford, Hart, Peugeot, Mugen-Honda and Honda engines, the car was called a Jordan because Jordan Grand Prix designed and manufactured the chassis. Even that changed for 2006 when, having been taken over by Alex Schnaider of Midland in 2005, the team and car name was changed to Midland.

The modern chassis is of unitary or monocoque construction, which means that it is effectively one piece, though in reality it is many pieces bonded together to form that single entity. Its primary purpose is to act as a bridge that connects all of the car's other components. It is mounting point for the engine and transmission, the suspension and steering, and all of the aerodynamic components. Its other great function is to house and protect the driver, which is why it is also known as a survival cell.

If the chassis is to perform these functions it must be extremely strong and robust, with very high torsional rigidity. If it isn't, all of the loads that the suspension feeds into it will not be relayed faithfully to the driver, and in turn he will be unable to relay them to the team. There are few things worse than a flexing chassis for misleading engineers into chasing other reasons for a car being off the pace.

The development of the carbon-fibre composite monocoque chassis in 1980/81, by John Barnard and his team at McLaren, and Colin Chapman at Lotus, revolutionised chassis manufacture. Composites took chassis strength another giant leap forwards from the strong honeycomb aluminium structures that had superseded Chapman's original sheet aluminium 'tub', which had itself supplanted the welded tube spaceframe when it first appeared in 1962. But there was another valuable advantage; composites eliminated the need for complex internal strengthening box structures, and this facilitated narrower monocoques. This proved very timely, as aerodynamic considerations required new shapes and the modular construction that composites permitted. Now, instead of designing cars from the inside out, designers started to design from the outside in. A team's aerodynamicists could outline the optimum shape they required, and it was then up to the chassis and engine designers to package all the necessary equipment within that smooth outer shell.

One of the other most significant influences is the size of the fuel tank. In 2003 the regulations were changed at very late notice to incorporate single-lap qualifying and the rule that forced teams to start the race on the fuel load with which they had qualified. The change came too late for cars to be re-optimised, so all of the teams went into 2004 with new cars. 'Obviously that was one of the first things we reviewed on the F2004,' Ferrari chief designer Rory Byrne admitted. 'That changed our thinking and our approach.'

The other great aspect of composites is that it is easier to repeat the production process faithfully, be it in chassis manufacture of the production of smaller components such as wings. Penske Cars' composites guru Don Berrisford lays a few carbon-fibre myths to rest. 'It actually improves with age, because the resins harden. And although you maybe don't specify gauges, like you did with aluminium in the old days, you can specify lay-up, thickness and direction. In CART we and Lola worked out the composite side of the regulations in conjunction with Kirk Russell from CART. Records are mandatory for each chassis. Drawings, curing times etc. Just like aircraft. It's actually a bit like building a spaceframe, you know. You can localise strength then fill in bits here and there.'

Berrisford also liked the repeatability. 'In the old days you could make a set of eight aluminium wings, and there'd be 40% difference between the best and the worst. Then we tried carbon-fibre and from

Opposite: By the 21st century the Formula One car was a complex carbon-fibre composite missile of immense strength and great structural rigidity and integrity. This is the 2009 Toyota TF109. (Toyota)

The tubular spaceframe chassis had largely been superseded by 1964, and the majority of teams relied on the bathtub-shaped aluminium monocoque which has greater strength for superior lightness and rigidity. (sutton-images.com)

then on wings have always been carbon-fibre. The drivers immediately found that the cars would repeat. Whatever you dialled in to one chassis would stay the same when you dialled it into another.'

These new design and construction philosophies did not alter the fundamental requirements of the process: commonsense, experience, knowledge and flair mixed with intelligence, and clear and logical thinking. But now methodology and the materials and the production process have evolved. By its very nature, the modern Formula 1 car is a complex confection that requires an army of people to create it.

When it began construction of its new R24 challenger for 2004, Renault began the work in late October 2003, less than two weeks after the final race of the season. The same thing happened with the R26 after the team won the 2005 championship with the R25.

Producing a new carbon-fibre monocoque does not happen automatically once its design has been finalised on the drawing office computers. The production phase cannot afford to leave anything to chance, and the technology used in the workshops at Renault's Enstone headquarters is cutting edge. The first stage of the process involves producing upper and lower moulds which will enable the team, after the laying up of the laminates, to produce the first chassis.

'The car begins life in the form of 50mm-thick epoxy sheets,' explains Colin Watts, composites manager at Enstone. The drawing office issues a very detailed plan which is then realised in the form of resin patterns that reproduce the form of the part to be manufactured. 'The technicians cut the epoxy by hand according to the designs provided, and place the sheets side by side. They are then glued together, with two metal stems running through them vertically to ensure they remain fixed in place. This whole assembly is placed in a big plastic bag, we extract the air, and then cook it in the autoclave at a pressure of 100psi. When the resin has completed this process, the whole assembly is as solid as a rock.'

By this stage, a little imagination allows the shape of the monocoque to be determined, in its three separate

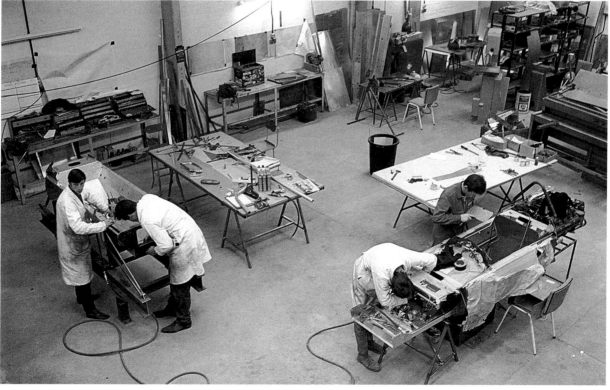

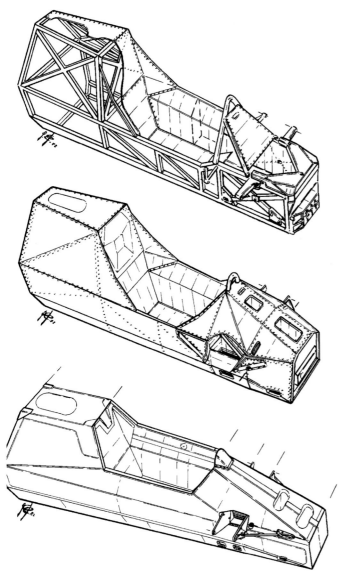

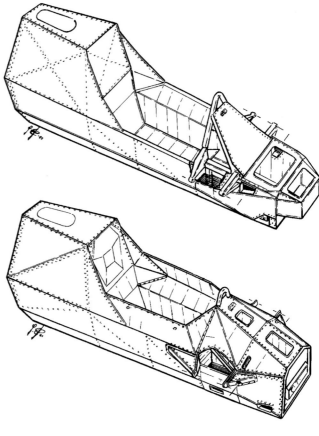

Ferrari's 126C and 126C2 chassis were a combination of very old and relatively new in 1981, when a basic spaceframe was clad in aluminium panels. By the mid-'70s most teams favoured the by now conventional fully clad aluminium monocoque chassis, and by the end of the decade aluminium honeycomb had also been incorporated. (Piola)

parts: upper left and right, and the lower half.

The second stage of the process is the machining. 'Two five-axis machines come into play,' explains operations director John Mardle. These machines work to a precision tolerance of 0.05mm, and programming the chassis machining alone requires 40 hours' work. 'They're computer-controlled, and grind and mill the epoxy assembly. At this stage, the main aim is to rough out the shape. Then, bit by bit, the tools used become more and more delicate, until the result is almost perfect. After 160 hours' work, what at the beginning of the process was a rough staircase of piled-up epoxy sheets has become a 90% accurate representation of the final result.'

Now it is time for the elbow grease. The moulds for the monocoque are produced from these final patterns, so the surfaces need to be millimetre perfect: the tiniest defect would be replicated on the six chassis produced during the year, and could cause a serious delay in the build of the new car. 'When we receive the finished resin assembly, we then need to prepare it for taking the moulds,' explains Watts. 'We use a very fine sandpaper to remove the last traces of the machining, paint the part black and then apply a high-shine polish. For some parts, however, we coat the resin in a very low-friction material instead. A little like you find on non-stick frying pans!'

At this point, the three parts of the monocoque are ready for the moulds to be taken, which is another precision job. By the time the process reaches the stage of taking moulds, the team possesses a chassis pattern accurate to 0.05mm. 'The following stage is much more complicated, as we need to decide how the moulds will be produced,' says Watts. 'Some large components, or those with very complex surfaces, for example, require more than one section mould.'

2008 Renault R28 monocoque. Malaysian GP.
(sutton-images.com)

A monocoque, for example, requires six different sections to produce the two moulds: four for the upper and two for the lower.

Once the pattern has been finished, painted and covered with a mould release agent, the Renault engineers cover each surface with sheets of paper cut to produce templates. These will then serve as patterns for the composites department in order that identical sheets of carbon can be cut. To the uninitiated, the raw carbon-fibre has the consistency of liquorice. 'The material we use is a type of carbon-fibre that is produced in big sheets. They are stored frozen, at a temperature of –18°C. The material includes a lot of resin to ensure that the surfaces of the moulds are completely smooth.' These cut pieces of carbon are then placed carefully on the resin pattern.

Once the sheets of carbon have been put in place, the whole is then put into a large plastic bag, from which the air is subsequently extracted to form a vacuum. This assembly is then taken to the giant oven called an autoclave, where it is cured under high pressure, around 100psi. Nuts and bolts are inserted into each side of the mould, in order to ensure that they can be adjusted to perfection during the subsequent stages of the process. After they have cooled, the moulds are then carefully removed from the patterns. The resin

pattern now has no function, and is destroyed. As for the moulds, they are machined to sand off the sharp exterior edges. They are subsequently used throughout the season to produce new chassis. Renault produces two sets of moulds for each monocoque, allowing the team to produce multiple chassis in parallel.

In order to streamline the forthcoming build process and optimise reliability, Renault creates a full-scale chassis. Ian Pearce is in charge of sub-assembly operations, and oversees each stage of the process as the team builds full-scale facsimiles of the mechanical components that will eventually form the new car. 'We reproduce absolutely every element of the car apart from the wishbones, bodywork and fuel system. We use a variety of different materials: carbon-fibre, wood, metal and even stereolythographic resin models, which account for about half the parts. Each piece is a 100% accurate duplicate of the real thing.'

This process means the team doesn't have to use its first pukka monocoque for prototyping work, but can instead free it up to be prepared immediately for track testing. 'We build a mock-up for a whole host of reasons,' Pearce says. 'First of all, we need to

Via computer-aided manufacture a specific number of cross-sections are cut out and then placed together, end to end, to form the basic shape of the monocoque chassis. (Renault F1)

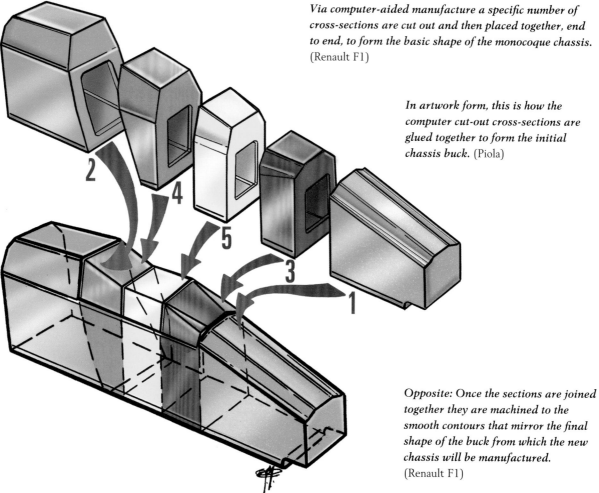

In artwork form, this is how the computer cut-out cross-sections are glued together to form the initial chassis buck. (Piola)

Opposite: Once the sections are joined together they are machined to the smooth contours that mirror the final shape of the buck from which the new chassis will be manufactured. (Renault F1)

know that all the components fit together perfectly. Once we've done that, we can cut all the cables and pipework to the right length. Components such as these often take a long time to manufacture and it's vital to make sure our measurements are accurate. There is so little physical space to accommodate all the parts that the manufacturing tolerances have to be incredibly precise.' The dummy monocoque comes from the same moulds that are used to build the race cars and are identical except that a different grade of carbon is used. It is easier to work with and thus saves a little time.

Once the dummy monocoque is ready it is placed on a four-sided flat bed to serve as a 'zero' reference point. All the subsequent drawings that emerge from the design department will be based around this. The most important thing is to get the lower part of the chassis ready. This is where the majority of components are housed because that optimises weight distribution. As parts arrive the team fits them together in turn. The second stage involves mounting the engine to the lower part of the monocoque. When the upper part

of the chassis is ready, the assemblers take care not to glue it to the lower half immediately. That way, they can take the monocoque apart whenever necessary to make sure that everything lines up correctly.

Despite all the cutting-edge technology used in Formula 1, measurements can sometimes be slightly wrong – albeit rarely. The use of a mock-up allows such problems to be eradicated as and when they occur. The drivers make use of the replica tub, too, to fine-tune the shape of their seat and its position within the cockpit. The team's chief mechanic also keeps a close eye on progress, to make sure that certain parts won't be too difficult to reach should they need to be replaced in a hurry during the course of a race weekend. The mock-up is usually ready about one month before the first race chassis. In the case of the Renault mock-up, however, it remains in service throughout the season so that development parts destined for the new car can be gauged for accuracy.

Once the moulds and templates have been produced, the production of the chassis proper begins in the operating theatre-like atmosphere of the composites department.

A Formula 1 chassis is not simply composed of one type of material: up to five different types go into producing the finished article, including carbon-fibre, resins, and aluminium honeycomb. The first step in cutting the carbon-fibre is to transfer the digitised files of each part to the Lectra cutting machines. Once this has happened, the software collects together all the

Opposite: Once the original buck has been fully prepared, female moulds are taken from it. The actual chassis will then be made from these (Renault F1)

Most modern monocoques are built using two female moulds, in which the two halves of the chassis are laid-up prior to being bonded together. (Piola)

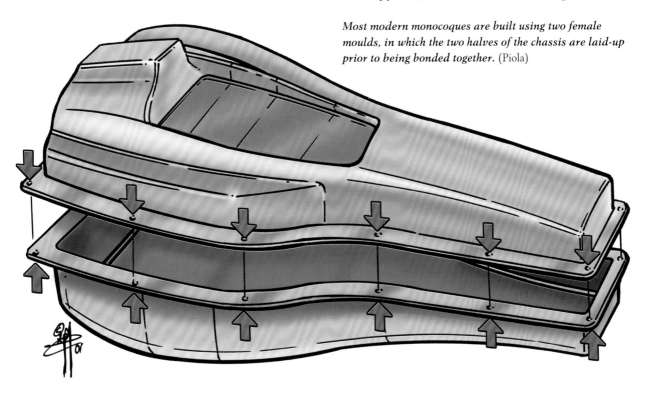

Above: Once the moulds have been produced, the meticulous laying-up of the chassis weave can commence within them. (Renault F1)

Below and right: At various stages during the laying up process, the carbon-fibre chassis is specially 'cooked' under pressure in one of these giant autoclaves. (sutton-images.com and Renault F1)

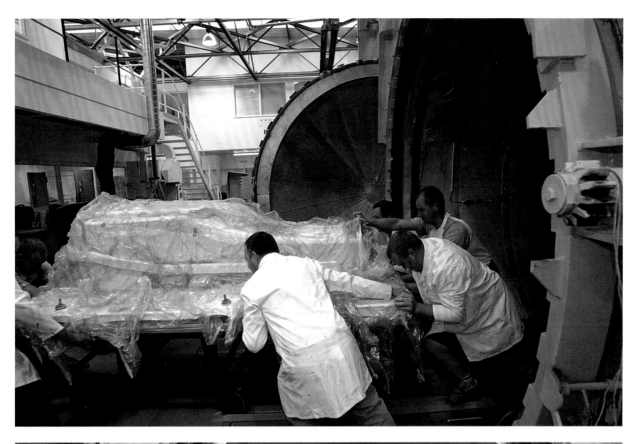

parts to be produced from a particular material, and organises them as efficiently as possible. One thing that can never be changed, though, is the orientation of material when it is cut: the fibres must run in a specific direction according to the forces the part is subjected to. The collection of parts is called a 'marker', and once this is ready the machine can begin cutting. For the upper part of the chassis, Renault cuts up to 500 different shapes which must then be laid up in the mould. Cutting all the markers for this part of the chassis takes between two and three hours.

The chassis itself is composed of three layers – the outer skin, the core and the inner skin – in a sandwich structure. The outer skin comprises between 150 and 200 plies, or cut shapes of carbon-fibre. The mould is assembled, and the procedure of laying up the plies begins according to the drawings received from the design office. Extremely careful attention is paid to the orientation of these pieces. Different types of carbon-fibre are applied in layers, and the amounts of material vary according to the location on the chassis: certain key areas, such as the engine mounts or the roll hoop, require more material to cope with the forces involved. During the preparation of the skins, the plies are cooked under pressure in the autoclaves in order to 'de-bulk' them, and squeeze the layers of

material together. Once the skin is finished, it is then cured in the autoclave before the core and inner skins are added.

Throughout the laying-up stage of chassis production, in the composites clean room, the autoclaves have a number of different uses. They come into play for what are termed 'de-bulks' and also the 'cure' itself. An autoclave is, essentially, a big pressurised oven in which the carbon-fibre is 'cooked'. Essentially, the construction of the chassis proceeds in stages, laying up the different cuts of carbon-fibre, and the autoclaves have a vital role to play at each stage. Parts are cooked at different temperatures and different pressures in a vacuum, to extract any air from the material. For every part that goes into the autoclaves, the process is the same: the carbon-fibre laid up in the mould must be covered in a breathable plastic layer, to allow the air to escape; this is then covered in a breather fabric, before being placed in a nylon bag which goes into the oven and has vacuum hoses attached to it.

The two principal processes with the autoclaves are the de-bulk and the cure. The de-bulk is used

The bare carbon-fibre composite monocoque chassis – even this two-seater – is an imposing piece of equipment, and can be lifted by one man. (sutton-images.com)

to compact and compress the material. The key is not to go as far as with a cure, which is designed to produce the finished, 'hard' material. With the de-bulk, therefore, lower temperatures are used to get the resin to the point where it flows and compacts the material down in the mould. For each skin of the chassis, two or three de-bulks might be necessary before the plies are ready for the cure. The latter is the process during which the carbon-fibre acquires its strength and stiffness. Typically, for the first cure of the chassis, it will go into the autoclave for three to four hours, at up to 180°C under a pressure of around 100psi. That pressure is then increased steadily as temperature rises, but the exact point at which this

is done is each team's closely-guarded secret, as it can realise a competitive advantage in the chassis' performance. Cures are run for the core and the inner skin as well, but at lower pressures.

Once the final cure has been completed, and the mould cracked apart to reveal the final part, the upper and lower chassis parts undergo final machining. The two halves are mounted in purpose-built jigs (in Renault's case on a Huron machine), and holes are machined through the carbon-fibre and into the various metal inserts for suspension pickups or engine mounts. Further work on a large JOBS machine allows detailing such as the obligatory camera mounting position, or areas around the fuel filler, to be completed, as well as

The FIA has introduced a mandatory template for the cockpit opening on all Formula One chassis, to ensure that drivers do not become so enclosed that they might not be able to evacuate it within the stipulated five seconds in the event of an accident. (Piola)

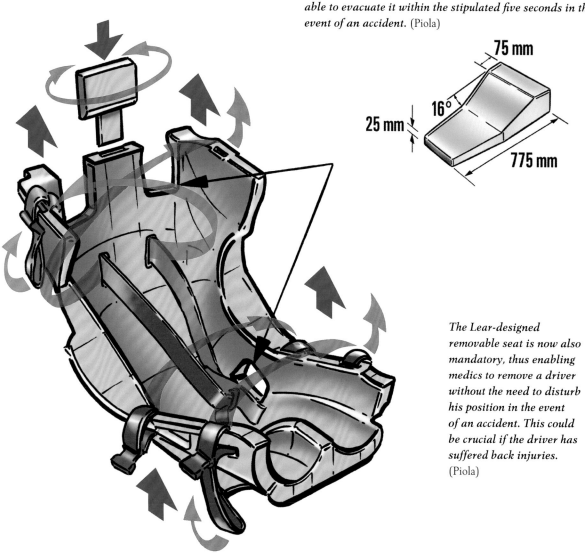

The Lear-designed removable seat is now also mandatory, thus enabling medics to remove a driver without the need to disturb his position in the event of an accident. This could be crucial if the driver has suffered back injuries. (Piola)

the internal profiles of the chassis. Once this has been done, the two halves are ready to be bonded together. The chassis is now virtually finished.

Machining the suspension pickup points and systems mounting points requires absolute accuracy so that the process can be repeated from chassis to chassis with 100% accuracy and confidence. It takes around three weeks on the prototype chassis, but about a week per chassis subsequently.

In designing and producing the chassis, designers must constantly balance the conflicting demands of weight and stiffness. The thicker the sandwich, the stiffer the chassis, but it is also heavier; a thinner core brings advantages in terms of weight, but will flex more. Controls are stringent: the sides of the chassis structure must be homologated with the FIA. Teams produce a sample of the chassis construction, which is then sent away and tested with an impact equivalent to having the nose of another car hit the chassis. Once this construction has passed the strength test, it is then frozen for the season.

During the winter, Renault's composites

A Jordan chassis, with the central fuselage still in carbon black, is readied for its mandatory FIA crash test.
(sutton-images.com)

department works night and day, literally, to produce the chassis. 'We have ten dedicated chassis laminators on day- and night-shifts,' explains Watts. 'We have two upper moulds and two lower moulds in the clean room at any one time, and lay up two chassis simultaneously.' Although the chassis may require the greatest manpower, it is actually an exception to how the composites department usually works. 'For almost all other components, a single technician will produce the entire part from start to finish. It is not the most efficient method, but our system is optimised for producing the best quality part. It improves consistency, and also gives the technicians a real pride in their work.'

As will be clear in all aspects of Formula 1 design and construction, that kind of attention to detail makes the difference.

It would be wrong to suggest that chassis design has stagnated, but the composite monocoque is now finely evolved. The last significant change to its specification came for 2008. After an unpleasant accident at the 2007 Australian GP in which David Coulthard's Red Bull speared across the cockpit of Alex Wurz's Williams, narrowly missing the Austrian's head, cockpit sides were raised 20mm and lengthened in order to enhance drivers' head protection.

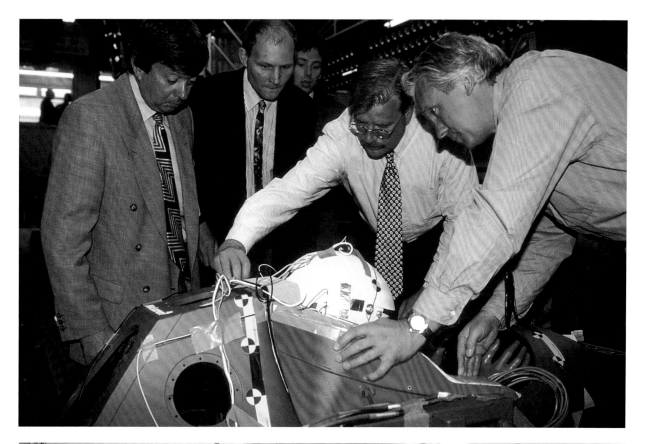

Not many of the men and women who manufacture these works of hi-tech art would ever want to witness the next stage, when a complete chassis is put through the FIA's mandatory crash tests (see pages 68–71), which are intended to provide the utmost means of safeguarding the drivers in the event of foreseeable accidents. Most are conducted, under FIA supervision, at the Cranfield Impact Centre in Bedfordshire, though overseas teams may specify more local sites

A group including Roland Bruynseraede, Gerhard Berger, Professor Sid Watkins and Charlie Whiting readies a fully-instrumented chassis for its crash test. (sutton-images.com)

of similar standard. They are rigorous in the extreme, but since they were introduced in 1985 they have been instrumental in saving lives and saving drivers from injury. They are one of the least-touted success stories of modern Formula 1 technology.

FIA Formula 1 structure crash testing – 1997 onwards

The mandatory chassis structure crash testing introduced by the FIA dates back to 1985, and consists of the following stringent tests:

TEST 1 – An impact test against a solid barrier (introduced 1985).
This is the head-on collision, the most nerve-wracking for the designer since failure can compromise the entire structure. The purpose is to ensure that the car can adequately protect the driver's ankles and legs.

Test structure: Nose box attached to a complete survival cell.

Impact speed: 12m per second.

Mass: 780kg.

Deformation: Limited to the nose box and no damage to the fixings of the extinguishers or seat belts. Driver's feet have to be at least 30cm from the front of the survival cell.

Max mean g: 25.

Conditions: Full fire extinguishers fitted. Fuel tank filled with water. Dummy, weighing 75kg, must be fitted with seat belts fastened. During the impact deceleration in the chest of the dummy must not exceed 60g for more than 3 milliseconds.

TEST 2 – A static load test on the top of the main roll structure (introduced 1991).
This is designed to assess the ability of the car to withstand inversion without its rollover hoop distorting or breaking under load.

Test structure: Main roll structure attached to a complete survival cell.

Test load: 72.08kN, which corresponds to a combined load of 57.39kN vertically, 42.08kN longitudinally and 11.48kN laterally.

Deformation: No greater than 50mm measured along the loading axis and no failure more than 100mm below the top of the structure measured vertically.

TEST 3 – A static load test on the side of the nose (introduced in 1990). Also known as the 'push-off test', this is intended to make sure that the nose, with its energy-absorbing deformable structure, remains intact during a glancing type of blow, as if the car has struck a barrier at a relatively shallow angle.

Test structure: Nose box attached to a complete survival cell.

Test load: 40kN at a point 55cm in front of the front wheel axis.

Time: Test load must be held for 30 seconds.

Deformation: No failure of the structure or of any attachment between the nose box and the survival cell.

Some idea of the unpleasantness of the nose-impact crash test can be gleaned from these photos, but there is no questioning the effectiveness of the FIA's safety campaign over the years.
(John Townsend)

Most cars use devices such as this horizontal shark's fin as the side-impact intrusion structure. This is from a Williams FW24. (Author)

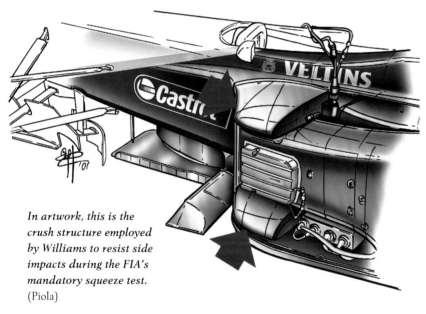

In artwork, this is the crush structure employed by Williams to resist side impacts during the FIA's mandatory squeeze test. (Piola)

in order that their weights may be compared. The first is weighed and all subsequent units must be within 5% of the initial weight.

Test load: 25kN on the first survival cell, 20kN on all the subsequent ones.

Test method: A pad measuring 10cm x 30cm is placed against both sides of the survival cell and the load applied.

Position: A vertical plane passing through a point midway between the front wheel axis and the front roll structure.

Time: Test load must be held for 30 seconds.

Deformation: No permanent deformation greater than 1mm after the load has been removed. Furthermore, on all subsequent survival cells the total displacement across the inner surfaces must be no greater than 120% of the displacement measured on the first survival cell at 20kN.

TEST 5 – A static load test on both sides of the survival cell (introduced in 1988). This is another part of the 'squeeze test', carried out at driver hip level.

Test structure: Every complete survival cell. All survival cells must be produced in an identical condition in order that their weights may be compared. The first is weighed and all subsequent units must be within 5% of the initial weight.

Test load: 30kN.

Test method: A pad measuring 20cm diameter is placed against both sides of the survival cell and the load applied.

TEST 4 – A static load test on both sides of the survival cell (introduced in 1992). This is the 'crush' or 'squeeze test', and is designed to ensure that the monocoque chassis will provide adequate protection against side impact. The tests are carried out at various points along the length of the chassis. (Gary Anderson tells the story of Jordan mechanics driving to Silverstone one morning coming across a damaged racing car monocoque lying in a hedge. It was F1 sized, and it transpired that it was the Life – née First – chassis from 1990 which, having failed its crush test, had simply been discarded!)

Test structure: Every complete survival cell. All survival cells must be produced in an identical condition

The FIA's stringent crash test rules have undoubtedly saved many lives. (Piola)

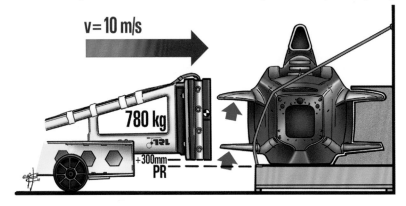

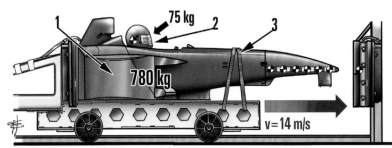

Position: A vertical plane passing through the anchorage point of the lap seat belts.

Time deformation: Test load must be held for 30 seconds.

Deformation: Maximum displacement of 20mm and no permanent deformation greater than 1mm after the load has been removed.

TEST 6 – A static load test on both sides of the survival cell (introduced in 1988). This is another part of the 'squeeze test.'

Test structure: Every complete survival cell. All survival cells must be produced in an identical condition in order that their weights may be compared. The first is weighed and all subsequent units must be within 5% of the initial weight.

Test load: 25kN on the first survival cell, 20kN on all subsequent ones.

Test method: A pad measuring 10cm x 30cm is placed against both sides of the survival cell and the load applied.

Position: A vertical plane passing through the centre of area of the fuel tank side.

Time: Test load must be held for 30 seconds.

Deformation: No permanent deformation greater than 1mm after the load has been removed. Furthermore, on all subsequent survival cells the total displacement across the inner surfaces must be no greater than 120% of the displacement measured on the first survival cell at 20kN.

TEST 7 – A static load on both sides of the survival cell (introduced in 1991). This is another part of the 'squeeze test', which assesses the ability of the chassis to withstand an impact on the underside.

Test structure: Every complete survival cell. All survival cells must be produced in an identical condition in order that their weights may be compared. The first is weighed and all subsequent units must be within 5% of the initial weight.

Test load: 12.5kN on the first survival cell, 10kN on all subsequent ones.

Test method: A pad measuring 20cm in diameter is placed against the underside of the fuel tank floor and the load applied.

Position: A vertical plane passing through the centre of the area of the fuel tank floor.

Time: Test load must be held for 30 seconds.

Deformation: No permanent deformation greater than 0.5mm after the load has been removed. Furthermore, on all subsequent survival cells the total displacement across the inner surfaces must be no greater than 120% of the displacement measured on the first survival cell at 10kN.

TEST 8 – A static load test on both sides of the survival cell (introduced in 1991). This is another part of the 'squeeze test', carried out at the front bulkhead level.

Test structure: Every complete survival cell.

Test load: 20kN.

Test method: A pad measuring 10cm x 30cm is placed against both sides of the survival cell and the load applied.

Position: A vertical plane passing through the front wheel axis.

Time: Test load must be held for 30 seconds.

Deformation: No structural failure of the inner skins of the survival cell.

TEST 9 – A static load test on both sides of the survival cell (introduced in 1991). This is another part of the 'squeeze test'.

Test structure: Every complete survival cell.

Test load: 20kN.

Test method: A pad measuring 10cm x 30cm is placed against both sides of the survival cell and the load applied.

Position: A vertical plane passing through the front wheel axis and the seat belt lap strap fixings.

Time: Test load must be held for 30 seconds.

Deformation: No structural failure of the inner skins of the survival cell.

TEST 10 – An impact test against a solid barrier (introduced in 1995 and upgraded for 1998). This is designed to assess ability to withstand side impacts.

Test structure: Side impact absorbing structure attached to both sides of a complete survival cell.

Test speed: 7m/s.

Mass: 780kg.

Position: 525mm forward of the rear edge of the cockpit entry template.

Deformation: All deformation must be limited to the impact absorbing structure. No damage to the survival cell is permissible.

Average deceleration must not exceed 10g.

TEST 11 – A static load test on each side of the cockpit rim (introduced in 1996). Another 'squeeze test', to assess integrity of the cockpit opening.

Test structure: All survival cells must be produced in an identical condition in order that their weights may be compared. The first is weighed and all subsequent units must be within 5% of the initial weight.

Test load: 10kN on the first survival cell, 8kN on all subsequent ones.

Test method: A pad measuring 10cm in diameter is placed against each side of the cockpit rim.

Position: 200mm forward of the rear edge of the cockpit entry template.

Time: Test load must be held for 30 seconds.

Deformation: No permanent deformation greater than 1mm after the load has been removed. Furthermore, on all subsequent survival cells the

total displacement across the inner surfaces must be no greater than 120% of the displacement measured on the first survival cell at 8kN.

TEST 12 – An impact test against a solid barrier (introduced in 1997). The rear-end equivalent of the head-on crash test.

Test structure: Rear impact absorbing structure attached to the gearbox.

Impact speed: 12m per second.

Mass: 780kg.

Deformation: All deformation must be limited to the area behind the rear wheel centre line.

Average deceleration must not exceed 35g and the peak must not exceed 60g for more than 3 milliseconds.

Below: The rear crash structure is the black carbon element in the lower part of the photograph. It is also part of the rear-wing mounting system. (Author)

Chapter 4
Engine
Air power

The engine is the heart of a racing car, but where the human heart pumps blood this mechanical heart primarily pumps air. In the overall technical package, and discounting the driver, the engine accounts for 25%, the chassis 50% and the tyres 25% of the car's overall performance.

In the past, for example when Lotus and Williams took quantum leaps forward as they harnessed ground effect in the late '70s and the early '80s respectively, it was possible for an underpowered car to beat one with a more powerful engine if it could generate significantly more grip. But when all of the major players had powerful turbocharged engines and broadly similar aerodynamics by the late '80s, this possibility was reduced significantly. Now, when cars are so closely matched technically because of even tighter regulations, it is almost impossible for a car with a really underpowered engine to make up with superior grip what it lacks in sheer grunt over the full course of a season. There are, however, always exceptions to rules. In 2003 Renault's wide-angle V10 was adjudged to be anything up to 100bhp down on BMW's narrow-angle engine, yet Fernando Alonso was able to exploit the handling advantage conferred by his power unit's lower centre of gravity (among other things) to win the Hungarian Grand Prix.

All Formula 1 engines are four strokes that operate on the Otto cycle. This is how they work. Pistons run in the cylinders, which themselves are located in the engine block or crankcase. The pistons are connected at their lower end to a crankshaft, which runs the length of the crankcase and is connected via gears to four camshafts, which are mounted in separate cylinder heads located atop each cylinder bank. There are two camshafts per bank of cylinders, one operating inlet valves the other exhausts. Ignition timing and valve timing systems are carefully designed to make sure that valves open and close at the right times, and that spark plugs ignite the air/fuel mixture at precisely the right moment.

On the induction stroke the descending piston draws air and fuel into the cylinder. The air and fuel are mixed in what is known as the stoichiometric ratio, 14 parts air to one part fuel. Current engines use four valves per cylinder, two inlet and two exhaust. These are more efficient and therefore generate greater power than two valves per cylinder, which had been superseded in all Formula 1 applications by the '70s. Under the current regulations a maximum of five valves per cylinder are allowed, three inlet, two exhaust. Among those who tried five valves without notable success were Yamaha and Lamborghini in the '80s.

On the induction stroke the camshaft opens the relevant inlet valves so that the cylinder draws in the air and fuel mixture. As the piston reaches its lowest point, bottom dead centre, it begins the second stroke, the compression stroke. Now the camshaft closes the valves so that the rising piston compresses the air/fuel mixture and heats it up. The ratio by which this mixture is compressed – the compression ratio – is one of the keys to engine power. In current engines it is usually not less than 14:1. As the piston reaches the top of its stroke, known as top dead centre, the ignition system triggers electric detonation via the spark plug, thus igniting the air/fuel mixture. The resultant explosion drives the piston back down the cylinder on the third stroke, the power stroke. The propagation of the flame and the efficiency with which all of the mixture is burned in the cylinder is another determinant of engine power. When the piston reaches bottom dead centre it rises again, this time with the exhaust valves opened by the exhaust camshaft so that the burned mixture can be exhausted from the cylinder. The exhaust pipe carries it away and expels it into the atmosphere. This is another area in which efficiency is a key to horsepower, so modern racing engines use a single exhaust pipe per cylinder which then mates further down its length with a maximum of three others.

Opposite: Complete with its exhausts, Toyota's RVX-09 2.4-litre V8 demonstrates just how compact, and therefore well-packaged, the modern F1 powerplant is.
(Toyota)

This is a continuous process when the engine is running and occurs at differing times in every cylinder in a stage known as the firing order. The order in which each individual cylinder fires is designed to create the smoothest-running engine possible. Generally 12-cylinders run smoother than eight, which tend to vibrate quite a lot, and that's another reason why the V10 is a good compromise.

The drive all this action generates is taken off the back of the crankshaft, where the engine is connected to the drivetrain (see Chapter Six).

Some 63% of the components are made of aluminium. The cylinder heads, the crankcase, the sump, the cam covers, the pistons and sundries such as water pump casings are all cast in this material. Steel accounts for almost 30%, for the long lead-time items such as the crankshaft, the camshafts, which are case-hardened, and the timing gears. Titanium is a very lightweight but expensive metal that accounts for 5% of the mix and is used for components such as the connecting rods, the valves and sundry fasteners. Magnesium, another lightweight material, is cast in smaller amounts for sundry housings. Carbon-fibre is also used to a small extent, for items such as the overhead airbox through which air is ducted into the intakes, and the inlet trumpets and their carrier.

Above: Typical of the modern Formula One engine is the piston with very shallow sides and cut-outs on the crown to facilitate clearance for the valves. (Piola)

Below: Precision engineering is everything. The BMW cylinder head below is a raw casting; above is the finished, machined end product. (BMW AG)

Below right: BMW's production block-based 1.5-litre engine of the Eighties was dominated by its turbocharger installation. (BMW AG)

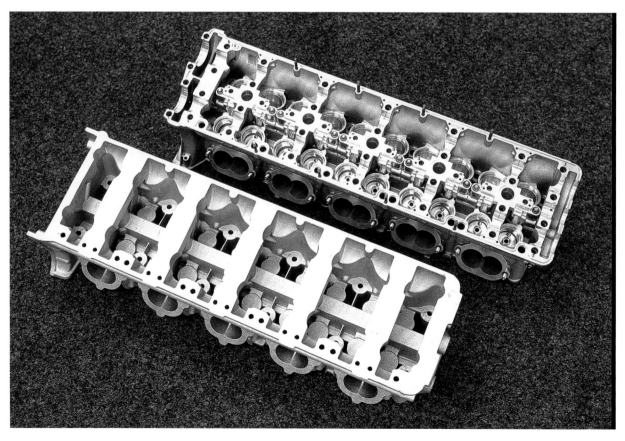

One material that may no longer be used is aluminium beryllium, which is very strong and lightweight but which one major team objected to and sought to have banned on the somewhat specious grounds of expense. That is thought to be one reason why Mercedes-Benz lost some of the dominance its engines enjoyed in the late '90s.

Ceramics were once predicted to be the next big step forward in engine materials technology, but there seems less likelihood of that now. Nor will there be oval pistons, another development of the '80s and '90s which has been banned from Formula 1 engine specifications by the FIA.

Former Mercedes-Benz engine guru Mario Illien believed that improvements in materials technology played a key role in enhancing engine performance. 'Today you get much better aluminiums and casting techniques are much better. Aluminium has better properties and so do the titaniums. You also get better finishing techniques and coatings. It's a lot of things in those areas that have improved, and because of that you have greater opportunities to make lighter components do the same jobs that heavier components used to.'

Up until 2005 the Formula 1 regulations stipulated that engines must be normally aspirated (not turbocharged), have a maximum cubic capacity of 3 litres, must run on what is effectively pump petrol (not the exotic toluene-boosted brews popular in the '80s) and have a maximum of ten cylinders. Since 2006 the rules catered for 2.4-litre V8s, with air-restricted V10s allowed in special cases in that first season only.

When the original 3-litre Formula 1 was introduced for 1966, replacing a 1.5-litre formula in which straight four-cylinder, flat-six and V8 engines had been the norm, and Honda's ingenious V12 the exception, engine designers explored various solutions to the need to generate high power and torque figures. While Repco and Ford opted for V8s, Honda, Ferrari, Maserati, Weslake and Matra all went with the V12. BRM joined them after a disastrous flirtation with a 16-cylinder engine which effectively comprised two of its 1.5-litre V8s with the vee opened out to a horizontally-opposed or 'flat' 180° angle, mounted one atop the other.

In the '70s Renault began to exploit a loophole that permitted turbocharged or supercharged engines of 1.5 litres. These used a crankshaft-mounted pump (the supercharger) or an exhaust-mounted pump (the turbocharger) to force-feed the engine its fuel and air mixture, dramatically enhancing its power.

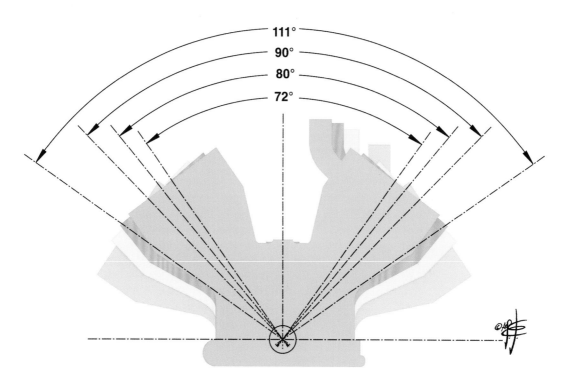

111°
90°
80°
72°

Four vee-angles have been tried in recent years: 72°, 80°, 90° and 111°. Overlaying them thus gives an indication of the merits and demerits. The narrower the engine the easier it is for the designer to package within the chassis, but the higher its centre of gravity. The wider the vee-angle the lower the centre of gravity, but when Renault tried 111° it encountered problems with packaging and vibration. Cosworth found the same with an experimental wide-angle engine. (Piola)

Eventually such engines became *de rigueur* until they were outlawed for 1989 in favour of 3.5-litre normally aspirated engines. Subsequently, to reduce speeds in 1995 after the deaths the previous year of Roland Ratzenberger and Ayrton Senna, the FIA mandated a new 3-litre formula which persists to this day. By then the V10 was almost ubiquitous, only Ferrari sticking faithfully to the V12. Though it was more powerful it was longer and heavier, used more fuel, and its crankcase was so much longer that it was fundamentally less torsionally stiff. There were more exhaust pipes to package, which was a significant consideration from the point of view of packaging and excess heat in the engine bay, and the unit's inferior heat characteristics – there was greater friction and therefore greater heat to be rejected – necessitated larger radiators, which in turn had a negative effect on the aerodynamics because they generated more drag. In the end, all of that was a high price to pay for slightly superior top-end power. In 1999 all the teams agreed that the FIA could outlaw engines with more than ten cylinders.

The number of cylinders was once the subject of debate in Formula 1, but from 1995 to 2005 all engines had ten, arranged in vee formation. It was the angle of the vee that varied, between 72° and 112° according to the philosophy of the engine designer. In the past he had free rein, but in the modern era he not only has to work very, very closely with the chassis designer, but often has to accede to the latter's wishes when it comes to choosing the vee angle and packaging the engine's accessories. This is because everything about the packaging of the car's components is critical to its weight distribution, balance and aerodynamics, and therefore its overall on-track performance.

How much air and fuel an engine can pump, and the calorific value of that fuel mixture, are two arbiters of horsepower. But both are rigidly controlled, the former by the capacity limit, the latter by the regulation mandating pump fuel of given calorific value. Thus the way to generate more horsepower in Formula 1 at present is to make the engine rev ever faster and thus pump more quickly. Revs, however, generate top-end power, and that is not all of the story. Bottom-end and mid-range power are just as important, because they influence a car's acceleration out of corners. This is another reason why eight and ten cylinders proved more popular than 12s in the past. Even when the latter were fitted with movable inlet trumpets in an attempt to enhance low-speed power and torque, the big multi-cylinder power units were still disadvantaged.

Nick Hayes, former engine guru at Cosworth Racing, explained the relative merits of the three configurations. 'In terms of more cylinders, 12 versus ten versus eight, in general more cylinders mean more valve area, so you can in theory get more airflow in an engine per revolution. More cylinders also tend to have lighter pieces for a given capacity, so you're often able to run them to a higher rpm. And both of those things mean more airflow, to which you put more fuel, and that means you get more base power. But what you do is take off some things too. More cylinders give you greater losses. Though you're producing more indicated horsepower, because there are more bits it takes more power to turn them all round, so in theory you get a situation where a 12 versus a ten, or a ten versus an eight, will each respectively have more power but a lot more losses, so that the actual brake horsepower number will be different. But there's obviously a lot more to it, because of the losses. More cylinders are less efficient, so you have to use a lot more fuel. In the end you've got a lot of things going against more cylinders and only a few going for them.'

The bore and stroke of an engine is also critical. The bore is the diameter of the cylinder (and hence the piston) and the stroke is the distance that piston must travel for each stroke. Generally speaking, the higher

an engine can rev, the more power it can produce. This was not always the case, particularly with V12s in the past, but modern improvements in engine design and electronics have helped. In the past the bore/stroke ratio was typically 1.3:1 for the Cosworth DFV. Today ratios of 2.25:1 are the norm, creating a large piston area thanks to a very short stroke.

An eight-cylinder 3-litre engine has a large bore, which is good for generating power, and a short stroke, which is also good for boosting revs because the piston has less distance to travel. An eight is also relatively short and therefore easy to package, and produces very good torque. A 12 can generate greater top-end power because of all its little pistons pumping up and down simultaneously, but historically 12s lacked torque in comparison to eights, even when Ferrari produced a legendary flat-12 in 1970. When he began designing the new normally aspirated engine that Renault would use for 1989, Bernard Dudot broke new ground by creating the V10. This was a compromise that harnessed the best aspects of an eight and a 12. It promised good power and torque, and was more economical and shorter than a 12 and had fewer frictional losses, and could therefore be packaged well. Renault set a trend that is now universal.

Prior to that, on the 1986 version of its turbocharged

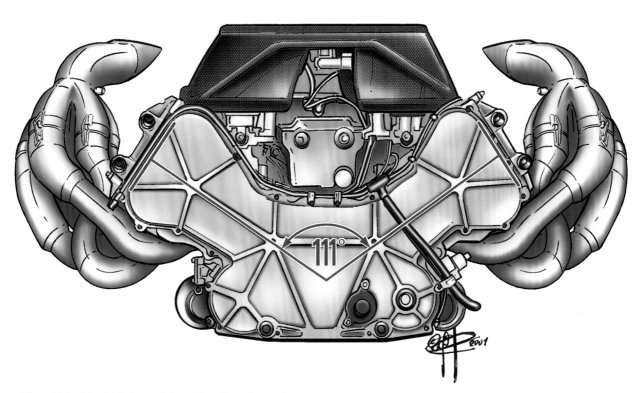

The width of the 111° Renault is evident here, but so is the remarkably low engine height. (Piola)

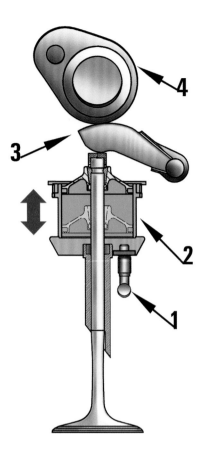

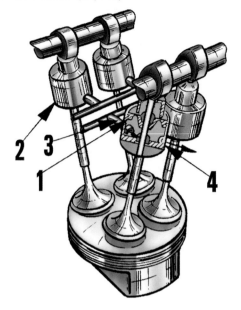

V6, Renault had broken more new ground with its valve actuation system. Rather than relying on old-fashioned coil springs to close the valves, Mercedes-Benz had introduced in 1954 a mechanical means of overcoming valve bounce – when the valve was moving at such speed that the valve spring lost its springiness and was no longer able to control the valve accurately. Later Dudot developed something that achieved the same effect but was lighter and even more efficient. He employed compressed air instead of the springs to close the valves. Without frail springs which were also prone to break if the driver abused the engine, the unit could rev far higher without the valve gear losing efficiency, and therefore develop greater horsepower.

Back in 1966 the new 3-litre Formula 1 was billed as 'The Return To Power'. None of the engines that ran in that first season truly generated the 400bhp that was the avowed aim, and the first unit to breach that figure was the 1967 Ford Cosworth DFV V8, which pumped out a healthy 405bhp. It was reasonably expected that with development the 3-litre racing engine might produce 450bhp – a then impressive 150bhp per litre – with as much as 600bhp as the ultimate target in years to come.

Towards the end of the 3.5-litre formula in 1994, Ferrari was generally reckoned to have the most powerful engine in racing, with 800bhp, but Renault's V10 was close on 780 and the similar engines of Mercedes-Benz and Peugeot had around 770. The Ford Zetec R in Michael Schumacher's World Championship-winning Benetton developed a maximum of 735/740bhp, proving that power was not everything.

Such figures were regained under the new 3-litre formula by the late '90s, when engines reached around 17,000rpm, as had their 3.5-litre ancestors.

When BMW re-entered Formula 1 in 2000 the stakes were raised again. The German manufacturer's 2003 P83 engine was generally adjudged to be the most powerful in the formula, with 920bhp. It generated this at a whopping 19,200rpm, or a fearful 320 revs per second. Such figures boggle the imagination.

Maximum horsepower isn't everything, however, even if it is the bit that most people want to know about. Mario Illien disliked the tabloid focus on outright power figures, and drew careful distinctions. 'If you take power, torque and driveability, I would say that driveability is easily the most important thing,' he said. 'Of course you need to have the top-end performance as well, but there are only two really fast circuits, Monza and Indianapolis, where the drivers are at maximum speed for longer over a lap than anywhere

Left: Stunning in its elegance and miniscule size, the Formula One engine is a work of art. This is Ferrari's 2003 052 V10 power unit.
(sutton-images.com)

Below: The modern Formula One engine cannot be divorced from its ancillaries. 2008 Ferrari F2008 engine, oil tank and radiators.
(sutton-images.com)

BMW's P83 engine was generally adjudged to be the most powerful in the formula, with 920bhp. It generated this at 19,200rpm. (BMW AG)

The exhausts of a BMW P84 V10 glow red hot as engineers in the dynamometer room in Munich take the unit to its maximum rev limit of 19,000rpm. (BMW AG)

else, where you really need it. All the other tracks are high downforce places where you really need to have a very driveable torque band which is as even as you can possibly get it. If you want quick lap times, that is the real key and is therefore very important.'

Axel Plasse, one of Renault Sport's track test engineers, held a similar view. 'We place significant importance on the driveability of our engine, and driver comfort. We are not obsessed with engine power. We endeavour to produce an engine which is driveable in all conditions and which gives drivers no reason for complaint. Our aim is to produce an engine which drivers can forget all about. It is often said that an engine on its own cannot win a race, but that it can lose one. An engine which puts out 10 or 20 extra horsepower will not change a car's overall competitiveness. However, an engine which fails does.'

To give some idea of the complexity of its baby, BMW released more information towards the end of that season than is generally expected in this day of super-secrecy in Formula 1. 1950 CAD drawings went into creating the unit; were they printed out and laid end to end, they would have covered 1.3km.

Idle speed was 4,000rpm, maximum race speed 19,000. It weighed less than 90kg. In an hour of flat-out race running it would ingest 1,995m³ of air and the maximum piston acceleration was 10,000g. Piston speed peaked at 40m per second and averaged 25m per second, each one accelerating from 0 to 100kph in a thousandth of a second. The exhaust temperature reached 950°C, the air in the pneumatic valve actuation system 250°.

Such figures place into even sharper perspective the fabulous reliability of modern Formula 1 cars.

By the end of the 2003 season, for example, Michael Schumacher's Ferrari had gone 38 Grands Prix without a single mechanical failure.

To give some insight into the gestation period of the highly complex modern Formula 1 powerplant, BMW engineers began conceptualising the P83 in November and December 2001, and the design process began in January 2002 and was completed in May that year. Model construction at BMW's foundry in Landshut occupied from March to May and component manufacture took from April through to July. Historically complex items such as crankshafts have a long lead-time of around three months.

Initial assembly of the prototype engine took place in July and the first bench test was conducted on the last day of that month. The first phase of test and development took the team through from August 2002 to January 2003, with the first in-car, on-track deployment taking place on 18 September 2002.

Final development to race readiness occupied from October to mid-February 2003, and further development occurred from mid-February to the final race of the season at Suzuka in October.

In 2003 BMW Williams won the Monaco, European, French and German Grands Prix and challenged for the World Championship, and by 4 September the 2004 P84 V10 engine was already undergoing its first track tests ready for the next season.

The whole subject of engine testing is an industry on its own. 'Generally speaking, testing is a means of validating a new development or a new component,' explained Axel Plasse. 'It is an indispensable phase of the development process and rare indeed are the fields of technology in which engineers can allow themselves not to test.

'Despite the importance of calculation work both within teams and at Renault Sport, nothing can replace testing. To be able to predict on paper what is likely to work and what isn't has effectively become increasingly important, but testing is still essential.

'Although bench testing attempts to reproduce real conditions as closely as possible, it has its limits. A Formula 1 car moves, turns and accelerates whereas an engine on the bench is fixed which means that a whole host of situations cannot be simulated.

'Having said that, the test bench remains a rigorous tool which is capable of determining, for example, whether a particular engine is developing, say, three brake horsepower more than another. This is something which a driver is incapable of doing. However, a bench test is a bit like a computer inasmuch as it can only quantify parameters that are quantifiable. Some parameters – such as the characteristics of a new type of fuel – are difficult to put into figures in order to evaluate performance gains. On the other hand, there are many subjective considerations – such as driveability and response – which can only be judged by a driver. Track testing is an intermediate phase between bench testing and race use. It's the final link in the chain before a part or a new development can be raced.'

All engine manufacturers have access to highly sophisticated testing equipment that can simulate conditions on the track. Renault, for example, has a three-phase system of engine testing that is used prior to the first track tests.

The first is the motored dynamometer. This is driven by electrical motors, and enables the engineering team to test the accessories on the new engine, such as the different pumps. As soon as the major components of the new engine are ready, this equipment is also used to check that specific areas of the powerplant are functioning correctly. As an example, the engine block fitted solely with the cylinder heads is tested to assess the distribution, according to head of dyno testing Stéphane Rodriguez. 'In this configuration, the engine is not fired up: the electrical dyno permits us to check certain technical solutions, or do short endurance runs. The tests are designed to ensure that everything is working correctly, and are therefore not particularly severe.'

Once this phase has been completed, the second is a visit to the thermal dyno.

This occurs around four weeks after the first phase, according to the arrival of the primary components and the adjustments that need to be made during installation. The engine will then be fired up for the first time. 'It is a pretty special moment,' said Rodriguez. 'The first aim is to ensure the engine starts! Then we check and measure dozens of parameters connected with the lubrication systems and temperatures. We also draw the first power curves.' The first fire-up is above all to reassure the engineers. At the beginning, the test is relatively undemanding: Renault's 2004 RS24 V10 (and all of its subsequent units) was thus analysed in its tiniest details for an entire day. After that the engine begins its pukka development programme, and the programme is separated into two sections. The thermal test benches chase absolute performance, testing engines with modified cylinder heads or valves, for example. Specific components and the performance of the engine are tested according to a number of precise parameters. Amongst this bewildering range of tests, only the parts which bring a significant performance gain are retained. From this point onwards, the three dynamic dynos at Viry-Châtillon are running all day.

Above and right: An engine is put through its paces at the Toyota F1 engine test facility in Cologne, while engineers monitor and observe its performance. (Toyota)

The dynamic dyno is the final phase and is regarded as the ultimate torture chamber for an engine. Once new designs have demonstrated an acceptable level of performance on the thermal dyno they are taken to the full dynamic dyno. One tests the engine on its own; another can test both engine and gearbox. At this point the aim is to check the engine's reliability, so the load on it is steadily increased so that it gets a thorough workout. The most demanding circuit on the calendar is reproduced in its smallest details using the onboard telemetry from the previous racing season: the engine must complete 700km at qualifying speed before it is passed. 'The process then becomes a continual exchange between the thermal dynos, which propose performance gains, and the dynamic dynos, which check their reliability,' said Rodriguez. 'It is a difficult balance to achieve: in developing the engine, we are constantly treading the fine line between performance and reliability.'

Dudot, who returned to Formula 1 with Renault in 2003, said: 'You have so many tools to control and check the engine and the running of the car, but all these tools bring us so many questions, and you need new areas in which to work to find the answers. It is very interesting, but due to the fact that you have lots of new questions, you also need to have lots of new people to analyse and

process all the data that you acquire. That is the reason why Formula 1 teams are growing so much.

'Back in 1989, when Renault Sport began with its normally aspirated V10, we had about 50% fewer personnel. I think that is the ratio for all the main teams. We generate so much data that you need all these extra people to go through it.'

When they have been passed raceworthy, all engines are set up specifically for the next circuit on the calendar, engineers ensuring beforehand that things such as the fuel mapping are correct for a given venue. All teams use their full or transient dynamometers for this work as well as reliability assessment. 'We can simulate race distances and certain conditions, as well as how well the engine picks up out of corners, its driveability,' said Illien. This way they can programme in the characteristics of different circuits, to provide empirical evaluation of various configurations, based on data acquired in previous races there. The majority of engine development is thus done on the test benches, though the final work must always be completed in the form of track tests.

This ceaseless search for optimum reliability became even more critical in 2004 when new regulations were introduced.

In bygone days engines were simply plugged in and out like light bulbs. If one broke, another went in. 'The days have long gone when you might try and make an engine work at the track,' said former engine builder Brian Hart in the '90s. 'When an engine arrives at the circuit today it's like a set of tyres. You just put them in and take them out.'

At one stage there were even 'grenade' engines specifically for qualifying, short-life units that were literally meant to produce fabulous horsepower increments over the normal race engines, for just enough laps to get the driver a decent grid place. The economic climate, and a general tightening of the regulations for 2003, tended to discourage such units. However, there was a return to the sight of engines being worked on in the paddock, as new rules allowed teams to replace some items when the cars were kept in *parc fermé* after Saturday afternoon's single-lap qualifying. On more than one occasion Mercedes-Benz received permission from the technical stewards to replace suspect valves on Kimi Räikkönen's engine.

As an indication of the development process during a racing year, BMW's P83 powerplant underwent nearly 1,400 technical modifications.

From 2004 onwards, however, new regulations demanded that teams could only use a single engine per car per race weekend. Any engine failure during that time would automatically mean that the driver whose car had to receive a replacement powerplant had to drop ten places on the starting grid.

The idea, though unpopular at first, was nothing new. Taking the wind out of the sails of critics who suggested that the FIA did nothing to try and contain costs, the FIA sought as long ago as 1993, at the height of the arguments over the ban on electronic 'gizmos', to introduce a limit on the number of engines teams could use during a season. The idea was that the same engine must remain in a car throughout an entire event subject to a maximum of 12 engines per team per season. Use of the spare car would count as an engine change, as would removal of the sump or the cylinder heads. The smaller teams proposed a limit of six to eight engines per team per race meeting, to try and counter the 'grenade' qualifying engines that were prevalent at the time.

That particular plan was unworkable, and predictably everyone forgot about it – until FIA president Max Mosley raised it again over the winter of 2002 when he and Bernie Ecclestone introduced swingeing changes to spice up the series after that year's Ferrari

Overleaf: Packaging is a critical part of Formula One design, and since the engine and transmission account for such a significant portion of a car, it follows that packaging the rear end is particularly important. Here are four variations on a 2003 theme, from Ferrari, Toyota, BAR Honda and Jaguar. (sutton-images.com)

domination. Mosley talked then of three-race engines, but Renault's Patrick Faure was among those who dismissed the idea of building 'tractor engines'.

At that time a typical Formula 1 engine was designed to run a maximum of 500km prior to a rebuild. Sometimes this would mean scrapping cylinder heads, or even blocks, depending on how deliberately marginal the design was. In 2003 BMW produced 200 of its P83 V10s, and BMW Williams would take ten to a race. Engines would usually be changed after practice and qualifying, and each was virtually priceless compared to the staple Cosworth DFV which had begun its extraordinary career in 1967 at £7,500 a shot.

For 2004 Mosley's regulation mandated that an engine must be capable of covering at least 800km, or one Grand Prix weekend. The idea was to reduce costs, but some argued that such a regulation would have the effect of increasing budgets as manufacturers sought the best way to bullet-proof their existing power units. This is easier said than done since it is quite clearly not just a matter of beefing everything up. There are some 5,000 inter-dependent components in a Formula 1 engine, and changing one often has a deleterious effect on others unless they too are changed to cope.

Then there was the matter of how much distance a team could expect to run during a Grand Prix weekend. Obviously those who took advantage of running three test cars on a Friday would cover more mileage and would therefore need a longer life long-life engine, which could put them at a disadvantage on race day. Equally, some teams might make the decision to do less running during a weekend, in order to keep their engines as close as possible to 2003 specification, winning an advantage that way while possibly depriving spectating fans of the sight of their cars and drivers. In extremis, the better-heeled teams might even consider building different life expectancy into their engines depending on the circuit. Different manufacturers would attach different lifing to various components too, depending on the inherent reliability of their powerplant. Another possibility was that a team could have fresh short-life engines ready for the race so that, when they swapped to them and lost their ten grid places, they had a more potent means of getting back up to the front on Sunday afternoon.

There was also the possibility that teams would develop 'quick-change' engine installations, so that in the event of a chassis problem the entire rear-end of the original race car could be removed and switched to the waiting spare car, which would not be equipped with an engine of its own. BMW's Mario Theissen said categorically that his team would not use such a ploy: 'It has not become more important and there have been no developments in that direction on the FW26,' he said. But Ferrari engine director Paolo Martinelli said: 'For sure the engine will be different in 2004. It will lead to a significant reduction in costs, which is necessary. The engine is the car now, not the chassis. There will be an impact on strategy, and we cannot discount quick-change engines. And one important point is that we must use the dynos even more to test

the engine via extended race simulations. That will save time developing the engine on the track, when the team needs to focus more on setting up the chassis and the aerodynamics.'

The need to focus on longevity took some of the impetus out of advanced development projects believed to be under way at both Mercedes-Benz and Renault to save even more weight and lower the centre of gravity further by doing away with the camshafts altogether. Both companies were thought to have embarked on research into engines where complete valve actuation was via electronic solenoids. Time will tell what future this concept has.

In 2005 Mosley mandated engines that would last two Grands Prix, and in practice the whole concept worked perfectly well and nobody really tried to do anything silly that was against the spirit of the rule. As costs and speeds rose early in the 21st century, however, he continued to seek further means of slowing the cars down. One such method had already been mooted in 2004: reducing engine capacity once more. Yet again, change was in the air.

Few proposals from Max Mosley have had quite the same incendiary effect as his diktat that engines should be reduced from 3-litre V10s to 2.4-litre V8s.

The first wind of it came at Imola in 2004, during the San Marino Grand Prix. As that weekend developed, cynics detected a pattern in the way things unfolded. First there was Michael Schumacher's recent visit to Dublin as part of his remit to act as an ambassador for FIA road safety initiatives. Then there was the question posed to him in Thursday's press conference about whether he saw a need for the current cars to be slowed down. Then Mosley's raft of proposed changes – including the change in engine capacity and configuration – was leaked to sections of the media, and when the full official list appeared on desks in the press room the following morning a governing body spokesman's suggestion that it had 'acted quickly to put out the correct story after all the media speculation' was seen as a disingenuous smokescreen to obscure all the politicking.

The clear intention was to peg horsepower back to 700–750bhp. At that stage the proposal also called for the engine manufacturers to be told what materials they could use and what manufacturing processes would be permissible. It also called for a standard engine control unit (ECU), something that Mosley had always been particularly keen on since it would mean that the FIA could make certain that electronic driver aids such as traction control really could be policed effectively enough to be outlawed. Manual transmissions and clutches were also part of the deal, together with the

need for every car to run with standard specification brake discs, pads and calipers.

The rules would also embrace chassis stiffness specification (to limit handling performance), an increase in minimum weight of at least 50kg to eliminate the need for ballast, and a combined tyre and aerodynamic package to achieve specific targets for cornering speeds, straightline speeds, grip and braking performance. To obviate the tyre war that had seen lap times drop so dramatically this season, only one tyre manufacturer would be allowed.

Subsequently, in anger at the proposals, the Grand Prix World Championship Holdings (GPWC) alliance of car manufacturers, which had already proposed a breakaway rival championship, pulled out of the Memorandum of Understanding with SLEC Holdings, the company owned by the Ecclestone family which at that time ran Formula 1, and out of negotiations about the sport's future.

A lot of double dealing ensued, and as GPWC metamorphosed into GPMA, the Grand Prix Manufacturers' Association, the situation softened. GPMA conceded that the engine rules had to change, while sticking out for other improvements.

As it became clear that Mosley wanted the smaller engines by 2006, the major sticking point was that two teams preferred the idea of staying with 3-litre V10 engines, reduced in power to last up to six or eight races by means of an air restrictor. However, the FIA believed they would still have too much power (800+ bhp) compared to the 2.4-litre V8s which were then expected to produce around 720.

'Most people I speak to are still enthusing about the motorcycle fight between Max Biaggi and Valentino Rossi in South Africa recently,' Mosley said in 2004. 'Most of them haven't got a clue what type of engine the Moto GP bikes run, or what an ECU is or who makes it. They want to see the human element in races, not a computer-controlled spectacle. The manufacturers are coming to realise that. Some teams, including their engine manufacturer partners, need 1,000 people to put two cars on the grid, at a cost of 150 million. They all know that is not sustainable, which is why they are prepared to talk. And cost savings will filter down to the smaller teams too, and they need to be kept in business.'

In the end the compromises resulted in 2.4-litre V8s arriving for 2006, with the old Minardi team, now owned by Red Bull energy drink magnate Dietrich Mateschitz and renamed Toro Rosso, allowed to use a restricted 3-litre Cosworth V10. From 900+ bhp, power outputs had fallen to 750 for the best V8s. The Cosworth V10 had more power and torque, but was limited to 16,700rpm by a 77mm restrictor under an FIA-calculated equivalency formula.

After all the hoo-ha died down, the change of formula proved quite painless, as it usually does. Behind the scenes, however, plenty of people had a lot of work to do. 'Of course, the V8 has been a completely new type of engine so it was quite tough and we have to work hard,' admitted Ferrari's engine director Paolo Martinelli. 'I think each of us is working hard, trying to develop as fast as possible, as usual in Formula 1, with a brand new engine. You can say that we have a different learning curve than we had with ten years' experience with a V10. Most of the job, or the majority of the very important or predominant factors, was well known. Here, sometimes, we find some new items, some new areas, where you can find performance and then you have to push hard for development.'

Renault's Rob White, however, was quite happy, even though the Regie's RS26 V8 was one of the last to reach the track. 'It's certainly true that we were the last on to the track, which came about from our explicit choice not to do a hybrid car in which we put an early version of the engine into a converted car of a previous generation. This was a thing we looked at, honestly, very, very briefly, and figured that for us it would not be best use of our resources. We looked at how to construct the project planning from the moment we knew what the rules would be until the date of the first race. We tried to build in the experiences from previous engine projects. Frankly, we did what we thought was right for our team in our context and we were, I think, reassured that it played out well for us.

'It's a new experience working on this family of V8 engines. They're not the same as V10s but they clearly have some very important family similarities. There's a lot of the genes of the previous V10 engines built into our V8. I think that's part of the way in which we approached the design of it. We tried to set ourselves aggressive performance targets. We tried to set ourselves clear reliability objectives that we thought would be worthy of a World Championship campaign. The difficulty of developing the V8 is, of course, due to the phenomena that are particular to V8s. There are some, but behind all of that the physics is the same, the engineering is the same and we're pretty confident that the people, the skills, the techniques that we have are portable between V10 and V8 engines.'

Though fundamentally the new V8 was a V10 with

The 2006 P86 was BMW's first V8 F1 engine, weighing in at around 95kg. (BMW AG)

one fifth cut off, and a now-compulsory vee angle of 90° degrees, it was an entirely separate concept with its own specific requirements. A V8 has a distinct firing sequence and demands a fundamentally different crankshaft design. Whereas a 72° offset crankshaft was used, for example, in BMW's P85 V10, V8 powerplants can feature crankshafts with either four throws spaced at 90° or four throws spaced at 180°. Standard production engines are fitted with 90° crankshaft variants due to their better dynamic attributes, but a 180° crankshaft is favoured in racing car engine design. The improved performance this allows offsets the disadvantages in terms of dynamics.

Mechanical dynamics and vibrations represent a particularly critical area of development for the new generation of V8s. They have different firing sequences and intervals to their V10 predecessors, and this leads to a different pattern of vibrations. The V10 entered a critical vibrational area between 12,000rpm and 14,000rpm. This was not really an issue as the engine did not spend much time in this rev band and smoothed itself out again as the revs increased. A V8, however, has different characteristics that take it into more dangerous territory as its vibration curve peaks later than a V10's – from approximately 16,000rpm – and continues to climb from there. It is therefore no longer possible for the designer to think in terms of getting through a difficult patch before everything is all right again. The problem of constantly increasing vibrations had to be confronted head on. If a designer fails to solve a V8's vibrational problems, the service life of the engine suffers and the loads exerted on the chassis and other components can also become a factor. In order to get on top of this problem, the

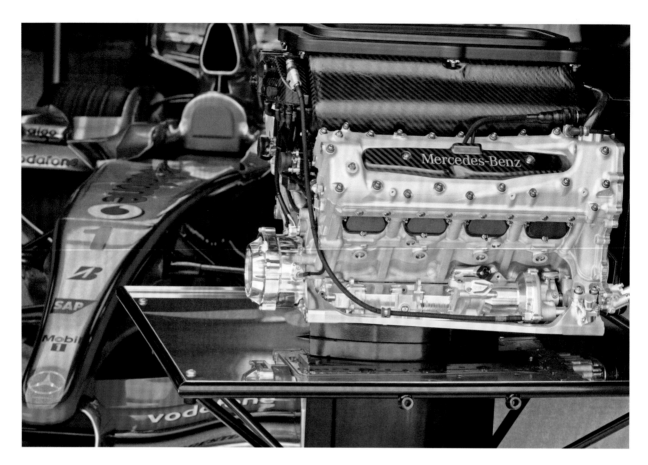

calculation and analysis of each individual engine component has to be totally reliable. This analysis is only part of a bigger challenge. Determining how they work with and against each other in simulations of the overall system is the main task.

The reduced mass inherent in the V8 should mean less in the way of 'bad vibrations'. However, the regulations have limited the designers' natural tendency to seek exotic – and therefore expensive – ultra-light materials. They can only work with conventional steel, titanium and aluminium alloys.

Interestingly, the new breed of V8s is heavier than its V10 predecessor, despite having two fewer cylinders. That's because the rules say that engines must not be lighter than 95kg, inclusive of the intake system up to and including the air filter, fuel rail and injectors, ignition coils, sensors and wiring, alternator, coolant pumps and oil pumps. It does not include liquids, exhaust manifolds, heat protection shields, oil tanks, accumulators, heat exchangers and the hydraulic pump.

The new regulations also stipulate that the engine's centre of gravity must be at least 165mm above the lower edge of the oil sump. Designers had previously managed to lower the ten-cylinder engine's centre of

Above: In the 2007 season, Mercedez-Benz's Ilmor FO108T engine powered Lewis Hamilton and Fernando Alonso to four victories apiece. (sutton-images.com)

Below: BMW's 2008 V8 was potent and reliable, and took victory in Canada courtesy of BMW-Sauber pilot Robert Kubica. (sutton-images.com)

gravity to the benefit of the car's handling. However, the longitudinal and lateral position of the V8's centre of gravity has to be in the geometric centre of the engine (+/–50mm).

The mandatory minimum weight and the minimum height for the centre of gravity meant that the V8 was much heavier than it actually needs to be, but in turn that enabled designers to create a more rigid crankcase, to the benefit of the cars' handling. And because it was no longer necessary to watch every single gram, they also made several static components such as the block and heads much more robust, and thus helped to increase the service life of the engines to meet the new rules demanding that each unit serve for two races.

Previously the dimensions of an engine's bore and stroke were a closely guarded secret. Now, however, the cylinder bore is limited to a maximum of 98mm. The gap between the cylinders is mandated at 106.5mm (+/–0.2mm), and the central axis of the crankshaft must not lie any less than 58mm above the reference plane.

Another critical change in the regulations was the ban on variable intake systems. Known as 'trumpets', these could previously be used to optimise the car's torque curve. The fixed duct lengths make achieving good engine driveability a more exacting challenge. Designers now have to strike a compromise between maximum power and good driveability. Where the best compromise for the pipe lengths is to be found depends on various factors. The track layout and the weather, for example, both play a role. Teams favour one set of intake pipe lengths for circuits with long straights – such as Monza, Indianapolis and Spa – where power is critical, and a different selection for twistier Grand Prix tracks such as Budapest and Monaco, where driveability is more important than raw power. The same applies in wet weather. The air intakes are, by definition, part of the engine and are included in its 95kg maximum overall weight, but they can also be changed up to qualifying.

Variable exhaust systems and variable valve control systems were also proscribed from 2006. The power supply to the engine electrics and electronics is limited to a maximum of 17 volts and the fuel pump must now be mechanically operated. Only an actuator may be used to activate the throttle valve system. With the exception of the electric auxiliary pumps in the fuel tank, all sub-components must now be driven mechanically and directly via the engine.

Architecturally, the V8 configuration was better than a V10. It was shorter, which meant not only that it could be packaged better for optimised weight

distribution but also that the rear end of the car could be cleaned up aerodynamically.

Then there was the fact that the configuration required less cooling, which in turn meant less radiator area and a further aerodynamic enhancement. The improved weight distribution also improved handling agility. Thus, though straight-line speeds fell compared with 2005, cornering speeds generally went up (hand-in-hand with tyre development) and often lap times fell. Generally, the drivers found the smaller-capacity cars more fun to drive round corners.

The one fly in the ointment, at least initially, was Toro Rosso's V10, especially when Vitantonio Liuzzi proved very quick in practice in Bahrain and Malaysia. The reasoning was that while Toro Rosso might be able to run more wing and thus have a small downforce advantage because of the Cosworth V10's greater torque and power, that would be balanced by the agility of its V8 rivals. Soon, however, Mercedes-Benz and Toyota were squeaking in indignant complaint.

Speaking for McLaren Mercedes, Ron Dennis said: 'First of all, all the teams who had committed to running V8s very much appreciated that there was going to be an advantage from running V10s and going down an equivalency route. We signed a document that undertook to each other that we would run V8s. The team that was given the concession to run V10s was Minardi, and it was given the concession for financial reasons, not for performance reasons. There are several parameters of the engine that must be addressed when achieving an equivalency. Horsepower is one, and it is something that absolutely you can achieve, but a V10 engine will always give more torque. It might or it might not form an equivalency, but it's important to remember that the reason for the engine issue in the first place was for cost reasons, not a formula by which people had a choice. That formula has been contracted out deliberately by people who wanted V8 engines. That is a clean, clear, analytical statement of fact.'

Patrick Head, however, believed the Cosworth V8 was a better bet than the V10. 'From what I've seen of power curves, run at its maximum, it's certainly below the V8 from Cosworth. The thing about it is that it's so under-stressed that it can be run at its maximum every lap of the race, every lap of qualifying, every lap of practice. That gives a certain advantage. The other thing is that it would have been a much bigger problem, I think, if one of the manufacturer teams had decided to go that route because the Cosworth V10 engine never had variable trumpets and, as I understand it, it has not been optimum-tuned for the lower revs, for the restricted intake. I'm sure that if any of the manufacturers had gone that route – because

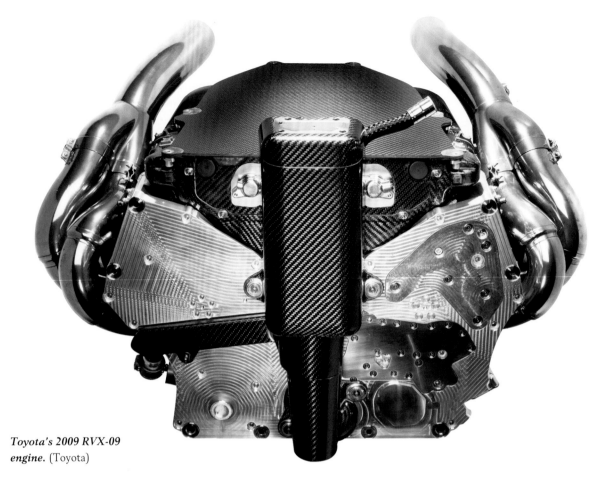

Toyota's 2009 RVX-09 engine. (Toyota)

you're allowed to run with those engines in exactly 2005 specification and they'd have had their variable trumpets and they'd have redone the camshafts and the ports and all the rest of it to optimise it for the new rules – then there would be a few people howling like hell now. Providing it's only the Cosworth V10 and it doesn't get optimised for that, then it brings another team out there which wouldn't otherwise be out there. I'm not sure that Colin Kolles from Midland feels the same way, but I don't have a problem with it.'

BMW's Dr Mario Theissen saw three advantages of a restricted V10. 'One is peak power. Even if you apply the restrictions in a very crude way by putting a plate into the air trumpet, I would expect it to have a higher peak power, though maybe not too much. Second one is higher torque, which should put you in a position at the start to overtake maybe one or two cars, and at the exit of a corner to accelerate much quicker. That's what we saw in Bahrain. And the third advantage is that this engine is good for several thousand kilometres and you can basically go at qualifying pace throughout the race. Those are the major differences from a technical perspective.'

Former racer Gerhard Berger, who had entered into joint ownership of Toro Rosso with Mateschitz, had the last word. 'I don't know about you,' he said at the Nürburgring, 'but I would think Mercedes-Benz has other things to think about than what we are doing with our engine. Like trying to win a championship… Besides, the system governing our engine is meant to be an equivalency formula, not a penalty.'

When the Toro Rossos had failed to score any points after six races, the bitching quietened down. By 2007 the team had done a deal with Ferrari to run its V8, bringing harmony once again. That year, the FIA mandated a rev limit of 19,000rpm.

For 2008 there was a minor revision to the two-race engine rule. This had had such a beneficial effect on reliability that teams would now get their first engine failure of the season free, with no penalty. Thereafter, other failures would attract the usual ten grid-place penalty. This went hand-in-glove with an 18,000rpm limit facilitated by the standard ECU developed by McLaren Electronic Systems (see chapter Five), to peg power around 800bhp.

For 2009 the engine lifing rules changed again. This time a team could use eight engines throughout the season, deploying them as and when it wished, for example using one engine regularly for Friday practice but replacing it with a fresher one for qualifying and the race. But the moment a ninth unit had to be used, a ten grid-place penalty would apply.

Oiling the wheels

Friction and heat are the traditional enemies of Formula 1 engines, and as specific outputs have again climbed closer to 1,000bhp after the halcyon 1,400bhp days of the turbos, lubricants have had to change to keep pace.

The basic function of the oil in an engine is not just to lubricate metal-to-metal interfaces, but to take heat away from sensitive spots. Engine oil must retain its properties at all temperatures. It must not evaporate too quickly, must protect against wear and, through so-called high-temperature viscosity, it must also ensure that all the components to be lubricated are continually bathed in oil. The forces within an engine, as we have seen, are simply so high that any failure in the lubrication very quickly leads to failure in the engine.

Teams have specific oil supply contracts, and the major players such as Castrol, Shell and Mobil use synthetically made oil mixtures developed specifically for their engines. The formulae for these are as closely guarded a secret as the bore and stroke measurements or tyre compound formulae.

Interestingly, far from being the thick fluid one might expect, Formula 1 oil is low-viscosity and therefore flows like water. This is because oil that was too viscous would create drag and therefore have a harmful effect on the engine's all-important ability to rev. 'The lubricant determines the so-called friction coefficient between the engine parts that slide over each other,' Dr David Hall, head of lubrication development at Castrol, explains. 'The lower it is, the easier and faster all the parts can move. Therefore, low friction results in higher speeds, along with lower friction loads on the components and a reduction in fuel consumption.'

The compromise between performance and reliability is crucial. An oil that is too thin can lead to premature failures, partly because it does not dissipate heat as effectively as a thicker oil. But an oil that is too heavy not only restricts revs but actually adds to the car's overall weight. An engine uses around ten litres of oil, of which seven are located in the crankcase and cylinder area.

During testing the engine oil is renewed on a daily basis, and often oil company representatives will experiment with oil levels and will take regular samples for laboratory analysis.

The optimum composition of lubricants is determined with the aid of computers, with factors such as the characteristics of the track affecting the format for specific events. At tight, tortuous tracks, such as Monte Carlo, high-viscosity oil is supplied because of the high loads imposed by the constant shifting between high-speed acceleration and braking, as that causes the temperatures in the engine to rise higher than normal.

Finding the ideal mixture is a lengthy process: the oils mixed in the computer are produced in small quantities for testing purposes. If these are successful, the lubricant has to be tested by the FIA to ensure that it complies with the regulations. Only then are larger quantities produced, which in turn are subject to constant purity monitoring.

The most important task for the oil engineers starts the weekend of the race, when regular samples are taken for analysis after each session of practice. Using sophisticated X-ray equipment they can detect any metal residue which makes its way into the oil due to engine and gearbox wear. This means that under certain conditions engine damage can be avoided. Depending upon the oil's degree of impurity, the engineers can then decide whether a part may have to be replaced straight away.

During the race computer telemetry continues to monitor the oil's performance, providing further notice of impending problems.

Typically, in the course of a racing season an oil supplier will provide around 30,000 litres of engine oil and 3,000 litres of transmission oil, and at each race a team will get through some 200 litres of the former and 75 litres of the latter.

As important as the oil is the fuel. This must also comply with the FIA's regulations, which make pump fuel mandatory. Formula 1 fuel is mixed in batches by each supplier, who must then supply the FIA with a 'fingerprint' for that batch. Even if a fuel matches the batch sample, if it doesn't have the same fingerprint as that homologated for each race it will be deemed illegal. Naturally, fuel plays a crucial role in the efficiency of the combustion process in an engine and thus in its overall power output, so the oil companies are continually introducing new fuels as a season progresses. A typical example was Shell introducing a new low-sulphur fuel for Ferrari at Indianapolis in 2003; this was a direct response to sporting director Jean Todt's call for every one of the team's partners to produce the maximum in the aftermath of the Hungarian Grand Prix, where Ferrari's titles chances hung in the balance. The success of everyone's efforts ultimately enabled Ferrari to win a record fifth consecutive Constructors' World Championship.

Chapter 5
Engine Management
Standard triumph

On the face of it, being tasked with providing every F1 team with exactly the same piece of electronic kit, to take away traction control and some engine braking management, was a mighty task, since everybody knows you can never please all the people all the time. When you had the name McLaren in your title, it was potentially harder still given the enmity with Ferrari that had sullied the 2007 season. But Dr Peter van Manen and McLaren Electronic Systems, working with partner Microsoft Corporation, did precisely that by the start of the 2008 season.

Perhaps the greatest control electronics exercise is over engines, and Max Mosley had long wanted a standard electronic control unit (ECU) so that the FIA could effectively decide what level of power and performance is acceptable, and eliminate things such as the vexed traction control. When he first proposed this it was as popular among the teams and manufacturers as a rattlesnake in a lucky dip, but gradually people mellowed. The problem was that car and engine manufacturers develop the engine and ECU together, and would rather keep doing that than have to use a third party's assessment of what they should use. One problem early in 2006 was that no definition of a standard ECU existed. Changing ECUs and all of the integrated codes associated with them was such a major undertaking that software teams would not have a great deal of time left before the proposed introduction of standard ECUs on 1 January 2008.

'I think in principle most of the manufacturers would prefer freedom with the ECU,' admitted Toyota team principal John Howett early in 2006. 'At least the actual cost of the ECU itself is not of an extreme magnitude. Okay, one would probably need to be more draconian in restricting electronic capacity to significantly reduce the cost area. I think there is an issue of actually ensuring that there are no artificial aids which are intended to be eliminated, such as traction control in the future, and therefore by having a standard ECU it may make it very easy to

police and avoid any rumours of a certain team having this capability or not, and I believe that's one of the reasons that the FIA wishes to integrate the actual standard ECU. But I think as a preference we would prefer to keep freedom.'

Williams's Patrick Head said that he was not convinced that it would automatically follow that having a standard ECU would eliminate the possibility of some sort of power modulation, 'But if we all get put to a standard ECU then those of us, few of us, with devious minds will turn their attention to other means. It's a change and I can understand that a lot of people, like BMW, building their own ECUs, will find it an interesting challenge which I'm sure will have some relevance and some knock-on to their road car development. It must feel very uncomfortable for engineers to be told "No, you can't do this, no you can't do a job in that area", and be given what will probably be a fairly middle-of-the-road type piece of hardware. It doesn't feel very Formula 1-ish. But anyway, that's what we're told we're getting and it seems it's still Max and Bernie's game so that's what we've got to play with.'

Opposite: Without traction control, it is far easier to get a car sideways, as Sebastien Bourdais proves in the Toro Rosso-Ferrari STR04. (LAT)

'As we understand,' said Dr Mario Theissen of BMW-Sauber, 'the original aim was to rule out artificial driver aids and we fully support that, even if road cars have it. We want to see the best drivers out here and want them to cope with the car at the limit and that is certainly more exciting without driver aids. We have had talks between the manufacturers and some teams, I think it was a year ago – at least a year ago – about how to achieve that, and we came to the conclusion that it should be possible to do that with a controlled section, accessible to the FIA, to make sure that there are not artificial driver aids. We would prefer to go along this route because today virtually everything comes with its electronics and virtually every functionality is controlled electronically. So in

Magneti Marelli's engine control unit was a compact, but nevertheless vital, component of several F1 cars, until the mandatory FIA standard ECU was introduced in 2008. (sutton-images.com)

order to have the possibility to test new functionalities, we would need to have access to the electronics and then you are immediately down to the question: what is standardised? Is it a certain area of the hardware, is it the basic software as well, even the application software? It's quite a difficult and tricky area, so, as I said, we would prefer to have a common standard which ensures that there are no driver aids and they cannot even be perceived to be there, but then to do our own stuff in order to use the same stuff for testing and racing.'

So that was the backdrop to the work that MES was tasked with. Van Manen admits that it was a tough commission when it was contracted by the FIA in July 2006 to create the new standard ECU.

'It was a question of understanding what the important requirements are for controlling an engine, gearbox, differential, throttle etc, and coming up with some application software that could cater for the different types,' he said. 'So the challenge really was in structuring it the right way, so that it could deal with all the differences without forcing teams to make mechanical changes to their powertrain. Once you have the structure right, then it's a matter of implementing it and providing sufficient detail early enough to the teams to enable them to comment upon that and also

to gauge the suitability to their own systems.'

Late in 2006 MES provided each team with a detailed specification. By March 2007 the first systems were ready so that they could start running simulations on their dynamometers. In the ensuing period, until winter testing started in Barcelona that November, MES worked on refining the prototype and dealing with issues that arose, such as sorting out protection strategies, etc. But the key thing was always having the structure correct in the first place.

The layman might look at the situation and say OK, they are all 2.4-litre V8 engines, what could be so hard about producing a universal electronic control unit (ECU) that would suit them all? But in F1 everything is bespoke to the nth degree, and much of what MES could achieve lay in the amount of information it was given by each individual manufacturer.

'As far as running an engine is concerned, the physics of how you manage the airflow, the fuel, the spark, is quite straightforward,' van Manen agreed. 'Where the differences start arising is how you deal with the transient effects as you accelerate out of a corner. Also, each of the engines had different protection strategies for the particular design. So you might have had an engine that had a certain fragility at the top end and you'd need software to help deal with that, while another might be strong in that area but require some support in other parts.

'The other thing that was important was dealing not so much with how an engine might run in normal operation but the sort of 'what if?' scenarios. What would happen if you lost one of the sensors, how would you deal with that? What would happen if something failed and you needed to continue to run? Then you would get into quite a subtle piece of engineering.

'Then how would you deal with the different requirements of the teams? One of the things that underpinned the whole process was the fact that the application software, how you control the engine, had to be visible to all of the teams. So whatever software we had in the unit, all the teams could see. So certainly during 2007 when you had teams competing in the championship, they had to take the decision themselves whether they asked for functionality, in which case the others teams would see that, or not ask for it, in which case they would go into 2008 without being able to use that. So it was very much a team

decision as to how open they wished to be. It was completely selfish from their perspective, and if they wanted to run it in 2008 they had to speak up.'

MES could scarcely have chosen a worse year than 2007 for this level of inclusive engineering, with the furore that surrounded McLaren at the height of the Stepneygate spy scandal, and trying to convince everybody that nobody would be disadvantaged.

'Yes,' van Manen conceded reluctantly, 'but to be honest the politics didn't really affect us greatly. Because it was quite an aggressive development requirement, both for us and for the teams, people just had to get on with doing it. And also we had been working with most of the teams anyway, they all knew us, so there wasn't a matter of anyone saying "Who are these guys who are coming in and doing this?" A combination of that and mutual engineering respect meant that the politics and the soundbites didn't really affect us that greatly.'

Could anyone now take a 2009 BMW ECU and stick it straight into a McLaren?

Though it looks innocuous enough, the ECU is a key component, and McLaren Electronic Systems faced a tremendous challenge in 2008 creating the standard unit on behalf of the FIA. (sutton-images.com)

'Yes. It's identical. What you've got is that all of the electronics are identical. Take one unit, and you can run it in any of the cars. They all run exactly the same software, so again you can take that program and run it in any of the cars. Where the differences lie is in the data used to tune that, and that is down to the teams. They have a piece of software and they have to tune their car to get the optimum performance. So there is no doubt that if a team does a good job on tuning the system and another team does a bad job, the team that does a good job will do better. But that's where the motor racing comes in.'

With no electronic aids to smooth engine braking, it was far easier to lock the brakes on a 2009 F1 car, as Nico Rosberg demontrates. (LAT)

That underlines the high level of responsibility for the MES engineers not to fail to spot how that could be done, as far as the McLaren race team was concerned, so that McLaren Group as an entity didn't get upstaged on its own software by, say, BMW, or, perhaps worse still given the events of 2007, Ferrari…

'It's worth pointing out that we don't have an "own" team, because we're quite independent from the racing team,' van Manen stressed, 'and although in F1 this is the first time that we have supplied all of the teams in the category, supplying a number of competitors in a racing category is not something which is unfamiliar to us. If you think of the electronic system as a fairly sophisticated piece of infrastructure that we're selling, it's then down to racing teams to extract performance from it. So we're giving them a tool and it's up to them to race it. From our perspective, a winning race is one where all the cars finish.'

Initially, there were suggestions that some teams had found a way to bypass the loss of traditional wheel sensors to sense imminent wheelspin, and hence activate traction control by cutting fuel flow or sparks, by measuring the speed and density of airflow into the airbox. Van Manen quickly scotched that notion. 'The short answer is that with the standard electronics and the software and the protection measures that we have, teams can't provide traction control.'

So everyone could be as confident as possible that there was no longer such a thing as traction control in F1, other than that provided by the driver's right foot?

'Correct. You just have to watch the way the cars dance around now.'

While the deletion of that aid was easy enough to understand, van Manen took time to explain the effect of the ban on engine braking management.

'With a racing engine, particularly an F1 engine, there is very little inertia, so when the driver comes into a corner and takes his foot off the throttle, the engine will slow down very quickly, so that will tend to brake the car. What we were doing in previous years within the electronics was controlling the torque being generated to smooth out that engine braking. So effectively that kind of settled the car in those conditions. When you remove that settling effect within the control system, it means that the driver has to do that himself – he can't take his foot off the throttle and slam on the brakes and let the system smooth it all out, he now has to blend the two.

'So what you've got, the combination of removing the engine braking features and removing traction control, is that the driver has to show a greater degree of control when he's slowing down into the corner, and also has to provide a greater level of control as he's accelerating out of the corner.'

The FIA-standardised ECU made its debut in Australia in 2008, coincidentally a race won by Lewis Hamilton's McLaren Mercedes MP4-23. It was highly successful, insofar as nobody really noticed. But drivers talked of 'developments' to sort out their cars to get the best from the electronics system.

'That was essentially a case of the teams improving the reliability of being able to deal with different things that come up rather than providing any sort of performance advantage,' van Manen explained.

'The biggest change with the standard electronics on the car was that all of the application software was completely new to everyone, so all of the teams had to deal at the start with a completely new piece of software, and then tune it. In some respects that took a lot of them out of their comfort zone. It was a big step, but it was the same for everyone.

'The standard ECU is a complicated system so there was a lot to do. But there weren't any major issues along the way. The nature of engineering and particularly of motor racing is that there is a lot of graft to do and you work through problems as they come up. The fact that we went into winter testing at the beginning of November and we had 11 teams going round and round the track, didn't happen by accident. There was a lot of work on our side and a lot of work by the teams and the FIA.'

He denies that hard work was necessary to avoid any suggestions of favouritism, however. 'To be honest, that relied on our own selfish human nature, if you like. We didn't want any of our systems to fail and equally we wanted to be completely fair and open to all the customers we sell to. That's our business. The moment that you don't do that, then you destroy your business.'

The first test in Barcelona generated over three days about 10,000 miles, or 50 race distances. The next test at Jerez in December the same again. Then came all the new-car running in January. It was some development schedule…

'It was very intense. Not wishing to be cheesy, getting it wrong wasn't an option. Sometimes, knowing the consequences of failure is good, because it keeps you focused.'

Nobody gives a second thought to the ECU on an F1 car now, and in many ways that is an ultimate tribute to the work that went into developing it.

'I have become a suspicious beast since working in F1 and I wouldn't for a moment become complacent about anything,' van Manen said. 'But the experience over the winter and then going to Melbourne in 2008 was positive.'

The ultimate recognition came a year later when, on 29 April, McLaren Electronic Systems was awarded the prestigious Queen's Award for Enterprise in Innovation, widely viewed as the UK's most prestigious accolade for business-related achievement and performance.

The lack of traction control means that drivers must now cope with the challenges of wet-weather driving unaided. (LAT)

Chapter 6
Transmission
Drive lines

The Formula 1 car's drivetrain comprises the engine and transmission, but it is always the engine that draws the attention. Everyone wants to know how much power an engine has; it is a sexy, vibrant, high-profile part of the machine. The transmission, figuratively and almost literally, lives in its shadow. It is a part of the car that is difficult to quantify in performance terms and therefore it receives little publicity unless something goes wrong. Nobody but the engineers and, possibly, the driver, is ever interested in which car has the fastest gearshift or the lightest transmission. It doesn't help that the gearbox is one of the most closely guarded technologies in the car, and that designers like discussing it even less than they do the engine or their overall downforce figures. Yet the best designs are as intricate as a Swiss watch.

Piston-engined vehicles need a gearbox because although the engine generates torque or twisting power, it cannot develop enough for the vehicle to move if it has a direct drive, or a drive ratio of 1:1. In other words, one complete revolution of the engine while the vehicle is at a standstill cannot generate one complete turn of the driven axle, and thus move the vehicle forwards. What is needed is a set of different ratios, which enable the vehicle to move from standstill, and then keep moving while matching the engine's speed to the vehicle's.

If there was only a first gear ratio of, for example, 3.4:1, the vehicle would move but pretty soon the engine would be screaming its head off at the top of its rev range, and the vehicle's outright speed would be severely limited. Even if there was a second gear and a third, with respective ratios of say 1.9:1 and 1.4:1, there would still be times – for example when the driver wanted to cruise on motorways – when there were insufficient ratios. He would thus need a fourth gear ratio of 1:1, and to provide relaxed driving once the car had reached cruising speed he might have an overdrive ratio of, say, 0.75:1.

Road cars and race cars differ in their requirements. Most manual road cars have five forward speeds (though some topline sports cars now have six), and their ratios are sufficiently well spaced to make maximum use of the engine's broad power band and to permit rapid acceleration and serene and frugal high-speed cruising with the highest ratio acting as an overdrive. Generally there is a gap of 1,000rpm between normal road car gears. The race car needs little of this. Instead it needs to maximise its performance. All Formula 1 engines have relatively narrow power and torque bands; the car must therefore be geared so that the engine operates within these bands in order to achieve maximum performance. For that reason they all use seven forward gears with relatively close ratios, so that the driver can always keep the power unit 'on the boil'. Gearing a car for the corners on a particular circuit is an art, and nowadays the engineers sort this out with the aid of computers and a wide range of ratios, long before a car actually arrives at the track in question. Thereafter only small ratio changes are likely.

Opposite: Ferrari's spotlessly clean transmission department at Maranello is more akin to an expensive private hospital.
(Getty Images)

A gearbox has an input shaft which transfers the power from the engine to the gearbox. This carries one set of gears, while another set is mounted on a separate shaft and is free to move backwards and forwards so that at different times different gears mesh with those on the input shaft, depending upon which ratio is selected by the driver. By changing the position of the gear lever, the driver moves gear selectors within the gearbox which dictate which gears will mesh to create the desired ratio. Drive is then taken from a pinion at the end of the second shaft, which is mated to a crownwheel so that the drive is turned through 90° to turn driveshafts which transmit it to the driven wheels. All Formula 1 cars are rear-wheel drive.

When a car is turned through a circle, the inside rear wheels turn through a shallower circle than the outer rear wheels. Therefore some means must be provided so that the inner wheel does not have to rotate at the same speed, or do as much work, as the outer as they

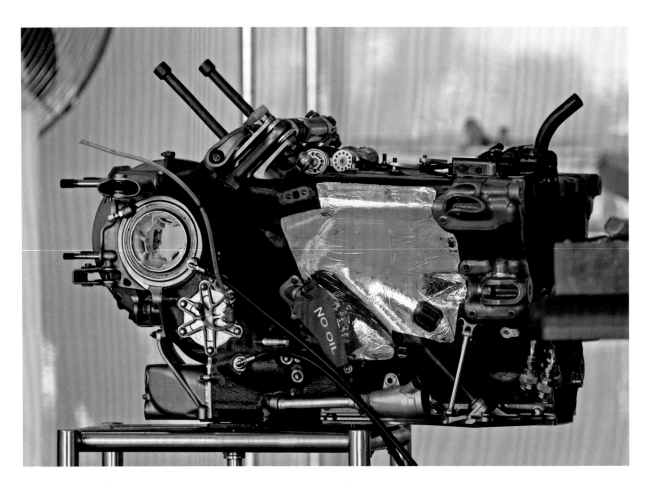

follow their different paths through a corner. Without this it would be extremely difficult, if not impossible, to make the car turn at all. The mechanism which enables this to happen is the differential.

Formula 1 differentials are highly complex components that are recognised by designers to exert significant influence over a car's handling.

Some differentials incorporate a mechanical limited-slip facility that helps to prevent wheelspin under heavy acceleration by locking the differential. A completely locked differential is ideal for acceleration, even in the wet, but of course a car with a locked diff would have great trouble getting round corners. It would always want to understeer, especially under power. Today Formula 1 cars use electro-hydraulic limited-slip differentials which allow either the engineers or the drivers to make constant small adjustments via buttons on the steering wheel. The electro-hydraulic differential can steer the car by controlling the differential torque across the axle. The torque distribution differs in different states, such as when the car is under power on acceleration, or when it is not, on the overrun under braking. Under these conditions the limited-slip

differential can induce a yaw or turning motion that will occur in addition to any steering input made by the driver, or it can resist yaw and enhance stability. The electro-hydraulic differential complies with the FIA's strict regulations and is easier for the engineers to set up to provide a given set of characteristics. The car's onboard computer controls a Moog valve, which in turn regulates the hydraulic pressure, which in turn regulates the torque going through each output shaft, while electronic sensors monitor differential wheel speed.

Another mechanism is also needed to pass the drive from the engine to the gearbox, and to enable that drive to be separated momentarily when the driver wishes to effect a gearchange. This is called the clutch, and without it the car could not be driven, nor could the gears be changed.

The clutch is mounted on to a round plate on the rear of the engine, which is itself bolted to the crankshaft and called the flywheel. The clutch has a pressure plate, which is part of its external cover, and a driven plate, which is mounted inside. The gearbox input shaft passes through them both.

When the driver wishes to change gear he must

Left: 2009 Renault R29 gearbox assembly.
(sutton-images.com)

Right: The wineglass and champagne bottle cork provide remarkable perspective for this Sachs F1 clutch. Though tiny (111mm diameter) it can transmit more than 900bhp.
(ZF Sachs AG, Germany)

interrupt the connection between the engine and the gearbox, which is maintained by springs in the clutch cover which force the driven plate into face-to-face contact with the flywheel. When the driver actuates the clutch pedal, hydraulic fluid pressure forces the clutch pressure plate into contact with the driven plate, momentarily forcing the latter away from the face of the flywheel. Drive is interrupted for as long as the driver operates the clutch, so he can change gear. When he releases the clutch, drive is resumed.

Formula 1 clutches use three or more carbon drive plates and are brilliantly compact units that are little larger than a man's hand-span. This is critical, as engine and chassis designers continually call for ever-lower crankshaft centrelines to lower the engine's centre of gravity. The diameter of the clutch is one of the limiting factors in this, but a typical AP unit is around 100mm. In the case of the Formula 1 clutch, the operation of the modern transmission is so smooth that the clutch does not need to be activated on upshifts. There is also less impact on the clutch on downshifts, when it is used, so it is race starts that impose the greatest loadings, and therefore components are carefully lifed.

In the past two decades the gearbox has become a key part of the Formula 1 car, and an area in which development has been expended. It is no longer simply regarded as the means by which the engines' rotating motion and power is converted into forward movement. It is a crucial component.

The gearbox has to withstand high loadings and temperatures, while also performing a structural duty. Thus the tolerance of components and the reliability of the gear assemblies play a critical role in the overall reliability of the car. This is why today's units are built with the attention to detail and precision excellence of expensive timepieces.

In the '50s the switch from front- to rear-engined cars necessitated the development of suitable transaxles – a combination of gearbox and differential that fitted on to the rear of the engine to transmit the drive. Previously, with front-engined cars, the gearbox had usually been fitted to the back of the engine, and this unit was connected to the differential on the rear

axle via a lengthy propeller shaft. Some front-engined cars, however, balanced their weight distribution (and therefore their handling) by mounting the gearbox with the differential at the rear. The new breed of cars from John Cooper's eponymous team and Colin Chapman's Team Lotus used proprietary Jack Knight, Colotti and, later, Hewland transaxles.

In those early days the transmission was merely there to transmit the power to the road. But with the 3-litre formula in 1966 came a fresh role as suspension components were mounted on to the gearbox, which thus assumed a structural duty on the car as well, as designs became more integrated. The fragility of ZF's transmission, however, was the Achilles Heel that cost Lotus the 1967 World Championship with Chapman's innovative Lotus 49.

In the '60s the American transmission genius Pete Weismann worked closely with Jack Brabham, experimenting among other things with automatic transmission long before it became a feature of the scene in the early 21st century. Another pointer to the future came when March designer Robin Herd, in search of a low polar moment of inertia, sought to make his March 721X less like a dumbbell with a

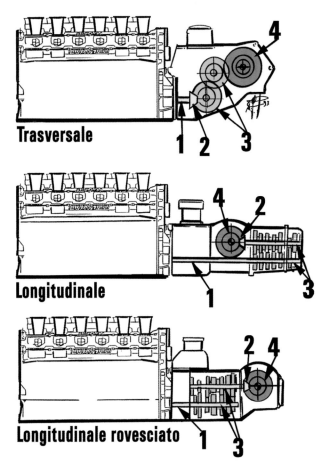

Trasversale

Longitudinale

Longitudinale rovesciato

weight either end by siting the gearbox in front of the rear axle line and thus packaging the weight along the shaft to make the car handle better.

The most significant development, however, came in 1975, when Ferrari mounted the gearbox transversely on its title-winning 312T. This was one of the first successful conscious efforts to package the gearbox, rather than leaving it pretty much as a passenger.

On engineer Mauro Forghieri's design, the gear cluster was mounted transversely – across the car – between the engine and the rear axle. This made the engine/gearbox unit significantly shorter and enhanced the car's balance and track performance.

Forghieri's design endured until 1987, when for other reasons of packaging Ferrari reverted to a more conventional longitudinal gearbox, where the gear cluster was once again mounted inline, behind the rear axle line.

The late '80s was a period of experimentation in the transmission field. Weismann was active again with McLaren's Gordon Murray when the South African designer collaborated on the design of the MP4/4, which went on to win 15 of the 1988 season's 16 races. Their gearbox was designed to optimise the very low crankshaft centreline on Honda's turbocharged

Below: In 1988 McLaren took maximum advantage of the low crankshaft centreline of Honda's V6 engine, and built a compact three-shaft gearbox especially for it. (sutton-images.com)

The 1989 Ferrari transmission, designed by John Barnard and Harvey Postlethwaite, revolutionised the sport by facilitating fingertip electro-hydraulic gearshifting. It is ubiquitous today. (Piola)

Left: A steering wheel from the 1989 Ferrari 640, showing the paddle shift levers,...

... still very much in evidence 20 years later (below left) on the rather more complex 2009 BMW-Sauber F1.09 steering wheel. (sutton-images.com)

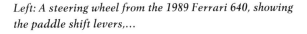

V6 engine. At Benetton fellow South African designer Rory Byrne came up with a longitudinal gearbox in which the gear cluster was ahead of the rear axle line. Separate castings for the bell-housing oil tank and gearbox facilitated faster ratio changes by splitting the two to provide access to the gears. Williams, meanwhile, produced its first transverse gearbox on the Judd-engined FW12. While all this work was going on, John Barnard and the late Dr Harvey Postlethwaite were undertaking experiments with the most significant gearbox development at Ferrari: the creation of a dramatic new means of shifting gears. In

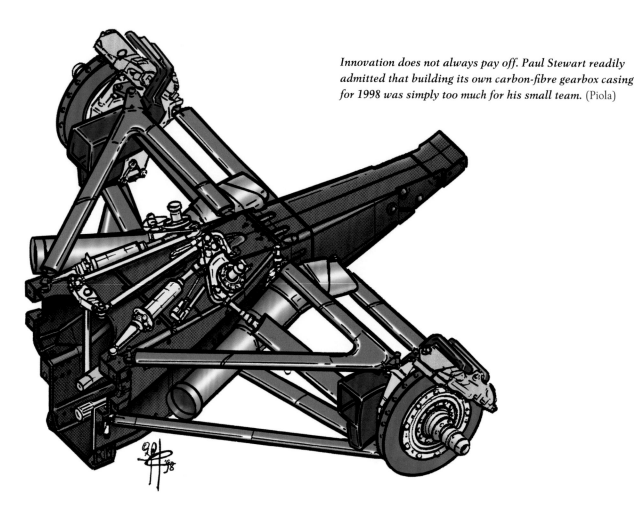

Innovation does not always pay off. Paul Stewart readily admitted that building its own carbon-fibre gearbox casing for 1998 was simply too much for his small team. (Piola)

1974 Chapman had experimented unsuccessfully on his new Lotus 76 with a standard five-speed Hewland FG400 gearbox, which was fitted with an hydraulic system for changing gear. The car used four pedals, a throttle to the far right, a standard clutch to the left, and two inter-connected brake pedals in the middle. This gave drivers Ronnie Peterson and Jacky Ickx the choice of right- or left-foot braking, Chapman firmly believing that two-pedal control was the way to go, the right foot dealing with the throttle, the left, braking. The clutch pedal was only necessary to get the car off the startline; after that the driver used a press-button atop the conventional gearlever to actuate the clutch when changing gear, which itself actuated the system via hydraulics run by a pump driven off the starter motor.

That system failed and was quickly withdrawn, as was an attempt on the 1978 Lotus 79, which used a German Getrag transmission, when again the technology was just not there to support the system, and it was abandoned.

Towards the end of the '80s things had changed. The same sort of electronic control systems that had enabled massive progress to be made in the field of

engine management, boosting power outputs, were also available for the transmission. At Ferrari Barnard and Postlethwaite set about utilising them to revive Chapman's concept of 'clutchless' gearchanging.

They achieved this with a revolutionary concept. The electro-hydraulic system featured steering wheel-mounted gear selector paddles which initiated signals to electronic valves in the gearbox, which in turn simultaneously activated hydraulic actuators and the clutch mechanism to select the individual gears. The gear cluster was an inline arrangement located behind the rear axle line. Thus, instead of lifting off the throttle momentarily while moving a gearlever backwards or forwards through a conventional H-pattern gate, all the driver had to do was keep his foot down while flicking paddles located just behind the steering wheel. In later years teams came to develop their own specific interpretations of this technology, and that can differ from car to car according to driver preference. At BAR in 2003, for example, Jenson Button preferred to activate the right paddle to downshift and the left to upshift, whereas team-mate Jacques Villeneuve liked to pull just one paddle forward to upshift and away to downshift.

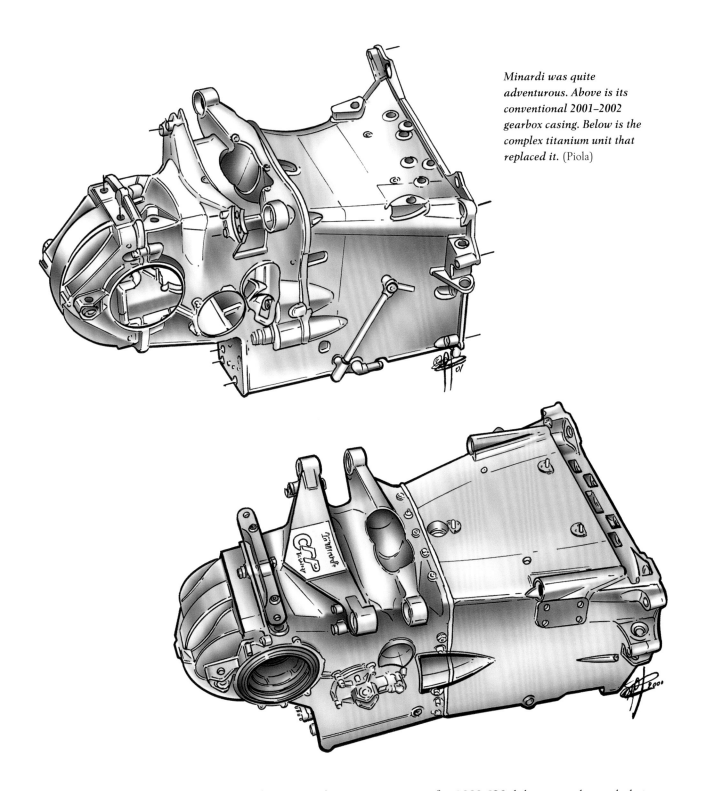

Minardi was quite adventurous. Above is its conventional 2001–2002 gearbox casing. Below is the complex titanium unit that replaced it. (Piola)

Ferrari's technology was so revolutionary that there were inevitable problems. Many times engines were literally split asunder when software problems initiated shifts from seventh to second gear, sending the revs sky high. Barnard and Postlethwaite were so convinced of the merits of their system – and history would prove them absolutely right as everyone came to embrace their idea – that the monocoque of

Ferrari's new-for-1989 639 did not even have a hole in it for the conventional gearshift linkage. When the car failed to do a full race distance prior to its debut in the 1989 Brazilian Grand Prix at Rio de Jacarepagau there were some grave doubts about Barnard's insistence on not designing in an emergency facility for conventional transmission, and driver Nigel Mansell even booked an early flight in expectation of swift retirement. Instead

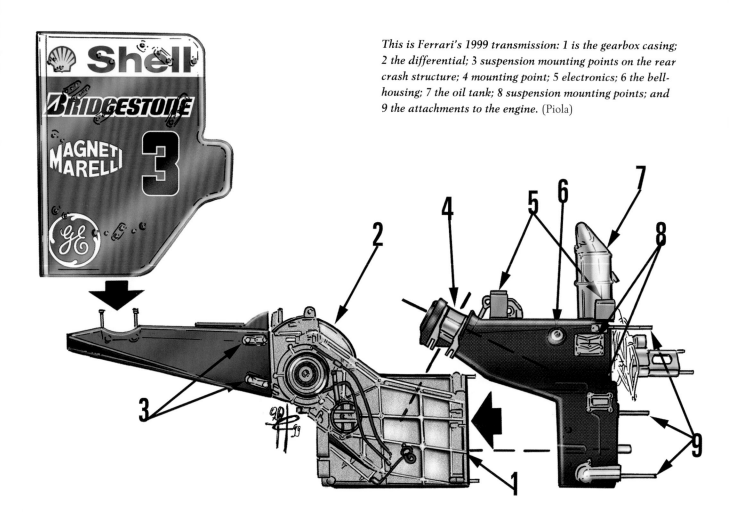

he won the race, and thus was the new technology baptised. Soon everyone began to employ it, some using pneumatics instead of hydraulics for actuation. Besides the speed of gearshifting, the beauty of the new technology once it was fully sorted was that missed gearshifts became a thing of the past, eliminating the spectre of over-revved engines.

The next step forward came with new materials for the gearbox casing. Predictably, it was the innovative Barnard who experimented with a fabricated titanium transverse gearbox on the 1994 Ferrari 412T1, instead of the conventional cast magnesium. On this unit he also reduced the number of electronic control valves from seven on the original 1989 design to just two. This led to further experimentation with materials and the actual structure of the gearbox casing, which was subject to very high power outputs as power outputs increased significantly and dynamic loadings as aerodynamic improvements enhanced cornering speeds. Thin-walled aluminium castings, similar to those used in engine technology, usurped magnesium

because, though slightly heavier, their superior stiffness offset any weight disadvantage.

It was not long before Barnard began experimenting with carbon-fibre composite casings on the 1998 Arrows. At a similar time Alan Jenkins was also at work on a similar concept for that season's Stewart. Both suffered cracking and stiffness problems, and Paul Stewart later admitted that such technology came far too soon for his fledgling team to handle properly as Stewart reverted to aluminium.

Ferrari next experimented with vastly expensive cast titanium, in conjunction, ironically enough, with the under-financed Minardi team which acted as guinea pig in 2000 and 2001. Initially this collaboration comprised a hybrid fabricated titanium gear casing with a carbon-fibre suspension mounting structure, before Minardi introduced a cast titanium unit in the middle of 2001. Subsequently Ferrari produced its own evolution of that with one-piece gear casing, bell-housing and suspension mount casting on its dominant F2002 in 2002. Its advantages were strength, stiffness and minimum weight, and they in turn led to improvements in the handling of the car because of enhanced weight distribution and rear-end packaging opportunities. With springing provided by torsion bars rather than coil springs, Ferrari's cast titanium gearbox situated significantly smaller dampers either side of the input shaft running from the engine to the final drive unit. This super-compact new unit, the work of Englishman John Sutton, also consumed less power and allowed faster gearshifting.

In 2003 McLaren ran its new MP4-18 in testing in A specification with a conventional longitudinal transmission and in X specification with a new carbon-fibre unit designed by Sutton. The car never raced, but the MP4-19 which evolved from it carried over Sutton's innovative new transmission.

The next major step forward came when Williams pioneered so-called 'seamless shift' technology. Was this effectively 'Son of CVT', the DAF-based continuously variable transmission with which it had experimented in the '90s until that technology was outlawed by the FIA? Patrick Head quickly dismissed that notion.

'No, there is no connection. CVT sought to maintain the same engine revs at all times. Effectively what seamless shifting seeks is zero interruption in the drive between the engine and rear wheels during gearshifting, by virtue of very, very rapid sensing and control of the gearchange.

'How it works is that you put a new gear into engagement while you're still in the previous gear. So while you're in the lower gear the system puts the drive into the higher gear as well. Just as this pulls the engine into backdrive on the overrun in the previous gear, as the new gear takes up the drive it pops the old gear out of engagement.'

This all happens very, very quickly, and not unexpectedly development of all systems included a period of what Renault's Rob White described as 'shrapnel time'. This was exactly what everyone went through while developing electro-hydraulic transmissions in the late '80s and early '90s, and was not unlike the problems that faced Anthony Fokker when he developed his synchronisation gear that enabled World War One pilots to fire through their planes' propellers.

'We are talking about milliseconds,' Head continued, 'and initially it was a matter of perfecting the synchronisation. Some teams have invested more

Nico Rosberg set fastest lap on his F1 debut in Bahrain, 2006, driving this Williams Cosworth FW28 with seamless-shift transmission. (sutton-images.com)

Above: Toyota engineers carry out rigorous testing of transmissions during development work at their Cologne facility. (Toyota)

than $6 million in transient gearbox dynos, but we didn't have one at Williams. Because of that we did a lot of damage to our winter testing programme as we learned things the hard way, out on the track.'

If anything, in terms of its concept the seamless shift owes perhaps more to the philosophy behind the old preselector gearboxes used in roadgoing cars such as Armstrong Siddeleys and in '50s racing cars such as Connaughts, whereby the driver selected the next ratio he wanted in advance but only activated it when he operated the clutch.

The aim of seamless shifting is simple and logical. 'There is something like a 30 millisecond period during the gearshift process when the engine is cut while the transmission goes into another gear and before the engine is reinstated,' Head explains. 'That is 30 milliseconds of stalled energy time in the drivetrain, and the overall influence of the shift on your lateral acceleration can be as much as 90 milliseconds by the time you've hit this spike and the system has recovered from it. So 90 milliseconds is the real damage, if you like, for each gearshift. That's 90 milliseconds in which

you're not transmitting drive. That can be particularly hurtful at a track such as Imola, where you're going up and down the gearbox. That's probably the worst-case circuit, and round there the seamless transmission can be worth up to four-tenths of a second a lap.'

When you consider that you'd need another 100bhp from the engine to achieve that sort of performance gain, seamless shifting is clearly worth having.

Williams investigated the concept for three years and worked on its actual system for 18 months before introducing it for the 2006 season on its Cosworth-powered FW28. Honda and McLaren also had slightly different systems ready to run, while Ferrari and Renault were also working on it. BMW had a system ready for introduction later in the year, based on Williams's after lessons the two learned during their 1999–2005 marriage, which ended in divorce in 2005 as BMW went on to buy Peter Sauber's eponymous team.

For 2008 the FIA began lifing gearboxes the same way it had engines, and now transmissions had to last four races. A failure would incur a penalty of five grid-places. At the same time, minimum gear sizes and weights were also mandated. This obliged most teams to redesign their gearboxes.

'Obviously there is an enormous amount of detail

Above: The compact design of a modern F1 transmission is evident in this view of a 2008 McLaren MP4-23 unit. (sutton-images.com)

Right: When it is necessary to change gear ratios at races or during testing, the transmission is separated from the engine complete with the entire rear suspension and wing assembly. (sutton-images.com)

to attend to, to get reliability for four races,' Williams' Patrick Head told *F1 Race Technology*. 'However, a lot of the work went into improving gear manufacture and gear steel to make the gears narrower and narrower and narrower – then suddenly we are told by regulation that we have to make the gears 12mm wide. That gave us a lot of headroom anyway.

'There has been a lot of engineering resource behind developing the gearboxes to do four races – some of the other teams have said that, as such it is costing them more than it was when they were working under the previous regime.

'I think people are finding that they have got to have more gearboxes in the pool and that they have to carry more around than they did before. So there are few people who really think this rule is saving them any money!'

Chapter 7
Electronics
Trace elements

There isn't a driver in Formula 1 who doesn't spend ages poring over the telemetry traces from his car after a practice session or a race, even though some of them profess to hate the modern-day spy-in-the-cockpit that has left them no hiding place when it comes to making excuses for poor performance or driving errors. In the distant past a favourite trick was for a driver to find out where the rev counter telltale was located so that he could zero it before an irate team manager discovered that his speed was the product of over-revving the engine, but today there is literally nothing that a driver can do in the cockpit of his car that his team cannot detect on the telemetry back in the garage.

Electronics, however, have also been helpful to drivers. In the engine they facilitate minutely controlled ignition timing and fuel metering. Fly-by-wire throttles mean that there is no mechanical link now between the throttle pedal and the engine; everything is done by electronics there, too, to achieve maximum efficiency. 'You know, it's amazing,' American F3000 driver Townsend Bell reported after sampling a BAR for the first time. 'They have actually developed a spring system so that the throttle still retains the same feel it would if it had a normal cable, even though it's really now only another button on the car.'

Then there is traction control, which has long been one of those bogeyman driver aids so detested by purists who believe that the driver should have to be the arbiter of the balance between throttle opening and grip level. It has undoubtedly helped lesser drivers over the years to keep up with their superiors, just as the electronics in the transmission have made the missed gearshift under pressure a thing of the past. It was outlawed for 1994, then allowed back in at the Spanish Grand Prix in 2001 as policing it proved almost impossible. Those who thought everything would be different were surprised to see that little changed as far as respective performances were concerned. 'I think to achieve 90% of what might be available from traction control is probably pretty easy and within the capability of all the teams quite readily,' Williams technical director Patrick Head observed at the time. 'So what you're actually seeing is whether one team's traction control is better or smoother or less damaging to the tyres than another's. It's probably quite a fine difference. In truth, on a new set of tyres, if you're actually looking at a grid position as opposed to track position, probably you might get just as good a lap time with the traction control switched off. It's only really helping to make the tyres last longer and look after them, although I think Michelin has already said that with traction control the wear is actually worse that it was. I think it's different for different teams.'

Some believed that the increased electronic freedom improved the morality of Formula 1, after allegations that some teams had been cheating with what amounted to traction control. 'Well,' Head said, 'there's less concern that some people might be circumventing things. I won't say cheating. There was all this talk that Ferrari had some clever system of traction control that was legal even though it was traction control. Well, if you actually look through the regulations there were so many different things in different articles up to Barcelona that were catch-all wordings, right down to as basic as the driver must drive the car alone and unaided. It was difficult to see how anyone could come up with something that was traction control but was legal. There was talk that Ferrari was varying the power of the engine around the circuit. In the places where the wheelspin was high it would make the engine less powerful. Well, I'd say it would be a pretty fine judgement whether that could be regarded as legal or not. But I have no idea what it was or was not doing. But now there is not so much talk up and down the pit lane that teams might be cheating.

'You've got to remember that certainly last year, and the year before, rightly or wrongly everyone had the view that Ferrari was being favoured by the FIA.'

Opposite: The age of the boffin: Toyota's pit is no different to any other in the 21st century, when telemetry and computers are crucial in running F1 cars. (sutton-images.com)

Traction control's role is to prevent wheelspin. It thus has three prime functions: it enhances traction out of corners; it reduces tyre wear; and it enables drivers to push to the very edge in the knowledge that their car will help them. If you dispute the latter point, Heinz-Harald Frentzen spun his Prost in Hungary in 1999 because the traction control failed him at a crucial moment when he had the car tweaked up in a nice four-wheel drift.

The system works by using sensors to monitor wheel-speed and cutting the power to individual cylinders when incipient wheelspin is detected. Sensors independently measure the difference in rotational speed of the front and rear wheels and collate the data. Formula 1 cars tend to be set up to oversteer since this helps the driver turn into corners better, but if the detected amount of slip falls outside this pre-determined window, the onboard management computer will cut the fuel supply to individual cylinders and reduce the power. That's why, when a driver is accelerating hard out of a tight corner, you will often hear his engine popping and banging as if it is about to blow up; it isn't, it is merely having the odd cylinder cut out to ensure that the rear wheels maintain maximum traction at all times. Like brake balance, the degree of traction control is adjustable via a control on the steering wheel.

Extensive tests are carried out to program the software precisely for the traction control. 'Only a perfectly functioning program ensures that the desired advantage can be achieved for the driver,' says Sam Michael, technical director at WilliamsF1. 'But at the end of the day the driver is the measure of all things. He has to coax the best out of the car using all the electronic aids at hand. Thus, a driver's skill will always be more important than the technology factor.'

Traction control's return was sanctioned again when an exasperated FIA finally admitted that trying to police it was all but impossible. There were suggestions that it should be banned again midway through 2003 – certainly for 2004 – but in the end everyone eventually agreed that it was better to keep it than to go through the aggravation and protests that would be the inevitable corollary of a new ban. Such is the progress of technology.

One of the prime arguments in traction control's favour, espoused by teams and drivers, is that it enhances safety, particularly in the wet. 'There's no doubt about it,' Toyota driver Ralf Schumacher suggested, 'it's safer with traction control. Without it I think there would be a lot more accidents.'

Part of the quid pro quo for the retention of traction control in 2003 was that for 2004 other driver aids such as launch control and fully automatic gearboxes were banned.

Launch control is another of those systems that get up the purists' noses. An electronic program took over the entire starting procedure for the driver, so all he had to do was instigate it via a button on the steering wheel prior to the start of the race and then hang on to the steering wheel when the car took off. A computer-controlled pre-set ideal engine speed and clutch engagement process did the rest. In 2002 David Coulthard won the Monaco Grand Prix from polesitter Juan Pablo Montoya after making a much better start. 'It was nothing to do with me,' the victorious Scot revealed. 'I'd like to thank McLaren's computer boffins back in Woking for this win.'

Purists always argued that launch control took away from the driver one of his key means of making up ground in a race, and the effectiveness of individual team systems in 2003 certainly backed up this view. Renault, in particular, had an almost bullet-proof system that enabled Fernando Alonso and Jarno Trulli to make ballistic dragster starts. Through into 2006, the Renaults were generally adjudged to have the best starting software in the business.

Since the semi-automatic electro-hydraulic gearbox gained favour in the early '90s, it had evolved to the point where gearshifts were pre-programmed via the onboard computer, thus relieving drivers of the need to make up or down changes. It ensured also that the driver did not stall his engine, either at the start of a race of during a pit stop. It was another example of electronics playing a decisive role and the technology was so sophisticated that each of the 10,000 or so sequential shifts that would occur during a race took a mere 20 milliseconds. That advantage would remain under the new rules, but from 2004 onwards drivers had to flick the gearshift paddles themselves to effect gearshifts.

The modern Formula 1 car is a mass of telemetric sensors located in strategic places to measure every component's activity, efficiency and status. Teams can literally run hundreds of sensors if they wish, and frequently do in testing. In races, however, up to 25 functions are usually monitored. All manner of parameters are monitored, such as engine revs, water and oil temperatures, oil pressure and the pressure of the pneumatic valve actuation system, throttle opening, fuel flow, fuel consumption, ground speed and the point at which the driver selects his gear, steering input, brake temperature, brake wear and retardation, suspension movement and loading, g-force, etc. If a team has been experiencing problems

David Coulthard put his win at Monaco in 2002 wholly down to the superiority at the start of McLaren's launch control. (sutton-images.com)

in certain areas, perhaps the temperature within the clutch bell-housing, this can also be monitored until a suitable cure has been identified and implemented.

The data that is gathered in this way is stored in an onboard recording system and then transmitted in three ways. In the first, each car transmits data to the pits in real time, so that there is a continuous flow of information the whole time that they are in action on the track. This way the engineers can assess whether the car is working within its defined parameters, such as the centre of aerodynamic pressure, roll stiffness, ride height, etc.

The second means stores the information and downloads it directly to the computers on each lap as a car passes a radar beacon that is usually set up a few hundred metres before the pits. This in turn activates an onboard transmitter whose signal is picked up by an antenna located at the relevant pit garage. This antenna is linked directly to the engineers' computers.

The final means is when the car stops in the pits. An engineer can simply plug his own portable laptop computer into the car's onboard system and download

as many as 12 million bits of data in moments. This third method is the safety net. The other two are not quite infallible as they rely on radio transmission from the car, and at times this may be compromised by fluctuations in radio reception due to buildings, changes in the elevation of the track, or interference from external electronic systems. This can be particularly problematic at street circuits such as Monte Carlo.

For the 1994 season the FIA banned two-way telemetric traffic, though it subsequently made a brief comeback for 2002 before being banned again for 2003. Pioneered back in 1993 by McLaren on its MP4/8, two-way telemetry facilitated a wireless connection between the car and the engineers in the pits and enabled data to be downloaded from the car, and for trackside engineers to upload data back to the car. Teams developed very sophisticated systems which enabled them to make changes to a car's set-up while it was still racing on the track, thus alleviating any set-up shortcomings and removing the final 'guesswork' from one of the most highly demanding aspects of racing.

In 2002 it worked like this. A team could intervene from the pits via a digital laser link to alter a number of the car's electronic management parameters. One laser on the car transmitted data, another in the pits

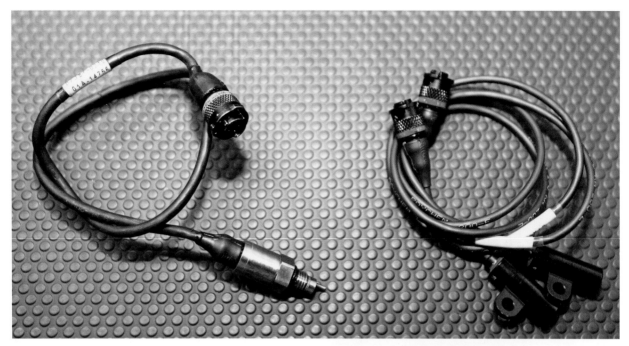

Above: Typical sensors fitted to a modern F1 car, in this case the Force India VJM01. (sutton-images.com)

Right: This sensor, connected to the pitot tube at the front of the car, measures the velocity of the air passing over the front of the car. (sutton-images.com)

did likewise. The rule, however, was that they could only use systems that were previously managed (and indeed still could be) solely by the driver.

This was an important distinction. Back in the '70s, for example, a driver could adjust things such as anti-rollbar settings from the cockpit. Mario Andretti indulged his Indianapolis-bred penchant for playing with the set-up of all his race cars while on the move by having the means of adjusting the rollbars this way incorporated on his Lotuses. But the rule in 2002 was that the only things that can be changed are electronically governed, rather than mechanically.

Zamman Ahmed, one of the engineers who has come into Formula 1 at Sauber Petronas via its strong Malaysian links, explained. 'The sort of things that we could adjust via two-way telemetry were engine critical parameters: rpm, pressures, temperatures, fuel mixture, traction control, engine braking, gearshifting. That sort of thing. The other thing that takes priority was chassis performance, mainly the hydraulic differential and brake balance.'

Two-way telemetry had two main functions over and above the ability to allow a team to take control away from the driver if and where necessary: it could help

simply to keep a car running if a problem that might otherwise have proved terminal arose, and it could enhance certain aspects of its performance. It allowed teams to anticipate problems. 'If on the last lap of a race, for example, you noticed the hydraulic pressure was falling,' Minardi engineer Andy Tilley suggested, 'you might have chosen to disable the gearshift. It was probably quicker just to do that than to try and explain to the driver what to do. By the time he'd done that he'd changed gear and broken something.'

Probably the most significant example of two-way telemetry helping in a race came at Monaco in 2002 when Mercedes engineers detected a slight problem with David Coulthard's engine, which then began to smoke visibly just over one-third distance. Suitable adjustments were made, just as everyone was sitting on the edge of their seats anticipating the imminent demise of the Scotsman as he led the race, and he was able to carry on and score a memorable triumph.

At Magny-Cours Nick Heidfeld's Sauber Petronas C21 developed a problem with its traction control when a sensor failed. He lost traction and therefore performance, but while it was a debilitating problem it was not terminal. For a while he simply turned the system off, but the team worked at finding a solution that at least alleviated the problem.

All of the big money teams were running in real time in 2002, and Peter Sauber invested close to $6 million to join them for 2003 when it was announced that two-way telemetry was banned again. The FIA was concerned because, as Tilley outlined: 'If you wanted to you could select a different differential map for each corner, working from the pits. You could actually be scrolling down your computer enabling just that while the guy is driving the car, if that's what you wanted to do. On the most sophisticated systems you'd have triggers and sensors to do that, but you could do it manually if you wanted to.' There were also fears that the facility might exist for one team to try tampering with another's cars, electronically.

So now teams are back to just relaying information from the cars to the pits. Most use a VHF radio link to provide 'ship-to-shore' communications between driver and the pits. The driver's helmet carries a microphone which is controlled by a push button on the steering wheel. The driver can only speak while activating this button but can receive at any time without recourse to separate movement. Communication is on a specific frequency, and usually

Below: The front of a modern F1 car is laden with various sensors. (sutton-images.com)

Communication is the name of the game. Throughout a race, senior team engineers and strategists (this it Toyota) monitor the data using screens on the pit wall to keep drivers informed. (sutton-images.com)

only the team manager will speak to the driver during the course of a race. All transmissions are encrypted to prevent rivals eavesdropping. The telemetric sensors provide around 100 impulses per second. Real time information flow is around 1Mb of data per lap, while the semi-real time download each lap provides the engineers with around 0.5Mb.

They are, however, completely at liberty to exploit real time computer connections between the racetrack and their factories. Thus engineers at the track can directly relay information to the factory while the cars are running, and if there is a problem, either with programming or set-up, the engineers at the factory can use the full might of the team's facilities to produce a corrective solution. They cannot do this, however, while their cars are in action.

Since the arguments of 1994 the FIA has initiated stringent checks on computer software, and all systems on board a car, or which can be connected to it, must be validated by the scrutineers before a race meeting. At the beginning of each season teams are given the choice of having their systems inspected on two different levels.

'Option 1' entails a full check of computer source code, to ensure that the system complies with the Technical Regulations. The FIA then copies the programs and holds them as a template, so that when programs are uploaded at race meetings they can be compared with the initial 'fingerprint', to ensure that no changes have been made to the approved software. Any updates must be re-inspected as an 'Option 1 recheck.'

'Option 2' involves a less detailed pre-season check on the control software but a detailed check of upload software. When programs are uploaded at a race meeting the FIA will take copies, which it keeps indefinitely. These may be inspected in detail at any time, even after the season has finished. Under 'Option 2' teams can make regular updates to their software without the need for continual reapproval.

If a team chooses 'Option 2' it may be subjected to a full source code inspection at any time, and in either case all hardware must be inspected and documented to facilitate monitoring of changes during the season.

Liverpool Data Research Associates Ltd (LDRA), the independent company that the FIA employed to investigate teams' computer software, explained source codes thus: 'Computer instructions are usually called machine code and are represented internally as a series of noughts and ones, known as binary numbers. This form of instruction is very difficult for humans to understand, so computer languages have been devised that enable us to express instructions in a form that is more natural to us. Programs written in these languages are known as source codes. A computer cannot use them directly but they can be translated into machine code that it can understand by using another program called a compiler. When the machine code is loaded into the computer's memory, the processor can then execute the instructions that are described in the source code.'

Electronics hold the greatest scope for teams to cheat, something that has long been a source of concern to the FIA after the controversial 1994 season. In the past teams have been fined for failing to divulge their source codes, arguing that such information is confidential. FIA president Max Mosley disagrees. 'Source codes are regarded by some people as confidential because there are big car manufacturers,

Some people never actually see their cars racing on the track. Here Renault engineers monitor the telemetry screens during a Grand Prix. (LAT)

for example, which use similar source codes on their road cars,' he says. 'Our position is simple. There are some things that we don't have to check: for example, suspension geometries. But in any area that we need to check, because it is an area that might conceal a breach of the rules, then our position is very simple: if you bring it to a race meeting, we are entitled to check it. So, if your source codes are so secret that you don't want us, or anybody, to look at them, don't bring those codes to a Formula 1 race, because we have to look at them in fairness to all the other competitors.'

Under Article 2.6 of the regulations it is the duty of the competitor to satisfy the stewards that his car complies. Thus they cannot avoid revealing information required by the technical stewards. Over the course of a season, the latter will probably carry out 100 random checks.

Electronics are also used to police the drivers: all cars carry sensors to detect any jump starts. However, on the flip side the driver has a special button on the wheel that engages the pit lane speed limiter during pit stops, so that the car simply cannot go any faster than the law allows. The latter have been known to malfunction, though, most notably when the Sauber Petronas team suffered three stop and go penalties in the 2002 Canadian Grand Prix...

Chapter 8

Suspension and Steering
Dampened ardour

The suspension is one of the most highly loaded and crucial parts of a Formula 1 car, and another one that's easy to overlook. But its structural integrity is one of the cornerstones of a car's performance. To appreciate that, just consider that all of the loads absorbed by a racing car – whether they be lateral cornering loads, vertical loads, or acceleration or deceleration loads – are initiated by the tyres' contact with the road and are then fed into the chassis via the wheel/tyre unit, through the axle/upright assembly, the suspension arms and then finally via the pushrod to the spring/damper units. The stability of the structure obviously also plays an important role in the manner in which the tyres interface with the track.

The suspension upright performs several tasks. Principally it provides the bridge between the chassis and the geometrically ideal position of the outer ends of the suspension arms. But it also houses the wheel bearing on which the axles rotate, and acts as a mounting point for the brake calliper, which nips the axle-mounted disc. It also has a brake-cooling function. It follows, then, that strength is the primary requirement in the upright, and one of the significant problems that Jaguar's R3 faced in 2002 was flexing in the rear uprights when the car was first launched.

The upright has to connect the points in space determined by the geometry chosen by the designer – the actual angles of the suspension arms where they are located and when they are operating. It is thus important that the unit is structurally strong enough to withstand forces acting upon it without distorting and thus influencing this geometry. If that happens, any flexure under load, either at the mounting points or across the structure, will not only affect the geometry but will also induce an undamped movement in the load path between the tyre and the damper. Thus there will be movement that is not specifically controlled by the damper, and this can influence response to steering input,

generate a lack of feel for the driver, reduce the car's inability to carry cornering load, and make it sensitive over bumps, or a combination of all of these problems. Wheel-bearing loads are also very high, under braking and acceleration and when cornering, so the upright must be strong enough to withstand these too. During braking the carbon-fibre discs glow red hot and generate temperature in excess of 1,100°C, so the upright must also deal with this hostile environment. At the same time it must either carry the brake cooling ducts or act as one itself, to ensure that the temperatures generated by the frictional interference of the brake pad against the disc are kept in the 500°C range.

The upright and calliper also have to resist braking loads when the driver requires the 605kg car to slow 300+ kph to speeds as low as 45 in the case of Spa's La Source hairpin. The forces here are enormous as the brake disc is effectively trying to twist the upright on its suspension arms. Any flexure here will make the car very unstable under heavy braking.

While the rear uprights have to deal with forces arising from the engine's power, the fronts have to incorporate mounting points for the steering arms which connect the wheels to the steering rack that is mounted atop the chassis. It is vital that there is no excessive movement or flexure here, not just because that might prejudice the driver's control but also because it would generate inaccurate feedback which he might then misinterpret while fighting on the edge of control in a race.

Like brake callipers, uprights these days are manufactured in metal matrix because it is so light

Opposite: Aerodynamic cleanliness is everything around the back end of a Formula One car, even if it means making geometrical compromises. The 2009 Brawn BGP 001 was particularly neatly packaged.

(sutton-images.com)

The front suspension of the 2009 Red Bull RB5 is typical of the current layout adopted by most teams. (sutton-images.com)

and strong. Previously wire-cit titanium and cast titanium were used, as uprights developed from the Triumph Herald proprietary road car components that were used in the '60s to the fabricated steel units of the '80s. Titanium fabrications proved unsuccessful for some time because the material is so notoriously difficult to weld. Failures of such units were believed to have caused the deaths of Peter Revson at Kyalami in 1974 and Patrick Depailler at Hockenheim in 1980. Eventually improvements in technology gave titanium its day, until metal matrix took over. Ferrari's metal matrix uprights are about 20% lighter than the titanium units and twice their price. To give some idea of the advantage, Ferrari's titanium front upright weighed 1.1kg, and its metal matrix upright weighed 900g, a very significant percentage saving.

Metal matrix components, a mixture of aluminium and carbon-fibre, are extremely difficult and expensive to manufacture and require significant care during the machining stages as the gases produced during the process can create serious health issues.

The important factor here is unsprung weight. Picture the vehicle's chassis effectively hanging between the wheels on the suspension arms: that is the sprung weight. The wheels and everything else 'outboard' of the suspension arms is unsprung. The lower the unsprung weight, the less likely a car's handling is to be affected when it is negotiating bumps and undulations.

A significant change was introduced by Ferrari in 2001 when it relocated the front suspension pushrod to a mounting point on the front upright, from its more usual position on the outer end of the lower front wishbone. This gave a more direct load path from the upright to the damper. It had been common practice on rear uprights, but they had no need to pivot as there was no steering function. The modification gave the driver much better feel through the steering.

Composites are also used in some suspension arms, as carbon-fibre units are some 400gm lighter than their steel equivalents. Today the use of upper and lower wishbones (so-called because of their resemblance to the shape of the notorious chicken bone) is universal. The arms are mounted by simple plates to the chassis

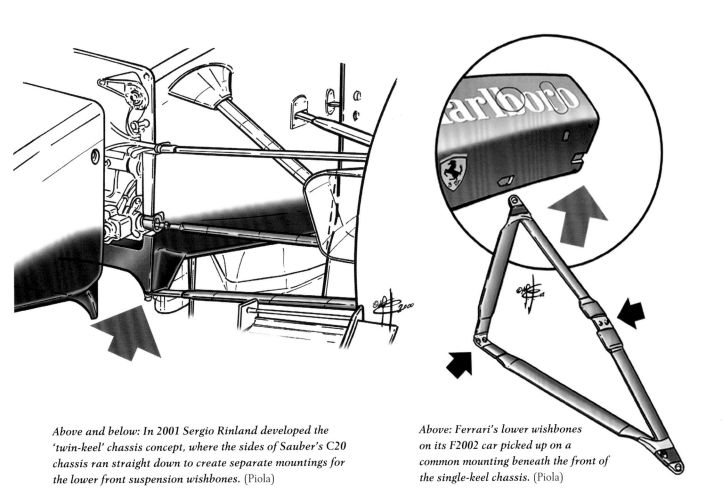

Above and below: In 2001 Sergio Rinland developed the 'twin-keel' chassis concept, where the sides of Sauber's C20 chassis ran straight down to create separate mountings for the lower front suspension wishbones. (Piola)

Above: Ferrari's lower wishbones on its F2002 car picked up on a common mounting beneath the front of the single-keel chassis. (Piola)

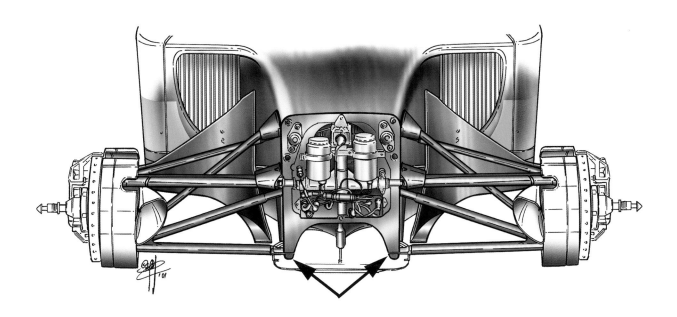

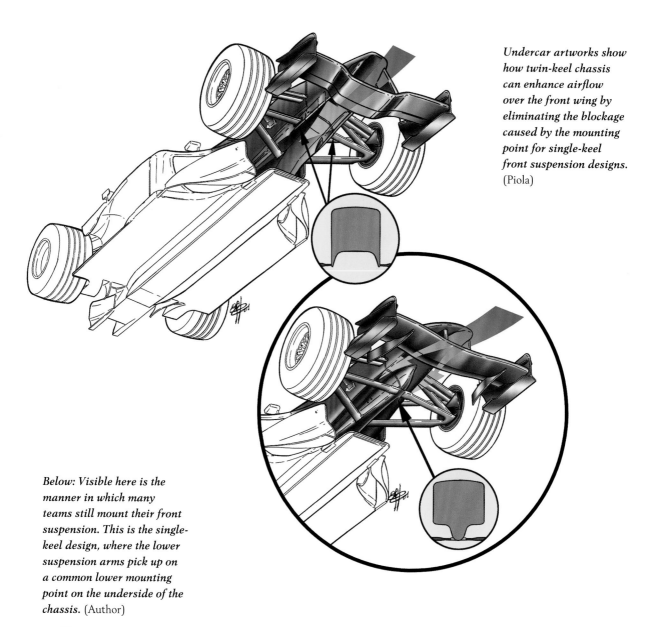

Undercar artworks show how twin-keel chassis can enhance airflow over the front wing by eliminating the blockage caused by the mounting point for single-keel front suspension designs. (Piola)

Below: Visible here is the manner in which many teams still mount their front suspension. This is the single-keel design, where the lower suspension arms pick up on a common lower mounting point on the underside of the chassis. (Author)

and in practice need only very limited upward and downward articulation. As the arms move up and down a rod mounted on the lower wishbone or on the lower section of the upright activates the springs and dampers that are mounted on the chassis. Because it operates at a diagonal angle and pushes the damper, this rod is called a pushrod. In previous applications where the dampers were mounted at the bottom of the chassis, since discontinued for reasons of efficiency and safety, the reverse pattern applied and pullrods were employed.

In order to maximise aerodynamic efficiency, the suspension arms have an aerofoil section determined by wind tunnel research, and these are tested for efficiency and strength on factory rigs. To make sure that the components are strong enough, they

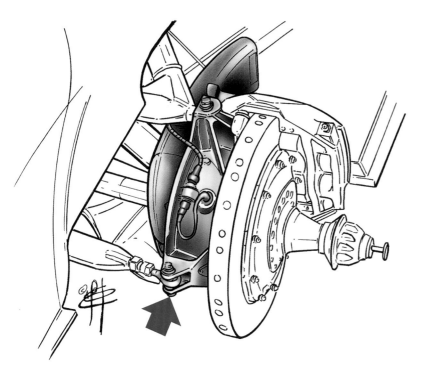

Below left: 2009 BMW-Sauber F1.09 front suspension. (sutton-images.com)

Below: 2009 Brawn BGP001 front suspension. (sutton-images.com)

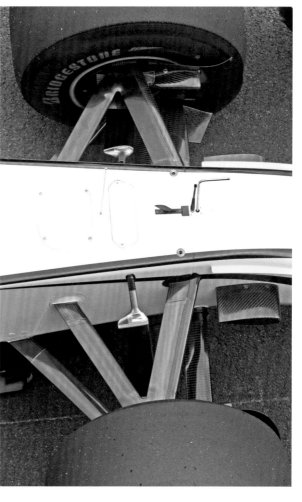

are subjected to loads far higher than they might be expected to encounter on the track.

The purpose of the springs is to provide necessary compliance as the car traverses bumps, while the purpose of the dampers is to absorb excessive compliance and damp it out. Teams will experiment with different rate springs until they find an optimal compromise. A spring's rate is expressed in terms of the amount of force it needs to compress or twist it; some springs have rising rate, which means their characteristics differ depending on the load imposed. There are two schools of thought in Formula 1; some designers still use coil springs, others, such as Ferrari, opt for the torsion bars – introduced by Colin Chapman back in 1970 on his Lotus 72 – for packaging reasons.

Damping is a key area of race car performance.

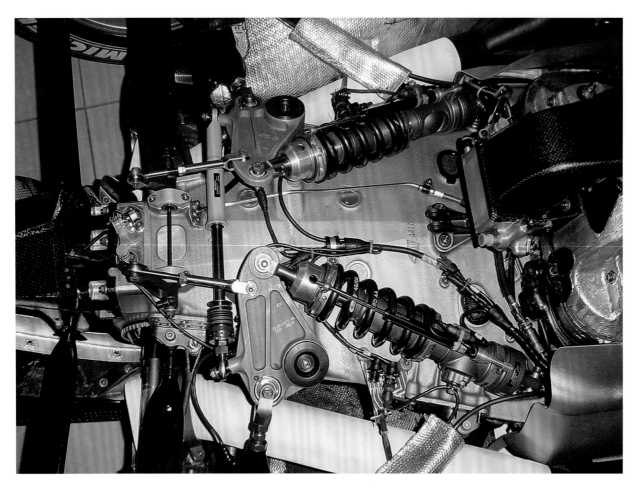

The rear suspension of the Williams FW24 is a masterpiece of cunning packaging, and everything fits beneath the engine cover, minimising the car's rear profile. Visible here are the pushrods, the coil-spring/damper units and their rocker links to the tiny rear anti-roll bar. (Author)

Dampers are highly sophisticated, and have a wide range of adjustments. In the interests of packaging, some have their own hydraulic fluid reservoirs.

The suspension pushrod activates a rocker which is linked to the springs and the separate dampers. The latter use hydraulic fluid which compresses as the damper rod is actuated. The viscosity of the fluid and the valving within the damper influence the degree of resistance and can be altered to provide different behavioural characteristics. Again, teams will carry out lengthy experiments to arrive at suitable damping specifications for given circuits, leaving fine adjustments open to the driver.

Another means of stiffening the suspension is the use of anti-rollbars, which these days take the form of torsion bars. These are activated when the car is cornering. If they are set up stiff, the car will resist roll during the corner. If they are set up to be more compliant, the car will be less resistant to roll. A further refinement is the use of 'bump rubbers' to restrict the spring travel. The springs strike against them and so keep the car from grounding as it bottoms out.

The suspension is one of the most adjustable parts

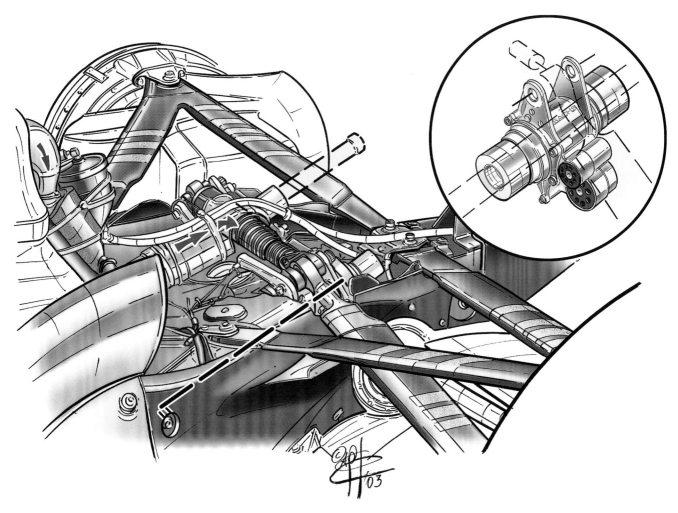

*Above: Ferrari's F2003-GA
rear suspension relied on
torsion-bar springs which
are compact and light.*
(Piola)

*Some teams mount their
front dampers atop the
monocoque, but Williams
opted to locate them
inside the chassis, down
in the foot-well, on the
FW24.* (Author)

of the car, and the manner in which the vehicle is 'set up' has a profound influence on its track behaviour, otherwise known as 'handling'. The aim is to set the car up perfectly for a given circuit. Perfect handling is when the balance of the car – the difference between front- and rear-end grip – is the same. In other words, the car tracks neutrally through a corner, and when it reaches its limit of grip does so equally at each end. The influencing factor in determining understeer or oversteer is the slip angle of the tyres. This is the angle at which the tyre is actually heading, compared to the angle at which the driver is pointing the car. It is said to be understeering when the front tyres' slip angle is greater than that of the rears, and oversteering when

the rear tyres' slip angle is greater than the fronts'. In practice, understeer means that the front end tends to wash out and the car runs wide turning into a corner; oversteer is when the back end steps out and the driver has to apply corrective opposite lock to prevent a spin.

The more neutral a car's handling, the quicker it is and the easier it is to drive at its maximum. It will also use its tyres better than a car that understeers or oversteers. In practice, a degree of either characteristic is to be expected.

An influencing factor is how 'soft' or 'hard' the suspension is set. On the one hand it must be soft enough to absorb shocks or uneven surfaces, or to allow the driver to vault kerbs. On the other hand, a certain level of stiffness is necessary to stop the car from grounding. A car that is set up too soft may have good traction and compliance over kerbs, but it will wallow and float in corners; a car that is set up too stiff will dart from bump to bump. Personal preference plays a

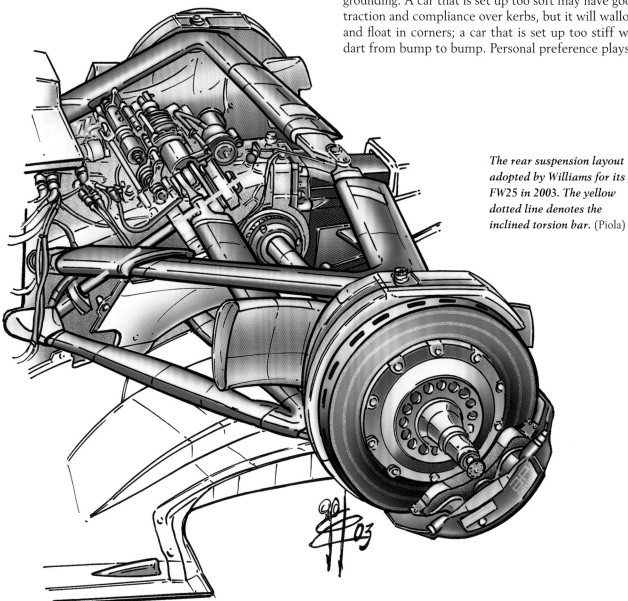

The rear suspension layout adopted by Williams for its FW25 in 2003. The yellow dotted line denotes the inclined torsion bar. (Piola)

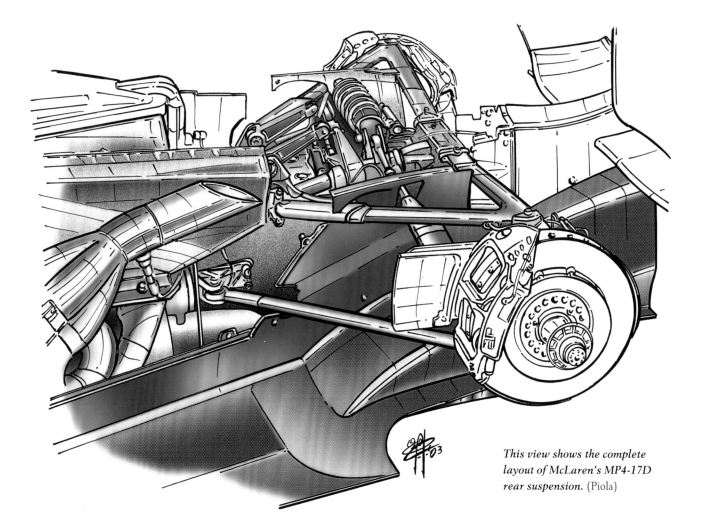

This view shows the complete layout of McLaren's MP4-17D rear suspension. (Piola)

large part in this compromise. Jacques Villeneuve, for example, preferred to have his cars set up relatively stiff so that they responded like a kart to his inputs.

The high cornering speeds at a circuit such as Hockenheim require a relatively soft set-up, to generate the necessary grip. Conversely, the best example of a hard suspension set-up is that used at Monte Carlo. The tight streets are best tackled with the precise handling generated by a stiff set-up.

So many factors come into play that, as BMW Williams discovered in the early part of 2003, failure to fully understand a car's set-up requirements can be costly in terms of results. Once engineer Frank Dernie had come on board with his vast race engineering experience, the team made rapid headway. But finding the Holy Grail is no easy undertaking at the best of times.

'The suspension is one of the most sensitive areas of a race car,' says Sam Michael, at that time chief operations engineer at BMW Williams. 'It has to react extremely sensitively. At the same time, it has to be extremely robust to be able to withstand the forces

generated. It is important to set the suspension so that all four wheels constantly have the same level of contact with the road, so that the car is as balanced as possible in any situation. This guarantees the manoeuvrability and ensures the ideal transfer of forces during braking and acceleration.'

The secret to mechanical grip is to control any rapid variations in the loading on a tyre's contact patch, and that's why there has been so much development in damping over the years.

The rotary damper, which acts in a similar way to the old lever arm dampers first used at the turn of the 20th century, proved very popular in the early Noughties as a sensible way of packaging the suspension, but in 2005 two fresh developments in damping had far-reaching consequences. Both came about as a result of the quest for stability, particularly when a car was driven hard over kerbs.

The first to attract the attention of paddock spies in 2006 was Renault's mass damper, which had actually appeared on the R25 at the Brazilian Grand Prix the previous year when it proved instrumental in assisting Fernando Alonso to the first of his World Championships.

Renault technical director Bob Bell had cleared the concept with the FIA's technical gurus, who agreed that it was legal. The team's 2006 challenger, the R26, was accordingly conceived with mass dampers as an integral part of the design, but where the R25 had only worn one in its nose, the new car used them front and rear.

The mass damper comprised a sprung weight enclosed within the nose of the R26 and one behind the rear suspension to dampen the pitching moment whenever it encountered bumps or kerbs. Curiously, it worked particularly well on Michelin-shod cars, once others had cottoned on and tried their own interpretations. Ferrari, for one, struggled to make mass dampers work with its Bridgestone tyres.

Renault began the 2006 season very strongly and had won four races in a row when it rocked up at Hockenheim at the end of July for the German Grand Prix. That was where the FIA had one of its periodic

A tiny adjustment to suspension settings can have a major impact on the handling of the car. Here a front suspension pushrod is being adjusted on a BMW-Sauber F1.09.
(sutton-images.com)

rethinks and decided that mass dampers were, after all, illegal, on the basis that they were effectively a movable aerodynamic aid. A ridiculous situation then arose in which the FIA stewards of that meeting ruled that the system was not illegal, and the governing body's insistence that its own stewards were wrong merely served to generate the belief, yet again, within paddock insiders that it was seeking to favour Ferrari. Cynics pointed to the 'reinterpretation' of tyre wear at Monza in 2003, which had worked against Michelin and in Bridgestone's (and Ferrari's) favour. And they also noted that the timing of the controversy sucked since the summer testing ban prevented Renault from being able to re-optimise its cars between races.

Renault appealed, but wisely ran without the dampers in the race, in which Alonso could only finish fifth in a car whose set-up had necessarily been significantly compromised.

Renault kept the dampers on the bench in Hungary, too, and on 23 August the FIA International Court of Appeal duly ruled that mass dampers were illegal under Article 3.15 of the Formula 1 Technical Regulations, since they really did constitute a movable aerodynamic device.

Observers were deeply unimpressed.

Renault lost around three-tenths of a second a lap

In 2006 Renault's performance suffered a glitch when the FIA abruptly decreed that mass dampers were illegal. (sutton-images.com)

and saw Ferrari take the upper hand in the remaining races of 2006, but it had the last laugh as Alonso hung on to clinch the title in Brazil after Michael Schumacher's engine had broken in the Japanese GP in October.

The fuss over mass dampers doubtless amused McLaren, which had come up with its own cunning suspension tweak which went all but unnoticed.

Part of the FIA's amended argument regarding mass dampers was that those on the Renault were not part of the suspension system. But McLaren's inertial damper used on the MP4-22 in 2007 – also known as an inerter or a 'J damper' in team parlance – *was*.

Professor Malcolm Smith was a Cambridge University don who approached McLaren in 2003. Parallels between electrical circuitry and suspension systems fascinated him, and he reasoned that a suspension system was just a big electrical circuit. In a typical suspension system the damper is the equivalent of a resistor, while the spring is the inductor, but Smith realised there was no equivalent to the capacitor. That bothered him.

That was when he came up with the concept of the inerter. McLaren liked the idea, and realised that it had to do all it could to keep their secret *their* secret. They called it the 'J damper', for jounce.

The idea of the inerter was for it to behave the same

way a mass damper did, evening out aberrations in the load distribution on the tyres to enhance and maintain grip. It had other advantages too. It proved a useful tool in managing the attitude of the car and giving a better compromise of suspension movement and a stable aero platform, to boost low-speed and high-speed grip respectively. McLaren engineers had found a cake and ate it as a means of maintaining the stiff suspension with limited movement that was an essential part of strong aerodynamic performance at high speed, and of reducing the variation of load on the tyre at low speed that would normally be an inevitable corollary. The inerter facilitated stiff suspension without as much penalty in slow corners.

McLaren developed Smith's idea and raced it for the first time, in the rear suspension of its MP4-20, in the San Marino GP in 2005. Later it incorporated an inerter in the front suspension too.

McLaren went to extraordinary lengths to conceal what it was doing, after entering into an exclusive rights deal with Cambridge University. The inerter was located in a casing within the rear transverse damper housing, where it comprised a moving weight attached to a threaded damper, with bearings on its outer face to facilitate its sliding up and down inside the housing. The weight opposed the changes in forces being fed into the tyres by the suspension. When the damper casing was removed, the only thing visible was another casing.

Different tracks required different levels of 'inertence' so the system had to be tuned to the frequencies likely to be encountered in order successfully to damp the cyclical behaviour in the suspension. 'We define the ideal inerter to be a mechanical, one-port device such that the equal and opposite force applied at the nodes is proportional to the relative acceleration between the nodes,' Smith said.

Normally this would be measured in kilograms per square metre, but in the interests of secrecy McLaren engineers adopted an internal code and measured inertence in 'zogs', their own arcane currency.

The key to the inerter, and the advantage that it conferred, was that it acted very differently to springs and dampers. They act after the event, reacting to external inputs. The inerter, however, operated in harmony with the natural frequencies of the suspension system, and could anticipate inputs. Movements and load variations could thus be cancelled out before they occurred. By doing so, the inerter stabilised load variations on the tyre's contact patch and thus enabled the rubber to generate its maximum grip.

Renault's mass in the R26's rear suspension had been wedge-shaped, with some 7kg at the front end and 3.5kg at the rear. The mass in McLaren's inerter was only about 1kg. As the mass was rotated upwards or downwards according to wheel bump or rebound, it

Right: Hidden among the brake master-cylinder fluid reservoirs at the front of the 2003 Williams FW24's chassis is the elegant power steering. (Author)

Below right: Power steering unit on 2009 McLaren MP4-24. (sutton-images.com)

Below: McLaren's inerter enabled its 2007 MP4-22 to perform particularly well when driven hard over kerbs. (LAT)

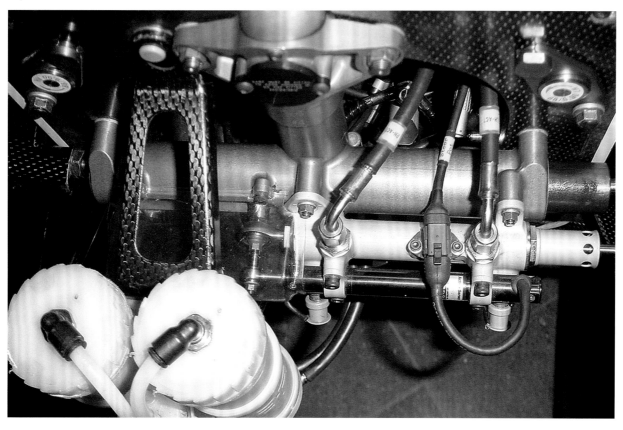

damped out oscillations created, particularly when the car was driven hard over kerbs. This was one of the reasons why the MP4-22 performed so well in such circumstances.

Eventually, other teams figured out what McLaren was doing, since it is impossible for such things to remain secret for long in F1 paddocks, where gossip is rife. Within a year or so Williams was developing its own inerter, and Ferrari had one in Turkey 2007. One race later, at Monza, the inerter on Felipe Massa's car broke and caused his early retirement. If the damper and the inerter operated out of synch, instant breakage of the damper was the frequent result. Seized bearings on the inerter were a common development problem and the sudden and extra loads that imposes on the damper were what usually broke it.

Subsequently, most teams adopted inerters. Unlike mass dampers, they were not deemed illegal.

The subject of mass dampers reared its head again

The steering wheel is one of the fastest-changing components on the modern Formula One car, as functions vary from season to season. This is the 2009 Ferrari F60's wheel, showing the complex array of buttons that operate systems such as radio, differential, fuel mixture and KERS. (sutton-images.com)

early in 2007. After Kimi Räikkönen had won the opening race, in Australia, an argument broke out between McLaren's Martin Whitmarsh and Ferrari's Jean Todt over the legality of the spring fixing device on the floor of the Ferrari F2007, which McLaren believed gave the floor of the car the possibility to act in the manner of a mass damper. Räikkönen's victory stood, but by Malaysia five teams – Red Bull, Honda, Renault and BMW, besides Ferrari – were required to modify the fixing systems which allowed their floors to 'give' as the cars hammered over kerbs.

Steering goes hand-in-glove with suspension. All modern Formula 1 cars use rack and pinion steering, where a pinion gear is attached to the end of the steering column and operates in a rack mounted on the top of the chassis. As the steering wheel is turned the pinion moves the rack. As the latter moves to one side or the other, depending on the direction in which the wheel has been turned, it in turn pushes the steering arms in one direction or the other and they turn the front wheels. The systems operate on Ackermann principles, which means that in order to help the car turn the inner wheel turns at a smaller angle than the outer wheel, rather like a differential helps the inside wheel to describe a smaller arc than the outer.

This view of Nick Heidfeld's 2009 BMW-Sauber F1.09 steering wheel shows just how complex modern F1 steering wheels have become, with a vast array of controls at the driver's fingertips. (BMW AG)

DISPLAYS
1 *Info of FIA/Race Control*
2 *Shift lights*
3 *Multi purpose display (i.e. gear indicator)*

BUTTONS
4 *N = Neutral*
5 *W = Activate front wing*
6 *Multipurpose button*
7 *K = KERS boost button*
8 *– = Presettings down*
9 *+ = Presettings up*
10 *Ack = Acknowledge*

11 *PL = Pitlane limiter*
12 *BB = Brake balance*
13 *R = Radio*
14 *Box = Pit stop*
15 *SC = Safety car*
16 *D = Drink*
17 *Pr = Problem marker button*

ROTARY SWITCHES
18 *Differential*
19 *Preload*
20 *Differential*

21 *Info to pit crew*
22 *Selector (i.e. KERS, Front wing, RPM*
23 *Tyre adaption*
24 *Wing = Presettings front wing*
25 *Pedal = Pedal map*
26 *Fuel = Fuel mix*

PADDLES
27 *Upshift*
28 *Downshift*
29 *Clutch*

In recent years power assistance has been something of a political hot potato. Today drivers benefit from systems which rely on hydraulics, like road cars, to provide greater or lesser degrees of assistance. Generally 30% is regarded as sufficient for a gym-trained racer, while still providing him with a reasonable level of feel. Teams also incorporate safety features, in case of power-assistance failure. All systems have built-in fault detectors and usually operate off a pump on the back of the engine that is driven by a shaft mounted in the gearbox. Electronic power steering has been banned.

The modern steering wheel has a distinctive D-shape and is custom-made for the particular driver. Besides being the most important component on the car, because of its ability to transmit instant messages to the man who controls it, it is also the centre of operation for the controls.

The yaw angles at which modern Formula 1 cars run are relatively low, so they can get away with limited steering lock and have such precise steering ratios – around 1½ turns lock-to-lock – that a driver doesn't need to work away at the wheel. That means they can have a surprisingly small diameter, around 250mm.

Chapter 9

Brakes
Disc jockeys

Every time a rookie driver first steps into a Formula 1 car, it is inevitably the braking performance and not the power and acceleration that makes the biggest impression. The sheer speed of the car rarely fazes good drivers, but getting used to just how late you can brake in a car with carbon-fibre brakes to Formula 1 standard takes a bit of learning. More than anything, it is a matter of the driver reprogramming his mental level of trust to cater for the awesome stopping power.

Ever since racing began, the ability to brake later than the next man has been a key part of overtaking. In the '60s and early '70s the Swiss driver Jo Siffert revelled in the nickname 'the last of the late brakers'.

The introduction of the disc brake in the '50s was a major step forward. Prior to that cars had used drum brakes. These comprised large cast-iron drums which were fitted on the end of the axles, so that they were covered by the wheels when the latter were fitted. Inside the drum were two semi-circular shoes, whose shape fitted the smooth internal shape of the drum. When the driver operated the brake pedal, hydraulic pressure from a master cylinder mounted behind the pedal, and smaller separate cylinders fitted inside the brake drum, pushed small pistons which in turn pushed the shoes outwards until they touched the inner face of the drum. The resultant friction slowed the rate of rotation of the drum, and thus slowed the car down.

Drum brakes were relatively inefficient, and had poor heat rejection properties. Despite copious finning on the outside of the drums, which came to be located in the airstream just inside the wheel's inner face, overheating was a constant source of concern and led to brake fade. This was a situation in which the brakes became so hot that they lost their efficiency. As the hydraulic fluid suffered heat transfer from the hot brakes it lost efficiency too and boiled, creating greater travel on the brake pedal. That is what a driver means when he complains about a 'long pedal'. Most drivers prefer the brakes to operate with very little pedal travel because it is a confidence booster. It's good to know that when you tap the brakes, they will react instantly, especially on tight street circuits such as Monte Carlo. There is nothing more off-putting than racing there with a long brake. In extremis, brake fade requires the driver to pump the pedal to restore hydraulic pressure and reduce pedal travel.

When Jaguar won the 1953 Le Mans 24 Hours after equipping its C Type sports cars with disc brakes, the motor racing world woke up, albeit slowly in some cases, to the new revolution. Discs are now universal in all forms of racing as well as on many road cars, although the cheapest road cars still use drum brakes on the rear wheels to complement discs on the front.

The primary benefit of the disc brake is that it is not enclosed like the drum, so the heat dissipation is much more effective. The disc rotates on the end of the axles, usually within the wheel, and is gripped under braking by a calliper which has a cylinder and a brake pad either side of the disc. When the driver operates the brake pedal, hydraulic pressure pushes the pistons further out of the calliper so that the pads are forced into contact with the disc to slow the car down.

Opposite: Carbon discs weigh far less than their cast-iron counterparts, and revolutionised Formula One braking technology.
(sutton-images.com)

Until the '70s cast iron was the choice of material for discs, with some reasonably exotic choices of material for the callipers. At times the latter have been mounted in the nine o'clock position, behind each wheel, at the six o'clock position to lower the centre of gravity, or the callipers have been doubled up, with a pair, one mounted at nine o'clock, and the other at three to offset braking forces.

Equally, designers have experimented with the number of pistons, or 'pots', per brake. Six-pot callipers became very popular because of their enhanced efficiency, as three cylinders each side of the disc pushed the pads into contact with the disc.

In the '70s that innovative designer Gordon

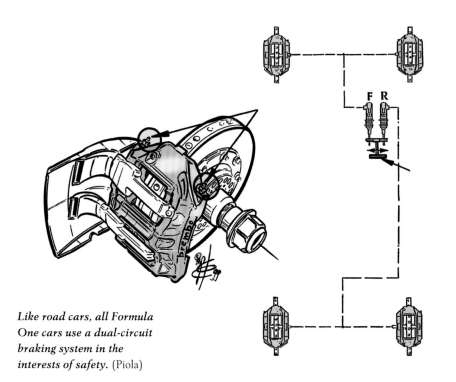

Right: Williams used two-pedal control on the FW24. The throttle is on the left in this photo, the brake on the right. Note carbon-fibre composite construction of the pedals in the interest of lightness, and the two master-cylinder pistons operated by the brake pedal. (Author)

F R

Like road cars, all Formula One cars use a dual-circuit braking system in the interests of safety. (Piola)

Below: Front brake assembly on Ferrari's 2008 F20008. (sutton-images.com)

Murray experimented with carbon brakes on Bernie Ecclestone's Brabham Alfa BT45, whose large fuel capacity and relatively high engine weight posed further braking problems as the South African sought to make a silk purse out of a concept that some believed to be a sow's ear. Once initial problems with wear characteristics were overcome, carbon brakes became *de rigueur* from the '80s onwards. Apart from their dull black colour (which glows cherry red under very hard braking), carbon discs look outwardly similar to their cast-iron counterparts, but they operate now in conjunction with high-tech composite carbon pads. Not only is the level of efficiency extremely high, they are also lighter than their conventional steel counterparts.

Many purists have blamed them for the lack of overtaking in modern racing, because their incredible efficiency has so reduced braking distances that one of the traditional passing opportunities of racing has been steadily diminished. Interestingly, however, Williams conducted experiments at Silverstone in 1995 with a car equipped with cast-iron brake discs, and found that the efficiency and feel were very similar to carbon discs, though the wear rate was inferior.

'There was very little difference between them and carbon brakes,' Patrick Head, engineering director of Williams, confirmed. 'Carbon brakes are more powerful, it's just that what we were running in the old days was a cast-iron disc with a fibrous pad, and what we ran during those tests was a cast-iron disc with a sintered

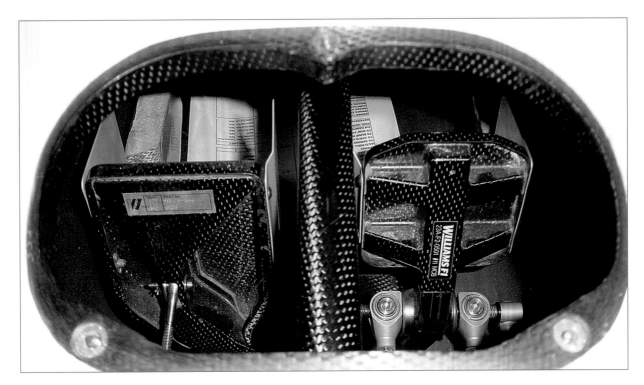

carbon metallic pad.' When something is sintered it has been turned from a powder state into solid state by the application of heat. 'It was a completely different pad, but the same sort of brakes that are on the touring cars. Very powerful, but a different deal. I don't think they would have lasted a race as well as a carbon disc, but as far as retardational power was concerned, they were pretty much the same.'

It is possible that cast-iron discs with special material specification to reduce their weight could prove as effective as carbon discs in lightness and operation, but today the latter are so good and so well established that it would take a brave man to seek to upset the status quo. Besides which, FIA president Max Mosley sounded a doubtful note when he observed: 'The problem is that it would be very hard to police what materials might be used. There are so many additives that one might then put into a cast-iron brake disc that, really, it would probably make little difference, both to cost and to efficiency.'

The braking system on a modern Formula 1 car naturally relies on a split hydraulic system, so that failure of one part of the system still enables the back-up to operate on three wheels. Since 1993 power assistance has been banned, but electronic brake balance mechanisms are permitted even though they appear to be a driver aid. The driver can operate the system to move the brake balance fore or aft according to circumstance, thus optimising braking efficiency. In the past he could do this using cable-operated adjusters. Today's systems are actuated via buttons on the steering wheel. The driver can thus press the relevant button before, or going into, a corner in order to shift the balance to the front or rear wheels. Since he has to do this and there is no automation, it doesn't count as a driver aid.

The toughest circuit on brakes is Monte Carlo, with its 14 corners and the need for thousands of gearshifts during a race. On its short straights the cars accelerate up to 290kph, but inevitably have to brake hard for the next corner. One of the toughest sections of any track is the run from the Portier corner through the tunnel and down to the hairpin. Cars reach their maximum speed on the approach to the chicane, before the

driver has to brake very hard and downshift through the gears from seventh to second. That means going from 290kph down to 80 in seconds. Not surprisingly, this subjects the brakes to enormous stress. On another section, Beau Rivage, the speed drops by a similar amount. The highest deceleration recorded in Formula 1 was 5.99g, but even today the telemetry often records spikes around 4.5g. That means that while braking a driver weighs four and a half times his normal body weight. When you consider that Formula 1 cars accelerate at only 2g and rarely exceed cornering forces of 3 or 3.5g, it puts the performance of the brakes into even sharper perspective.

'High fours are a good figure,' suggested former

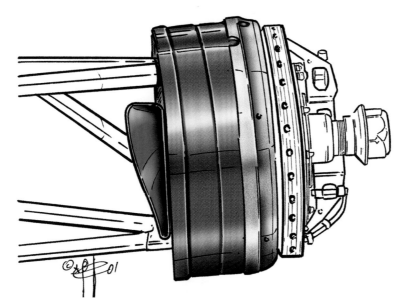

Left: In 2001 Ferrari once again showed its innovative streak when the F2001 appeared with drum-shaped ducts designed to enhance brake cooling. Before long everyone else followed suit. (Piola)

Above right: 2007 Ferrari F2007 rear brake assembly, with rear mounted calliper. (sutton-images.com)

Right: Front brake assembly on 2007 Toyota TF107. (sutton-images.com)

Left: A front brake assembly on the 2006 BMW-Sauber F1.06. (sutton-images.com)

Force India's Adrian Sutil locks up the front wheels of his VJM02 under braking at the British Grand Prix. (sutton-images.com)

Jordan, Stewart and Jaguar engineer Gary Anderson. 'If you were pulling 4.5g on a big stop, that'd be pretty good. Not bad at all.' And that is not the end of the extremes. The brakes reach temperatures of 1,000°C, there is 1,200psi in the hydraulic fluid lines (which have special outer braiding to prevent the possibility of them bursting), and the drivers needs to exert some 150kg on the brake pedal every time they apply it, over 300km races…

Within limits, Formula 1 discs operate better the hotter they get, which is just as well given the temperatures they are subjected to. As it has always been, overheating is thus still a problem that requires some cleverly thought-out solutions. Teams change their brake cooling specifications from circuit to circuit, depending on how hard each track is on braking. All Formula 1 discs are ventilated, which means that slots cut into the disc help to circulate cooling air to ensure that the brakes do not operate outside their specified temperature range. They are also fitted with sensors that inform the team of impending problems. This became important after shattered discs affected some

AP's calliper is a fine piece of casting and the disposition of its six pistons is clearly evident. (Piola)

teams in the late '90s, but even so Kimi Räikkönen's McLaren-Mercedes suffered a rear disc failure in the closing laps of the 2003 French Grand Prix at Magny-Cours.

Today's cars have to use aluminium callipers. The FIA has attempted to place some limit on braking performance by specifying aluminium, a maximum of six pistons and two brake pads per wheel. Most callipers are manufactured in MMC – metal matrix composite – strengthened and stiffened some 20% by the presence of a silicon carbide particulate in the aluminium. For a time some teams favoured stiffer callipers manufactured in Albermet, the trade name for aluminium beryllium metal, an alloy which has a remarkable performance. Since these were 30% lighter than standard units there was a considerable saving in unsprung weight overall, but aluminium beryllium has since been banned by the FIA.

There is a price to be paid for all this efficiency, and that is that the brake discs on a Formula 1 car have to be replaced as a matter of routine after each race.

Tyres are also part of the braking efficiency equation (see Chapter 10), since it is ultimately all about the coefficient of grip. Slick tyres have a wider tread surface and therefore put more tyre into contact with the road. When grooved tyres were made mandatory for 1998, the level of grip fell by some 20% since there was less rubber on the actual road surface. While this slowed down cornering speeds it naturally also affected grip under braking. For a while, as intended, they opened up braking distances, but soon the tyre manufacturers developed better tyre construction and compounding which restored the lost grip.

The aerodynamic set-up also influences braking. Generally speaking, the more downforce in a set-up, the more drag that is created, so that when a driver lifts off the throttle the car will already start to slow itself because the engine power is no longer offsetting the drag. This can also reduce braking distances.

'The braking procedure in a Formula 1 car is an extremely complicated one,' said Gavin Fisher, former chief designer at WilliamsF1. 'It is the interplay between brakes, tyres and aerodynamically generated downforce that guarantees ideal deceleration.'

Arguably, it is still down to where the best driver can brake later than his rivals, but we are now talking such small distances that their effect on overtaking has for many years tended to be minimal. Braking is thus another area in which technology has robbed the driver of an area in which his own feel, courage and expertise might be exploited to generate an advantage on the track.

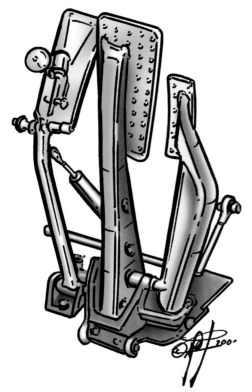

David Coulthard preferred three-pedal control. This was his set-up at McLaren. (Piola)

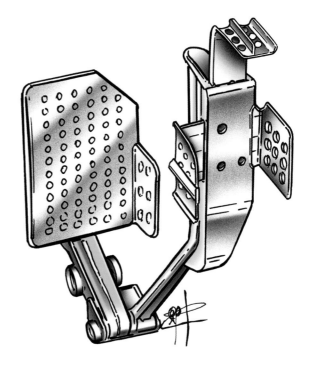

This is the pedal set-up used by Ferrari, with side-plates to stop the drivers' feet slipping off the pedals. (Piola)

Chapter 10

Tyres
Daylight rubbery

All of the sensations that a Formula 1 car relays to its driver come primarily from four little rubber contact patches. The tyres give the car its footprint on the track, and while you need a lot of other things going for you too, if your tyres aren't up to it you are never going to get the job done. Failing to get the best out of them can have a similar effect, as BMW Williams and McLaren Mercedes showed in 2002 when they didn't make the best use of their Michelin tyres and Ferrari and Bridgestone romped away with the World Championship.

'The four tyres dictate everything, and unless you are kind to them and don't take too much out of them, you're going to be in trouble,' said former Jordan designer Gary Anderson. 'They are the biggest thing, to be honest, the biggest individual component on the car, which gives you grip. You must look after them. It's what this is all about.'

The old adage is that tyres are round, black and boring, but not in Formula 1. They are the mechanical prima donnas. Their compound (the mix of the rubber) and their construction (the precise way in which they are made) exert major influences on their behaviour. They are also sensitive to temperature, track surface and driving style, not to mention the car's handling characteristics, grip level and traction. But when your tyres are working in your corner, fighting for you, there is no cheaper or better way to make a big jump in lap speed.

Since 1998 the FIA has made grooved tyres mandatory in Formula 1. Prior to 1971 tyres had been treaded, but development in various areas of the sport saw the pure slick tyre evolve. Effectively this had no tread; put another way, its tread extended across the whole surface of the tyre. This enhanced grip significantly – unless, of course, it was raining. Then the tyre had zero ability to sipe away water, and the driver was in trouble. In the 1975 British Grand Prix at Silverstone a breakers' yard developed at Club Corner when a late rain shower caught out driver after driver running on slick tyres.

In 1997, anxious to curb cornering speeds and spotting a cunning way of bringing tyres out of the area of the technical regulations (where any changes required unanimous agreement of the teams) and into the sporting regulations (where changes could be made on safety grounds without unanimity), FIA president Max Mosley hit on the idea of introducing grooves. This would effectively reduce tread area again, and therefore cut cornering speed.

'Stirling Moss started me thinking along these lines,' Mosley admitted, 'when he was talking about historic cars and said that you should never allow historics with treaded tyres and historics with slicks to race at the same time, because the performance gap is so enormous. This set the whole thinking in train. What actually happened was that slicks and aerodynamics came in around the same time, and one has always thought that the enormous climb in performance was due to aerodynamics, but in fact the quantum jump was slicks.'

Opposite: To show support for the FIA's environmental campaigns, Bridgestone added green differentiating rings to its softer slicks and 'extreme-wet' tyres in 2009. (sutton-images.com)

The idea worked initially, but the tyre wars between Goodyear and Bridgestone, and latterly Bridgestone and Michelin, generated such a high level of development that soon cornering speeds went up again as softer, more durable, tyres evolved. Had slicks kept developing, however, it's fair to say that cornering speeds would now be even higher.

Whether it is a racing tyre or a road tyre, the basic manufacturing principles are the same. Once the rubber has been taken from plantations, it is blended with carbon black (which gives the tyres their colour), sulphur and other materials such as oils, resins and plasticisers to form a compound predetermined by design engineers working with sophisticated computer programs which take into account previous on-track testing experience. In Formula 1, tyres are usually built within a two-week lead-time (even less than that in 2003 when Michelin had to modify its front tyre design after complaints by Bridgestone).

Once extruded rubber sheets have been formed from the basic materials they are laid up on circular formers, where other materials such as woven nylon or polyester and bead rings are laid up to form the basic carcass on which the rubber is then wound. The way in which the various materials are laid up, in particular the angles of each ply, have a critical effect on its ultimate performance. The end result of this process is the creation of the 'green' tyre, which is barely recognisable as the real thing. It is then placed in a two-part metal mould, where heat and pressure are applied for a specific period to cure it and give the tread its pattern.

Formula 1 tyres are constructed along similar lines to roadgoing radials. Their sidewall stiffness is of paramount importance in determining their influence on steering input, feel and response, and is a function of the construction design. They fit 660mm diameter wheels. Dry weather grooved fronts fitted between 305 and 355mm rim width wheels, the rears 365 to 380. Both front and rear dry weather tyres had four 2.5mm deep grooves which are 10mm wide at their base and 14mm wide at their contact surface. There was 50mm spacing between their centrelines. The front tyres weighed around 9kg and had an overall tread contact area of 280cm^2; the rears weighed 11kg and had a tread area of 440cm^2. F1 tyres are tubeless, and are inflated by specially processed air converted into nitrogen-rich gas which thus ensures that they retain constant properties. They do not operate in a benign environment, for the temperatures across the tread of a slick could reach 120°C, at operating pressures lower than the usual 30psi of road cars. Typically, front tyres run at 20–24psi, rears at 17–19.

Over a race weekend each driver is allowed ten sets (40) dry weather tyres and seven sets (28) of wets (excluding 'monsoon' wets), which have a much more distinctive tread designed to clear away gallons of water a second when the car is travelling at maximum speed on a wet surface. There may be two types of wet: a full wet for 'monsoon' conditions, and an intermediate better suited to less wet conditions. The choice of two was reintroduced shortly after the 2003 Brazilian Grand Prix: for the new season the FIA had allowed teams only one type of wet tyres; when Bridgestone and Michelin gambled on intermediate tyres and were subsequently faced with monsoon conditions there was general outcry and the one-wet rule was rescinded on grounds of common sense.

A wet tyre is designed to be 'soft' enough to provide as much grip as possible in slippery conditions, but the moment the track begins to dry out the movement in the tread can quickly start leading to overheating.

Above: This display of Bridgestone tyres shows the different patterns available for use in Formula One in 2009. From left to right; 'extreme-wet' rain tyre, wet-weather tyre, 2009 slick and 2008 grooved tyre. (sutton-images.com)

Typically a manufacturer will send 1,400 tyres to each race, and the fit and very well trained fitters from Bridgestone and Michelin can fit 100 tyres an hour. On the Thursday prior to a race they will fit around 750. In the course of a season, a tyre manufacturer will make between 50,000 and 60,000 covers.

The two most critical factors in the interface between car and tyre and tyre and track are the rubber compound, and the temperature at which it operates. Compounding is an art, and not surprisingly the rubber recipes are closely guarded secrets. When Lucky Strike BAR Honda switched from Bridgestone to Michelin for the 2004 season, the Japanese manufacturer ensured that the British team did not retain any of its tyres that the French manufacturer might then have been able to dismember and analyse.

Prior to 2009 teams tested continually. One of the purposes of this was to determine the right tyre compound for a given circuit, and how long a tyre was

effective before degradation robbed it of performance. Generally speaking the softer the tyre, the more grip the tyre will generate, but its longevity will be relatively less than that of a harder compound. Harder tyres, by contrast, last longer; but their inferior grip generates lower cornering speeds. At races drivers had a choice and could leave it until qualifying to make it; after that, however, they had to stick with that choice. Cars were placed in *parc fermé* after the single-lap qualifying session. They had to start the race on the tyres with which they qualified, and had subsequently to fit replacements of similar compound during their pit stops.

With the reintroduction of slick tyres in 2009, drivers had to use each of supplier Bridgestone's two chosen compounds over the course of the race.

As far as operating temperature is concerned, tyre engineers must select in advance of a race the two compounds they believe are best suited to a specific temperature window. In testing and even at races tyre engineers continually take temperature readings at the most varied points in the pit lane, in order to record the temperature of the asphalt as accurately as possible. This provides a reference point, and unless it is raining the temperature rarely drops below 10°C. However, even a difference as small as one to two degrees in track temperature (which is more relevant to tyre performance than ambient temperature) is enough to change the window in which a tyre performs to the best of its ability. 'The tyre pressure is then matched to the asphalt temperature,' explains Sam Michael, technical director of Williams. The front tyres run between 1.14 and 1.2 bar; the rears at 1.02 to 1.08 bar. If the temperature is cool and the tyre too hard, then the car will slide around as much as if the temperature was warm and the tyre too soft. As little as 0.1 bar either way, or even a difference in pressure between each tyre, can be enough to compromise a driver's chance of achieving the ultimate lap time. Interestingly, drivers of the calibre of seven-time World Champion Michael Schumacher can detect such minor discrepancies.

Teams go to great length to ensure that the drivers get tyres at the right temperature. They are inflated to the specified pressure, and are also pre-heated for up to two hours to their optimum operating temperature around 100°C. Special electric tyre warmers are wrapped round the tyres to achieve this since it is vital that the tyre performs to its optimum from its first lap. One of the things a driver learns early in his career is the importance of generating sufficient heat in his tyres; spinning on the opening lap on cold tyres is a

The manner in which wet-weather tyres clear water away from beneath the tread is superbly illustrated as Sebastian Vettel's Red Bull Renault RB5 heads for victory in the 2009 Chinese Grand Prix. (LAT)

frequent reason for retirement in junior formulae.

Formula 1 tyres often need careful nurturing. In 2001 Michelin's tyres did not perform to their best unless the driver had scrubbed them in; this entailed putting several relatively gentle laps on them until the shine and the sprigs of rubber known as 'sprue pips' from the moulding process had been worn away. The contrast in performance between scrubbed and unscrubbed tyres was thrown into stark perspective that season at Spa. On scrubbed rubber Giancarlo Fisichella thrust his Benetton Renault into second place and eventually finished third; team-mate Jenson Button, who had not been allowed out to scrub his tyres in the morning warm-up, struggled down the field with understeer as a result.

Tyres that are too cold will create oversteer as the car slides around; in extremis this can cause the rears to oversteer and blister, as the rubber tread starts to separate from the tyre's carcass.

The modern Formula 1 tyre lasts about 150km, though this is dependent on the precise blend of compound, operating temperature and the driver's driving style.

In the overall package of the Formula 1 car, a question is frequently asked: which is more important, power or handling? Distilled to its basics, is grip more important than grunt?

The simple answer, of course, is that both are important. But in Formula 1 nothing is ever simple. There are different percentage returns for the same effort from the respective chassis and engine designers. A poor chassis can disguise a strong engine; equally an excellent chassis can flatter an average engine.

Tyre performance is the single fastest way to improve lap times. An improvement in grip will result in an improvement in lap time. An improvement in an engine's power output will also achieve this, but not to the same extent. It requires a much larger percentage increase in horsepower to achieve the same result.

'The most important thing for a designer is to understand where you should be concentrating your efforts, and that should be what makes the biggest difference to lap times,' says senior Williams development engineer Frank Dernie. 'We have had simulations for a number of years and even with the simplest of simulations you can look at which things make the most difference, and at the absolute top of the list is the tyre. It's never been different. The fact is that the laws of physics haven't changed, the facts have always been the same but not everyone realised what the facts were, and that includes people who were designing the cars.'

If you made a comparison between two widely differing circuits, such as the tortuous Hungaroring and the much faster Monza, an increase in horsepower would have a much more significant effect on the lap time at the latter rather than the former. A 5% increase in power at Monza would reduce a theoretical lap time by 0.8 seconds while a 5% increase in grip would reduce it by 1.25 seconds. If you were to apply the same performance improvements for engines and grip at the Hungaroring, the respective improvements would only be 0.4 and 1.94 seconds. For Hungary the grip/engine performance ratio is 485.00%, while at Monza it is 156.25%.

While this is simple, achieving increases in either power or grip does not come without a price. However, manufacturing a better tyre is the cheaper

The tyre manufacturers set up finely equipped depots in the paddock, where the tyre fitters work flat out over a race weekend in all weather conditions to ensure that each team has its allotted share of rubber. (sutton-images.com)

alternative and has fewer knock-on effects that need to be taken into consideration. Generally speaking, an improvement in the tyre is just an improvement in the tyre, and the lap times drop as a result. An improvement in engine power, however, can have all sorts of hidden effects – such as a corresponding reduction in reliability, narrowing of the power curve or the need for larger radiators to maintain the cooling, which might result in an increase in drag.

Aerodynamics also play an important role in getting the tyre to work and, just as importantly, allowing it to survive. 'A typical simulation will show that losing a bit of drag in the same way as gaining a bit of power makes a difference to the lap time but far less than you expect, whereas a bit more downforce makes a huge increase,' Dernie says. 'In the simulation you tend not to have tyre degradation, so if you just take downforce all on its own you go faster as it helps the tyre enormously, particularly in medium-speed corners. By comparison the tyre is better everywhere, it's got better traction, better braking. The tyre is probably the least glamorous part of the racing car but the most important, and it was just as true in 1980 as it is today.'

If a tyre manufacturer gets its compounding and construction right, it is then a matter of the team and

Tyres only last a finite time in the heat of Formula One battle. This photograph shows how the tread tends to smear across the tyre when it gets really hot. (LAT)

driver honing the set-up of the car to exploit it to the full. But if they get it wrong, the durability of a race tyre can always be compromised by even the smallest degree of understeer or oversteer.

Williams's director of engineering Patrick Head has no doubts about how critical tyre performance is to lap time, but knows it is also just one of many factors. 'People love to know how important the engine is relative to the tyre, and what percentage the engine provides and what percentage the tyre provides, but the reality is if you want to be quick you've got to have everything working the best you possibly can.'

At Indianapolis in 2005, Michelin got things spectacularly wrong in the USGP. Bridgestone, via its Firestone involvement in the Indy Racing League and the Indianapolis 500, knew that a new 'diamond grading' surfacing in the Speedway's Turn One had a deleterious effect on tyre wear during the 500. Accordingly it did its homework prior to the Grand Prix there in June the following month, where Turn One would become Turn 13 as the direction of the circuit was reversed. Michelin did not do this, and in practice on Friday it soon became apparent that it had a serious problem on its hands. Ralf Schumacher crashed his Toyota very heavily in Turn 13 as a result of a left rear tyre failure (it was the second year in succession in which the young German had crashed there). A weakness in the sidewall, exacerbated by the diamond grading, prompted serious concern about the durability of the French tyres.

Michelin initially believed that Schumacher's tyre failed because of Toyota's combination of suspension camber angles and tyre pressures. Practice and qualifying went ahead, with all of the Michelin teams adopting fresh recommendations from the tyre manufacturer regarding those parameters. However, these recommendations changed the wear rates and performance of the tyres, so some Michelin teams headed into the race with less data on predicted performance because what they spent their time gathering on Friday and Saturday has been rendered academic. Higher tyre pressures, for example, led to oversteer and higher wear and there was no way to predict with suitable accuracy what this would be. With increased wear came the increased risk of tyre failures.

Michelin had some tyres with supposedly stiffer sidewalls sent over from its base in Clermont-Ferrand ready for Sunday (it transpired that they were not stiffer, being tyres of the type last used in Spain), and in the meantime the Michelin teams spent all of Sunday morning arguing with Bernie Ecclestone and the FIA about the best course of action. Michelin put its hand up and confessed that its tyres were not suitable for the track, which has the longest full throttle run of any on the calendar and includes the two banked corners, Turns 12 and 13. 'Having collected the results of our in-depth analysis from France and the USA,' it said, 'we confirmed that with the tyres on which we have qualified we are not able to sufficiently guarantee the total safety of the drivers.'

As a compromise, Michelin asked the FIA to install a chicane before Turn 13. The response from FIA race director Charlie Whiting, at Max Mosley's behest, was unequivocal: 'Your teams have a choice of running more slowly in Turn 12/13, running a tyre not used in qualifying (which would attract a penalty) or repeatedly changing a tyre (subject to valid safety reasons). It is for them to decide. We have nothing to add.'

Nine of the teams said, 'No chicane, no race.' Ferrari, sensing its first victory of 2005, said, 'No problem.'

Slowly a ludicrous situation worsened, and little by little Formula 1 at the Indianapolis Motor Speedway went from critical to needing life support. There were suggestions of imposing a 280kph speed limit in the banked turns, or, even more stupid, letting cars race, but behind the safety car. But on a day that called for strong governance, innovation and compromise, or at least a decent back-up plan, nothing happened.

Right: The difference in sidewall deformation between Bridgestone (top, on a Jordan) and Michelin (below, on a Toyota) is evident in this shot taken as the cars negotiated Turn 13. (sutton-images.com)

At 12:30 Jordan's Tiago Monteiro left the pits, followed by the Ferraris and his team-mate Narain Karthikeyan. As the brinksmanship continued, it was another five minutes before Williams, Renault and BAR sent their cars out, followed by Minardi, Toyota, Sauber and McLaren.

'The future for F1 and Michelin in the US is not good,' Bernie Ecclestone conceded as he worked the grid, and not even his legerdemain could rescue the situation. The world soon learned just how bad the situation was. All 20 cars appeared on the grid after the formation lap, but after the green flag lap all of the Michelin-shod cars pulled straight into the pits and were pushed straight into their garages. It was unprecedented.

On the grid, the two Ferraris were joined by two Jordans and two Minardis, the latter two teams obliged to race by their Bridgestone contracts, and the suicide act was complete. Bitterly disappointed fans gave what passed for a show a major thumbs-down. As Michael Schumacher led team-mate Rubens Barrichello around in what was meant to be a race, the crowd were on their feet – leaving. There was more action in the car parks than on the track. Irate fans reacted by throwing drink cans. '$ back' signs proliferated. Schumacher won from Barrichello, and

for the first time since Zandvoort 1961 all starters finished. 'We went out there to have fun, and that's what we had,' Schumacher said. 'It was not the right way to win my first race of the year, but it wasn't a disaster.' It might not have been for Ferrari, but on its deathbed in the US Formula 1 slapped its fans in the face. 19 June 2005 was the sport's bleakest day since Ayrton Senna was killed. Not one soul profited from a victory so hollow you could hear the wind whistling all the way through it.

Describing events at the track, IMS president and chief operating officer Joie Chitwood III said it was a 'major setback' to F1's future in the US but that talk of voiding the contract with Bernie Ecclestone's FOM company (it ran out in 2006, but though there was a race at IMS in 2007 the US GP disappeared again from the calendar from 2008) was premature. 'What occurred today was something we were not prepared for. We invested a lot of time and effort in

In the 2005 US GP at Indianapolis, Ralf Schumacher crashed his Toyota as a result of left rear Michelin tyre failure. The damage to the car indicates why, in the absence of more suitable rubber, the teams running the French tyres had no option but to pull out at the start of the race. (sutton-images.com)

preparing this property for a world-class racing event. The inability to have control over the actions today… to say it's a disappointment is an understatement. Everyone here at the Indianapolis Motor Speedway prides themselves on producing world-class events. The fact we had no control over what occurred is our greatest disappointment. No one at the Indianapolis Motor Speedway is proud of what occurred today.'

Allegedly, George was denied his right by promoter's option to have installed a chicane. It would not have been perfect, but it would have been the best compromise, and precedent for it existed with the chicane in Spain that the drivers had insisted on back in 1994. As for the Michelin teams, they had no option under Indiana State Law but to withdraw. Had any of them raced on tyres acknowledged to be unsuitable, they could have faced prosecution even had there not been any further incidents.

Mosley was accused of trying to use the situation to force independent-minded Michelin out of the sport, so that Bridgestone could have supply monopoly, and of obliging Indianapolis Motor Speedway boss Tony George not to use his promoters' option. There was talk of action against the seven teams, but thankfully common sense prevailed and things settled down once more. Later Mosley became bullish again, until in September the so-called rebels fired a fresh salvo across his bows with the announcement that they were continuing their plans under the Grand Prix Manufacturers' Association for a separate racing series. It was not until May 2006 that this spectre finally disappeared as ongoing negotiations were concluded, to their satisfaction.

Edouard Michelin's company would not be around to see the Brave New Dawn. Having bitten its self-constructed bullet and made financial reparation to all of Indianapolis's disappointed fans, Michelin withdrew at the end of 2006, giving Bridgestone a supply monopoly again for 2007.

Tyres: round black and boring? Not in Formula 1.

One of the major factors influencing the race at Indianapolis that year was the FIA rule change which banned tyre stops. This generally worked extremely well to enhance the spectacle, notably at the Nürburgring where leader Kimi Räikkönen nursed a badly vibrating flat-spotted right front Michelin on his McLaren, only to have his suspension break as a result on the very last lap. However, for 2006 tyre stops were permitted once again for reasons that were not entirely transparent. The FIA argued against itself that free-for-all tyre changing in races would enliven things further by eliminating the 'slow-burn' nature of 2005 races, and increase the level of competition.

Elsewhere, drivers were still only permitted seven sets of tyres over a race weekend, with no more than two specifications to be provided by the supplier. Tyres used in qualifying and the race had to be of the same specification.

For 2007 Bridgestone, now the sole supplier, brought two choices of dry-road compound to each race, but now teams had to use each during the course of the event. The softer tyre was distinguished by a white stripe in the centre groove. Since one compound would inevitably confer faster lap times than the other, they had interesting choices to make regarding which tyres they would start a race on. The key would thus not simply be how long each driver could go on their chosen fuel load, but how long they could make their tyres last. In extremis, it was not impossible that harsher than anticipated tyre degradation might force a driver to pit sooner than planned, upskittling carefully calculated strategies. Several teams reported that Bridgestone's soft compound rear tyres grained quite quickly.

For 2008 only minor evolutionary changes were made to the control tyres, which led to a welcome measure of continuity for teams and drivers. In a new development, however, Bridgestone marked its extreme wet weather tyres with a white line down the centre groove in order to assist spectators and media by making it visibly distinguishable from the wet weather tyre.

Hirohide Hamashima, Bridgestone's director of tyre development, noted at the beginning of the season: 'Most teams have new cars so they have the additional challenge of finding the best set-ups to maximise performance from our tyres on cars they are still learning about. For drivers, the lack of traction control will make a difference.'

Extraordinarily, however, Bridgestone discovered that deletion of traction control was actually beneficial to rear tyre wear.

Hamashima told *F1 Race Technology*'s Ian Bamsey: 'The lack of traction control improves the wear rate at the rear. Everybody thought that without traction control the car would be oversteering more this year, so they made a car with more understeering tendency and that is why the front tyre wear rate can be higher this year.'

The lack of engine braking management, massaged out that year by the standard ECU, also put a heavier workload on the fronts.

Everything changed for 2009, when slick tyres made a welcome return to Grand Prix racing for the first time in over 11 years. The FIA's idea was to use the greater contact patch of slicks to increase mechanical grip to make up for the anticipated reduction in aerodynamic downforce.

While purists applauded the return of slicks, the tyres presented some significant challenges as far as balancing the cars was concerned. Getting rid of the grooves that had been a feature since 1998 increased the area of the narrower front tyre by a greater percentage than it did the wider rear, which had the effect of reducing understeer and increasing oversteer. Making Bridgestone's control tyres last over long race stints would thus be a key factor in winning. Jenson Button proved that on his victorious run in the opening race in Australia when he nursed his Brawn through its final stint on the supersoft rubber which, as Sebastian Vettel proved in a Red Bull that was less benign to its rubber, was prone to graining the moment the car began to slide around.

Bridgestone introduced a new method of marking to designate between compounds, as the previous convention of painting one of the grooves with a white line no longer applied. To show its continued support for the FIA's 'Make Cars Green' campaign, it identified the softer of the two dry compounds available for each race with green sidewall markings.

The now renamed 'wet' tyre (formerly the 'extreme' tyre) also featured a green line in a central groove.

As before, two compounds of tyre were available for every Grand Prix, with the requirement that both should be used in the race. Bridgestone's dry rubber arsenal ranged from hard and medium to soft and super soft.

'The move to slick tyres is significant,' Hamashima said, 'although Bridgestone have a lot of experience with these tyres from many different race series so we are confident that we can produce good racing slicks. We are making these tyres to the same sizes as we had with grooved tyres, but this means there is a new front/rear grip balance. The teams will therefore have to work hard to get a good set-up.

'We received many requests last season to make the difference between the two compounds greater, so we have attempted to do this by not only having a different compound stiffness, but also varying the temperature working range of the tyres. We have sought to allocate one tyre which has a lower working range and one which has a higher working range. This means that, even more than before, competitors will have to think long and hard about how they use their tyres, and there will be good rewards for those who make the best choices.'

The supersoft tyre was not universally popular, and in Malaysia Fernando Alonso was moved to describe its selection as an option by Bridgestone as 'crazy.'

BMW-Sauber motorsport director Mario Theissen said in China: 'Generally speaking we found out that with the new set of aero regulations and the new tyres you need a very much forward weight distribution, even more than expected. We have a very strong front end with a powerful front wing and relatively wide front tyres and a weak rear end with a small rear wing and not big enough tyres, so you need to put weight on the front axle.'

There were also some interesting developments in the wet.

In the rain in China Jenson Button's hitherto dominant Brawn struggled to generate tyre temperature whereas the winning Red Bulls of Sebastian Vettel and Mark Webber, which worked their rubber harder, had an advantage. 'I was just really struggling with the tyres,' Button reported. 'They were shuddering. They shudder because you can't get temperature into them, front and rears. It was a difficult race and every lap you thought you were going to throw the car off.'

Tyre design is, of course, a significant factor in wet races, and the Bridgestone full wet sipes away huge amounts of water via its deep tread. But the type of road surface is also critical, and Shanghai's tends to retain water.

Button made another interesting point, with regard to Shanghai's surface. 'The scary thing was that normally when you follow a car you see the two lines in the water and you know exactly where they've been and you can follow that line because there's less water there, but I never saw any lines on the circuit. That was the amazing thing. The water doesn't seem to clear and that was the worst thing about it.

'There's always been a lot of spray in Formula 1. I don't think that has changed. But for some reason we seem to be having a lot of wet races over the last couple of years which I think stick in our memories more. The problem with getting temperature into the tyres is more of a new issue for me. You know we didn't have that so much in the past. The tyres don't seem to work as well as previously in the very wet conditions. We don't seem to be able to break through the water. Obviously these guys [the Red Bull pilots] could get it to work, so it wasn't such a bad problem for them, but it's something that's very strange, that we're struggling so much with aquaplaning and tyre shuddering which we didn't used to have four or five years ago. I don't remember having such big issues.

For dry races, slicks are here to stay, but as early as April 2009 there were whispers that the FIA might seek to alter the front to rear grip/balance equation on the cars by mandating a narrower front tyre from Bridgestone.

Chapter 11

Simulation Techniques
The power of virtual reality

Early in 2009 the publicity department at McLaren circulated a remarkable little piece of viral marketing that demonstrated conclusively just how far the world of virtual reality had progressed since the first edition of this book was published.

It began innocuously enough, with a couple of guys playing at driving their remote control McLaren round a complex course in their office. Contact with the race team followed, which led to them being present as the reigning World Champion, Lewis Hamilton, stood alongside a McLaren MP4-23 in the garage at Portimao circuit. Lewis was twiddling with his Blackberry Storm mobile phone, and it soon became clear that he was controlling the engine, as its throttle note was rising and falling. The link came via the phone's Bluetooth connection.

Extraordinarily, he then 'drove' the car out of the garage, without even sitting in it, purely by using the remote control medium of his phone.

It was FIA president Max Mosley's fear of the remote control F1 car, expressed back in 1993, come to life…

It's no secret that F1 teams use very advanced simulation technologies. It's the technology itself whose secrets are so closely guarded. Today, computational fluid dynamics, wind tunnel development, transient dynamometers and seven-post test rigs are all standard fare for any self-respecting team. The goal of all of these expensive tools is to ensure that the cars are as competitive as possible – and as reliable.

Simulation techniques in F1 go far beyond that, however. Computers crunch away to work out every conceivable race strategy and increasingly teams are realising the value of driver-in-the-loop simulators. This means that rather than engineers playing with computers, as happens with other simulation, the drivers sit in 'virtual' F1 cars.

There may be a belief that the F1 simulators are simply glorified computer games, which have a value

in teaching drivers circuits that they have never visited, but the story is much more complicated than that. Simulator technologies arrived as teams recognised that they could make money by working with computer gaming companies to create entertainment for the public.

The first racing computer game was *Gran Trak 10*, a single-player racing arcade game released by Atari in 1974. The first big success was *Pole Position*, a Namco game in which a player had to complete a lap within a prescribed time to qualify for a race at the Fuji Speedway. If successful, their car would race with others. As home computers developed in the '80s the first true F1 game appeared. *Formula 1 Grand Prix* (F1GP) was released in 1992.

Opposite: Kazuki Nakajima explains the details of Williams's simulator to motorcycle racer James Toseland at the team's Grove factory in 2008. (Williams F1)

Nowadays anyone can sit at home and drive F1 cars, playing with many different parameters such as fuel loads, tyre wear and so on. But home computers, no matter how sophisticated, can only do so much. One may have a steering wheel and pedals, but there are none of the real sensations of what it is like to drive an F1 car.

In the last decade F1 engineers have come to realise that advanced simulation can be a tool not just for driver training, but also to work on technical solutions and set-up conundrums. Simulation can improve lap times and at the same time save time and money by giving the team a way to test without needing to put the cars on the racetrack.

Virtual testing is now a reality.

Modern simulation technology can be traced back to the '20s, when American engineer Edwin Link, who had begun his career as a builder of organs and nickelodeons, used his knowledge of pneumatic pumps and valves to create the first flight simulator in Binghampton, in upstate New York. At the time teaching new pilots to fly in cloud, using only their instruments, was both expensive and dangerous and Link felt that a machine could do the job cheaply and safely. The result was a device which became known as the Blue Box, an enclosed aircraft cockpit. The pilot sat inside and used the controls to 'fly' the device using instruments alone. The Blue Box generated pitch, roll and yaw motions controlled by the pilot. The prototype appeared in 1929 but Link's business did not take off until 1934, when the US Army Air Force purchased four machines after a series of trainee pilots died while doing instrument training. World War Two created a boom for Link's ever-improving machines. He provided 10,000 of them, and more than half a million aircrew from different nations learned to fly on them. The development included large-scale systems aboard which entire bomber crews trained together.

The boom in civil aviation after World War Two led Link to develop simulators for the new generation of jet engines. By the '60s the technologies had changed, with hydraulic actuators replacing their pneumatic predecessors, and new simulators were built to include the 'six degrees of freedom', which meant that the platforms on which the cockpits were mounted were able to generate roll, pitch and yaw plus surge (longitudinal), heave (vertical) and sway (lateral). Visuals were also introduced. The earliest versions used cameras that filmed models of the ground; in the '70s came wide-angled screens with film footage; later still came curved mirrors and ultimately plasma screens with virtual imagery.

The development was not restricted to planes, with the advent of gaming and a diversification into ground-based machines, notably armoured vehicles. These simulators enabled the army to create battlefield environments to train its crews. The automotive industry also started looking at the potential of simulators to help the companies involved understand how drivers behaved in different situations, thus enabling designers to improve dashboard ergonomics and strengthen safety features based on accidents that might occur because of drivers becoming tired or distracted. Military demands meant that development was constant, with innovations such as g-seats, belt-tightening devices and pneumatic cushions, all of which

Flight simulators have been an essential part of commercial pilot training for many years, but are aimed at procedural training rather than replicating the 'feel' of an aircraft. (sutton-images.com)

helped to create the impression of the pressures that a driver would feel at certain speeds, in addition to 360° domes to create a totally virtual environment.

Today there are reckoned to be 1,200 professional flight simulators in the world, designed and developed by companies such as Canada's CAE, France's defence giant Thales and US firms such as Flight Safety International and Northrop. The majority of these use motion platforms known as Hexapods or Stewart Platforms, which feature six independently-actuated legs, the lengths of which change in order to orient the platform. Sound and imagery add to the environment created.

The accuracy of simulators is an area in which there has been much controversy between the mechanical engineers and advanced medical researchers, who argue that it is not very realistic because of the way in which the human body reacts to stimuli. This is a very complex question because of the wide range of

The Williams team simulator is thought to be one of the most realistic in Formula One. Here Formula BMW Asia driver Jazeman Jaafar views his performance in 2007 with a Williams engineer using the system's replay and analysis facility. (sutton-images.com)

sensory inputs that the brain integrates. The medical men argue that the reactions of the muscles and joints (the proprioceptive system) do not tie in with the others and also believe that the vestibular system (the balance mechanism in the inner ear) is also affected. They argue that this means that depth perceptions are not always correct.

One of the problems with some of the simulators is that they induce sickness because of a discrepancy between the perception of visual motion and the corresponding motion cues. This led the engineers to look at ways to overcome the problem and to the development of what are called dynamic simulators,

Recreational and gaming Formula One simulators are becoming ever-more sophisticated, and F1 teams have recognised that there is a market for commercial versions of their systems, such as this system designed to provide a realistic simulation of the proposed new Donington Park Grand Prix circuit. (sutton-images.com)

which have the entire hexapod moving around to meet the body's need for the sensation of real motion.

The bottom line is that there is no such thing as a standard simulator. Each one is a prototype and the most interesting element in their use in F1 is that most of the systems have been developed in-house by the teams, rather than being developed with specialist partnerships. One thing that is clear is that the experts on simulators have also been moving, as other teams realise the value of what they do not have.

There is general agreement that the two best systems in 2009 were those that had had the most development.

McLaren was believed to have spent as much as $40 million on its system and used British Aerospace technology, developed for the Eurofighter aircraft. At Woking the driver sits in a full-size F1 monocoque, in front of a large, curved plasma screen. The whole device is mounted on a hexapod which moves around an area about the size of a professional basketball court, in response to the driver's steering and pedal inputs. This was the only dynamic simulator in F1 at the time.

It was believed that the best of the fixed-base units was Williams's, where the development had been amazingly cost-effective, with a budget probably a tenth of what had been spent at McLaren. Williams was able to stream data back to its factory after a practice session so that it could use the simulator to try out other set-ups, which could then be run 'virtually' overnight to ensure that the cars had the optimum set-ups based on absolutely current data.

Up to that point Ferrari had been using a fairly

simple unit, housed at the Fiat Research Centre in Turin. In 2009, however, it announced a partnership with the US firm Moog to create a state-of-the-art dynamic device.

'The dynamic driving simulator is a new step for us in developing virtual tests that give drivers the true feel of a real environment and direct feedback on their actions,' said head of research and development, Marco Fainello. 'It will support the new breed of tests we are planning to launch.'

Red Bull Racing tried a relationship with a specialist company but went on to do its own thing, intending to create a dynamic unit as soon as possible. As Honda F1 became Brawn GP early in 2009, new owner Ross Brawn planned something similar. Renault had an arrangement to use a system created by a local specialist firm but declined to impart details, albeit admitting that its system was not on par with other teams'. Force India had its own very basic system but tried out a facility at the old Upper Heyford airbase which was owned by Wirth Research. Proprietor Nick Wirth had been the man behind the ill-fated Simtek F1 team in 1994 before becoming technical director at Benetton before it became Renault. Some suspected that this was also Renault's secret facility. Oddly, Toyota and BMW said that they were not using any simulators midway through the 2008 season, though both firms have advanced road car simulators. Toyota has the world's largest driving simulator at the Higashifuji Technical Centre in Japan and BMW has a similar unit in Munich.

What is clear is that most teams believe that the F1 simulators are the most advanced of all.

'I think they are better than the best flight simulators,' said former Red Bull Racing engineer Geoff Willis. 'Those are now more about training and not so much about performance.'

And do they work?

'It's pretty useful,' said Williams's Patrick Head, although he won't say more than that.

The estimated lap time from simulation for the Grand Prix of Europe, the inaugural race at Valencia, in 2008 was 1m 37s. In Q1 on Saturday afternoon Jarno Trulli lapped his Toyota in 1m 37.948s. Sebastian Vettel cut that to 1m 37.842s in Q2, with Felipe Massa, Nick Heidfeld, Trulli and Lewis Hamilton all in the same bracket...

The teams believe they will find a way to make money from the systems. In the world of computer gaming the race is on to create cost-effective simulation systems that could be sold to the public. The Nintendo Wii is a move in that direction, with sensors that transform the movement of the players into actions in the game. The next leap forward will probably be a device to give players the same sensations as those being simulated. Since the end of 2006 an astonishing 30 million Wiis have been sold. They cost around $250, which means that it is a $7.5 billion market. The first company to get to the markets with simulation technology as seen in F1 stands to make even bigger profits. In the meantime, money can still be made. Recently the Costa cruise ship line bought a series of F1 simulators from a Dutch company called VESC to try to attract customers. The full-scale machines, complete with hexapods, are now cruising the world.

An artist's impression of the planned Red Bull Racing F1 simulator, initially developed in 2006 with specialist company cueSim. (QinetiQ)

Chapter 12

The Art of Reliability
In order to finish first...

By the end of the 2003 World Championship season, Michael Schumacher's Ferrari had gone 38 races – more than two seasons – without a mechanical failure. That was a stunning record, and is a testament to just how reliable the modern Formula 1 car can be if there is sufficient time, money and intelligence behind it to render it bullet-proof.

Remember that old axiom: 'In order to finish first, first you have to finish…'?

The so-called 'small-part breakdowns', which have for so long robbed drivers and teams of expected success, have become increasingly rare. When he visited the Australian Grand Prix in Melbourne in 2003, former Ferrari driver Chris Amon could only smile philosophically at Schumacher's remarkable car. In his day he lost Grand Prix triumphs for the Prancing Horse for reasons ranging from differential failure to trivia such as a blown fuse in the fuel pump.

This progress has not happened by accident. It is a blend of choosing the right materials for the job, and implementing stringent quality control programmes.

As we have seen, the Formula 1 car is a confection of state-of-the-art materials: carbon-fibre composites; metal matrix; thinwall aluminium; titanium; magnesium. Nothing less will do in the never-ending search for lightness, efficiency, durability and reliability.

Prototypes of individual components are made at great expense, then tested thoroughly on factory rigs until they are passed as satisfactory. They then provide the templates for mass production as a team's latest challenger comes on stream. In the longer term, derivatives of the components themselves, or their manufacturing processes, may filter down to road cars. Such is the manner in which Formula 1, the greatest category of motor racing, helps to improve the breed. Today's advantage on the circuit may be tomorrow's revolution in vehicle manufacturing.

This technology transfer is what lies at the heart of major motor manufacturers' investment in Formula 1; they are not merely there for the publicity benefits and image enhancement. The processes and the philosophies that generate the successful Formula 1 car can also be utilised in road-car production. This is especially true in areas such as tyres, electronics and materials.

Three important factors lie at the heart of materials sourcing. They must be light enough not to jeopardise ideal weight distribution. They must be capable of withstanding extreme forces during races, without allowing defects to arise. And the car must comply with the FIA's safety standards and crash tests.

'Apart from this,' says Brian O'Rourke, chief composites engineer at Williams, 'production time has to be kept as short as possible. Our parts have to be supplied to us very quickly. Indeed, sometimes modifications have to be ready for use at the next race. This means the parts have to be made quickly. Overall, meeting this requirement profile means that we have a hi-tech level that is comparable to that of space research.'

Opposite: In 2009 more cars than ever were finishing races, thanks to the incredible reliability of the modern F1 car. This could be problematic for small teams such as Force India, which struggled to score points.

(sutton-images.com)

High load-bearing capabilities, fast availability and reliability at low weight – this demanding combination can only be achieved by using modern hi-tech materials.

Carbon-fibre composite is a good example. Approximately 60% of a Formula 1 car comprises carbon fibres embedded in epoxy resin (also known as CFRP). This includes the monocoque chassis, the crushable nose assembly that plays such a key role in safety, the front and rear wings, parts of the suspension, the clutch and the brake discs, and some of the engine's ancillaries. Carbon is clearly an extremely versatile material. Carbon-fibre layers, consisting of individual fibres woven together, can be shaped to suit almost any requirement. The carbon layers are formed and then baked to match the intended application. Carbon only weighs a quarter of a comparable quantity of steel, but can withstand twice the load and has impressively high rigidity.

Testing is another means by which teams try to ensure that their cars are as reliable as possible, although the amount that is permitted is now severely restricted.

(sutton-images.com)

Titanium has similar properties for Formula 1 application, though like metal matrix, which is a mixture of carbon-fibre and aluminium, it is very expensive. Its main advantage is that it weighs only half as much as steel, but when used as an alloy it can match steel's strength while remaining almost corrosion free. It is widely used in engine manufacturing, as well as parts of the suspension and gearbox.

Even lighter and also mainly insensitive to external influences is magnesium. Formula 1 wheels are made solely of this light alloy, which guarantees maximum strength with minimum weight. Apart from this, magnesium is also used in gearboxes or in combination with aluminium for the onboard computer's casing. Its one disadvantage is that it burns so fiercely that magnesium fires are notoriously difficult to extinguish, but fire is much less of a danger in modern Formula 1 than it used to be thanks to significant advances in design and safety.

Aluminium is primarily used in engines and transmission casings, and in conjunction with carbon-

fibre in the chassis. As a material it demonstrates how the technology transfer between Formula 1 and road-car production works, but it highlights some of the associated problems. Aluminium is a popular metal because of its low density (2.7g/ccm in comparison to iron's 7.86g/ccm) and its durability. Now aluminium-bodied road cars, such as Jaguar's latest XJ series, are becoming increasingly popular too because of the metal's resistance to corrosion and its light weight, and the beneficial effect that the latter has on fuel economy and performance. However, aluminium is much more difficult to process, particularly to weld, because it has a lower melting point than steel, and like titanium it can only be welded when air is excluded. This requires a painstaking and costly design, which in turn increases costs.

Cost, of course, is much less of a consideration in Formula 1 than it is in road-car manufacture, where unit cost is all-important. One is effectively a series of perhaps ten limited-run prototypes, while the other is a mass-production run that will run into many thousands. In the latter instance cost is a key factor as even the slightest increase in unit cost will have serious repercussions. For example, the fact that a Formula 1 carbon brake disc can cost between €1,300 and €4,000 is immaterial. Indeed, units are changed after

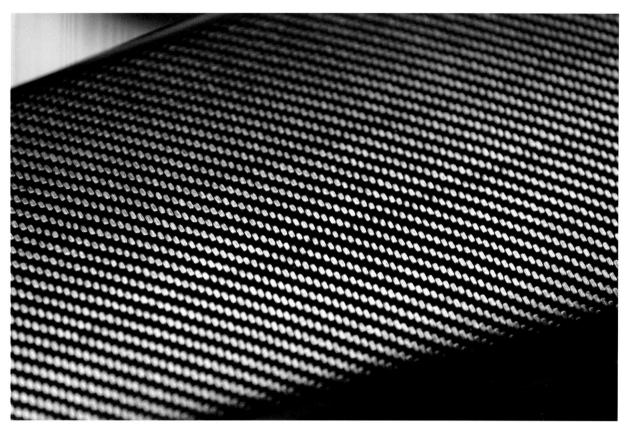

Carbon-fibre composite material has its own very distinctive appearance. (sutton-images.com)

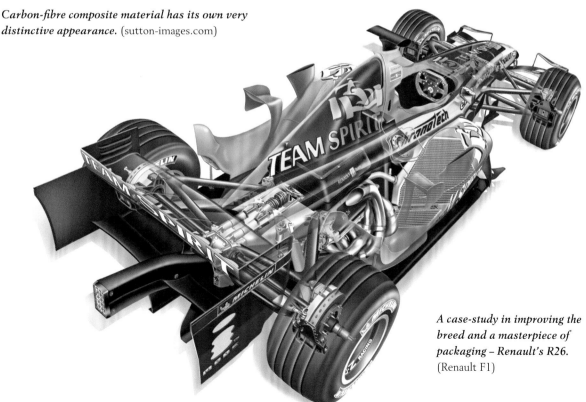

A case-study in improving the breed and a masterpiece of packaging – Renault's R26. (Renault F1)

Carbon-fibre is the perfect material for things other than monocoque chassis, such as brake discs and suspension components, and ancillary items such as brake cooling scoops. (sutton-images.com)

each race. But such materials could only be used on the most expensive road cars. There is no doubt, however, that exotic materials will continue to make inroads on production cars in the future. Aluminium will become even more popular as it is fully recyclable: it can be remelted and used again in high-grade applications. Even carbon, which is extremely expensive because of its production method, is now being used in the manufacture of upper-market sports cars.

Safety experts from the Allianz Centre for Technology in Munich expect carbon-fibre materials to make their way into low-volume passenger-car production soon. 'Examples here are ceramic brake discs, which are reinforced by carbon-fibres, or individual carbon-fibre components, ranging from plenum chambers to roof modules, as used in sports cars,' says Dr Christoph Lauterwasser from the AZT. 'Progress in production technology is naturally decisive in terms of mass production, although fundamentally carbon-fibres have a series of highly appealing properties – next to weight, these include crash behaviour and corrosion resistance.'

Both of these properties will enjoy increasing priority as the road-car world becomes ever more conscious of the need to conserve, and the need to enhance safety even further. FIA president Max Mosley's initiative with the European NCAP crash

testing will also lead to further technology transfer from Formula 1 to road cars.

Titanium also has excellent corrosion resistance and high strength and its limitations are its high cost and the difficulty of processing it cost-effectively. It is, however, used in medical technology, spectacle frames and some motorcycle exhaust pipes. In the meantime, Formula 1 continues its role as its test-bed.

Building reliability into Formula 1 cars also teaches manufacturers valuable lessons that can have direct applications in the road-car world, where reliability is also essential. BMW Williams, for example, has implemented a multi-stage quality management programme to guarantee the greatest possible reliability. Every one of a car's 10,000 or so parts is subjected to its specified control checks.

High temperatures, humidity, vibrations, incredible acceleration and braking forces: Formula 1 is a hostile environment that pushes everything to the limit. It's why most teams apply the basic principle: 'Trusting

is good, but checking is better'. It's not too fanciful to suggest that in Formula 1, quality control can be a matter of life or death. 'That is the reason why we do not allow suppliers to construct safety-related parts: we produce all of the critical parts ourselves,' says Alex Burns, General Manager at WilliamsF1, who is responsible for quality control.

Excellence is the watchword of every team, from the conception of a car all the way through the design and production processes to final operations. The standards are higher than in any other undertaking outside aerospace. Everything has to be co-ordinated perfectly. When BMW and Williams were working together, between 1999 and 2005, there were 450 personnel whose lives were dedicated to that pursuit at Williams, and a further 220 at BMW Motorsport. Their safety net had an extremely fine and intricate mesh. Computers helped quality management in the field of conception and design, but the next stage could only be carried out by hand. The designers began working on the development of the chassis and engine for the 2003 BMW Williams FW25 at the beginning of 2002, and the first components were delivered in the summer. As a result, the team was able to test the engine on the test bench in September, before taking it to the test track for the first time in October.

'Product Lifecycle Management' or PLM, supervised the quality monitoring of individual parts at BMW Williams. In a workflow that was a true logistical masterpiece, the life cycle of every component was tracked and constantly documented. Regardless of whether it was a seal, a damper or a suspension

wishbone, the quality engineers recorded all data, such as: the production and processing date, the delivery deadline and the result of quality checks. A record was kept of every single part of a Formula 1 car; if a fault occurred, it could be identified and fixed immediately. Components also had marks so that the staff member responsible for making it could be identified. Other teams use similar systems.

The art of troubleshooting and avoiding problems is perfected on the racetrack. As an example, all of the sensors on the BMW-Sauber F1.06 in 2006 were used to monitor the track's features and deliver data on the performance and state of the engine, transmission

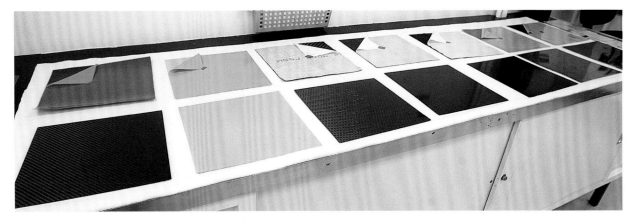

WISHBONE PATTERN AND SHUTTERING

Once a component has been designed and drawn a pattern is required; this is usually CNC machined directly from the CAD system.
The pattern needs to be dimensionally accurate allowing for the expansion, it also needs to withstand 90-psi pressure during the mould cure. The surface finish needs to be the same as is required on the finished item, usually highly polished.
The shuttering provides a surface for a flange on the split mould, which is required for complex shapes.

Left top: Composite materials are laid out prior to selection. Quality control is paramount at all times. (sutton-images.com)

Left middle and bottom: Suspension wishbones and their moulds are checked for quality at all times. All teams operate systems where the individual maker of each component can readily be identified. (sutton-images.com)

Right and below: Components are finished to very high tolerances, and the use of computer-controlled tooling is essential to ensure accuracy. All components are rigorously tested before they are certified for use on a car. (BMW AG)

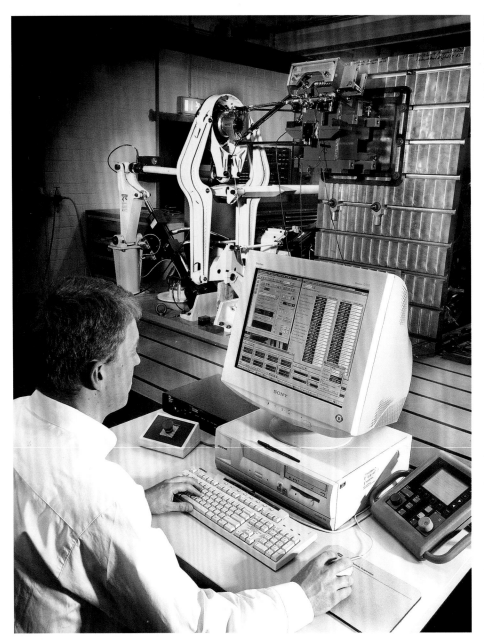

and other units to the team's pit-lane control centre. Two BMW engineers continuously monitored the engine online and the team communicated with the driver on the radio. This intensive data gathering and monitoring enabled the team to identify and react immediately to any problems that arose. Once all this data had been gathered, further detailed fault analysis could begin, either after a test, a practice or qualifying session, or a race. The cars were completely dismantled and subjected to more than 200 diagnostic checks. Minor defects could be remedied before the next Grand Prix. If, for example, problems had arisen in a fabricated component during a race, by the following Tuesday a designer could already be at work devising a remedy that could be produced on the Wednesday. This could in turn be tested on Thursday. Even changes in the software could be made from one day to the next by modifying the parameter settings. More significant modifications, for instance to the aerodynamic components, could be implemented within weeks, once all the stages of the quality checks had been completed.

The final means of imparting quality, long before a Formula 1 car gets anywhere near a racetrack, is to check out many of its systems on test rigs well before it leaves the factory. It is another key part of the process.

No matter how good the design process is, being able to prove it before a car runs is critical. Multiple component test rigs are thus used to measure things such as stiffness and ultimate strength. The latter may entail an impact, or else fatigue simulation. Long before it goes off for its mandatory crash tests the monocoque is subjected to torsional load tests, while suspension, steering, dampers and electro-hydraulic systems are also tested on purpose-built rigs before assembly. In the case of suspension, some teams use a single-corner rig, which takes up minimal space and can be put to work while the full-size car is needed elsewhere. The sprung mass of the rear car is suitably represented, as is downforce, and the rig can be used to measure efficiency or longevity. Likewise dampers are also put through their paces on specially calibrated rigs. A Kinematics and Compliance (K&C) measuring rig enables cars to be given a full workout at the factory, to make precise measurements of the kinematic and compliance characteristics of suspension and steering systems.

Brake and tyre manufacturers also have their own test rigs, which again help to prove and develop the product before it goes into battle.

The most important rig is the seven-poster road simulator. Teams mount a complete car on this expensive piece of equipment, so that they can subject the vehicle to a fully representative cycle of what it will encounter on the track. This will be based on data gathered previously, and the cycle can be varied to cater specifically for all types of circuit.

The hydraulically-powered seven-poster rig comprises four vertical electro-hydraulic actuators, one beneath each wheel. Three tension struts linked to downforce actuators pull the chassis down to represent downforce, roll, pitch loads and load transfer.

This system is so accurate that the team can reprogramme dampers, suspension and wing settings to compare results, or it can let drivers practise their art. When BMW Williams tested young upcomers Nico Rosberg and Nelson Piquet Jr at Jerez in December 2003, they let each of them 'drive' the simulator for eight hours apiece on a simulation of the Spanish circuit.

In the merciless crucible of Formula 1, perfection remains a utopian goal. But therein lies one of the great appeals of this highest echelon of motor sport, in which everyone in a team, from the principal to the production-line worker, has their eye focused solely on the attainment of excellence.

Chapter 13

The Recovery of Energy
Improving the breed

It's been a long time since F1, or motorsport in general, could lay genuine claim to improving the breed of road cars that we will drive in the not too distant future. The disc brake, the most famous example of racing technology being developed to the benefit of the everyday motorist, won the Le Mans 24 Hours as long ago as 1953...

But the advent of Kinetic Energy Recovery Systems (KERS) in 2009 – the brainchild of FIA President Max Mosley – changed all that. Even though doomsayers in the paddock would have had it otherwise.

The latter had a field day in the summer of 2008 as the teams which embraced the technology early began to test their systems. In Jerez in August a BMW test engineer received a very public electric shock which was quickly broadcast on YouTube. Around the same time, Red Bull Racing's experimental department had to be evacuated when a lithium battery caught fire, and there were rumours of a battery explosion chez Toyota.

Mosley always made it clear that KERS would be optional, and while its main proponents insisted that they would continue development and would run it as soon as they could, others planned to steer clear. Mosley, of all people, should have realised that the only way to get teams in F1 to play ball was to make them, but curiously he chose the more benign route of encouraging them. Not everyone could see the clear and crucial value in adopting such systems in order to establish the sport's green credentials and give it a fresh chance to contribute something highly significant to the automotive world.

There are three basic concepts: the electrical supercapacitor system favoured by BMW, the normal battery-powered systems of McLaren Mercedes, Ferrari, Toyota and Renault, and the mechanical flywheel from Williams.

The electrical systems are more compact and employ an electric motor generator (EMG) which charges and releases energy from the very latest state-of-the-art lithium ion batteries every time the driver brakes. This is managed by the KERS control unit which is linked directly to the car's standard electronic control unit (ECU).

In BMW's case, the supercapacitor is a device that creates an electro-static field as a short-term means of storing energy. The next step from that is the ultracapacitor, still currently under development.

The mechanical system relies on a carbon-fibre flywheel which spins at speeds between 60,000 and 75,000rpm within a vacuum chamber, which is connected to the car's drivetrain by a continuously variable transmission (CVT). As it accelerates and decelerates, the flywheel stores and releases energy.

There was another potential system which was activated hydraulically. This was conceived by McLaren, but was not ratified by the FIA.

This is how KERS works.

Under braking the rear wheel brakes act as generators and the kinetic energy that is created as electricity is stored in the batteries (or flywheel) ready for the driver to exploit via a push-button on the steering wheel when he needs extra grunt. Actuating the button makes those generators behave like powerful electric motors to add thrust to the power of the V8 engine.

BMW's motorsport director Dr Mario Theissen, a very keen proponent of the technology, said: 'For us KERS is an extremely exciting project and a great opportunity. We are standing at the threshold between

Opposite: Kimi Räikkönen maximises his Ferrari's speed by pushing the KERS button on the climb to Les Combes at Spa. The extra power was crucial in helping him to beat Giancarlo Fisichella's Force India. (LAT)

a conventional package of engine and independent transmission and an integrated drive system. KERS will see Formula 1 take on a pioneering role for series production technologies going forward. F1 will give a baptism of fire to innovative concepts whose service life and reliability have not yet reached the level required for series production vehicles, and their development will be driven forward at full speed.'

That was the single most important aspect of the new technology, because it would legitimise F1, and give it genuine impetus in its quest to be seen to be green.

Toyota's technical director Pascal Vasselon, however, saw little application for road cars from spin-off technology. That was interesting, given the Japanese manufacturer's devotion to hybrid technology.

In April 2008 Williams F1 acquired a minority shareholding in Automotive Hybrid Power Limited. Renamed Williams Hybrid Power Limited, the company, led by engineer Ian Foley, was already developing a hybrid power system based on a composite flywheel rotating at speeds of up to 100,000rpm that would capture energy generated under braking.

Patrick Head, Williams F1's Director of Engineering, said, 'High-energy flywheel technology is a challenging field of engineering. We fully support the FIA's positive initiative in energy recovery systems which we hope will allow Formula 1 to make some contribution to the development of an environmentally beneficial technology that could help to reduce the carbon emissions of vehicles.'

Foley, WHP's managing director, said: 'As AHP, we had begun to develop our own advanced flywheel technology for application in vehicles. As Williams Hybrid Power, we will make use of the higher profile and Formula 1 development programme to accelerate development and bring it to market more quickly.'

Foley had absolutely no doubt that the flywheel KERS system had significant benefits in the outside world. 'We see it having numerous applications in road transport,' he said, 'from trucks to buses to trains. The flywheel has enormous potential as an energy-saving device.'

The FIA was careful to frame the regulations so that different KERS systems did not prove more advantageous than others, but nevertheless the aim was clearly to create a performance benefit no greater than 80bhp.

Toyota's engine designer, Luca Marmorini, hit on the most likely advantage of the system, however. 'KERS will not make a massive difference to lap time as the extra power will only be available for around 6.5s per lap,' he said. 'So a time benefit of around 0.1s and 0.3s per lap is realistic, without considering the weight distribution and packaging implications. But an additional benefit KERS could offer is a chance to overtake. On one-lap performance it is questionable whether it will provide an advantage compared to a non-KERS car when you take into account the weight distribution issues but, providing that you have traction, you could have a better chance to overtake.

'It is expected that our car with KERS would still be at the minimum weight as defined in the rules because at the moment our car is significantly lighter than the 605kg minimum but we comply with the regulations by using ballast. If KERS makes the base weight of the car 25–35kg heavier, then you have less ballast to move around and this could have a performance impact as it limits the opportunities to change weight distribution.'

A typical KERS system weighed in at 30kg early in 2009, something that could easily be accommodated given that most teams carried 50kg of ballast to meet

the 605kg minimum weight. However, it was not quite as simple as that. In 2009, with the return to slick tyres, teams were doing all they could to make the most of more powerful front tyres by bringing more weight on to the front axle. Typically, 2008 cars had 46–48% of their weight over the front, and many teams struggled to improve on that.

Choosing KERS meant accepting a reduction in the ability to juggle tungsten ballast to fine-tune weight distribution, in return for that likely advantage in overtaking. But for many teams which opted to run it, it was a circuit-by-circuit decision. And, as some drivers could be up to 20kg lighter than their rivals, it could also favour them. BMW-Sauber, for example, ran Nick Heidfeld on KERS for the first four races, but after trying it on the Friday in China and finding no advantage, his team-mate Robert Kubica only used it in Bahrain.

The electrical systems were the only ones to race as these words were written, and though they were generally deemed easier to package than the mechanical, they still posed problems. Generally, it was reckoned that for every 10mm increase in a car's centre of gravity a tenth of a second could be lost on a typical track. This was something that affected Renault, which sited its KERS components, including the batteries, beneath the fuel tank. Ferrari, however, had its batteries in the undertray and, according to informed rumour, in the front wing, to bring weight further forward. Williams's system, with the mechanical flywheel, required the CVT to be mounted on the nose of the crankshaft right behind the fuel tank.

Safety was the 'hot' story of KERS in 2008, particularly after BMW's excitement in Jerez. What concerned observers was that a team of race-winning calibre did not know immediately what caused a potentially highly dangerous situation.

'I think all the teams are taking the safety aspect very, very seriously,' said Ferrari's Aldo Costa in Hungary that season. 'You have to remember that first the system has to be managed on the bench, in-house, in testing, so the safety aspect is the first priority. You cannot use a system in-house, on the test-bench or in testing, that you believe is not safe enough. Safety, of course, is the first aspect. I don't think anyone would use a system in the race that they don't believe is safe. And in terms of when it should be decided whether or not to use the KERS in a race, this is still very early days. We think there is potential, we think we can have a performance advantage, so we will push in that direction, and at the very last moment, if the whole package is faster, we will use it. Otherwise not.'

Toyota's technical director, Pascal Vasselon, addressed the issues of battery fires and explosions. 'Going through the possible failure modes of the KERS system is just what we have to do,' he said. 'We will all be trying to overheat or overcharge batteries. We will all be trying to crash flywheels for those who will use flywheels. We just have to do that, so it will be all about making sure that we keep these failures under control on the test bench, and later on the track. So for sure, yes, you will hear about battery fires and things like that, simply because we will have to gain experience in this direction.'

Mike Gascoyne, who was at that time in technical charge at Force India, was his usual pragmatic self when he said: 'The safety issue is one that's being stressed but it's just an engineering problem and an engineering challenge. At the end of the day, we carry 70 kilos of fuel around at 200mph and go round corners. It's just a similar engineering safety issue to address.'

Mosley, predictably, defended his baby. 'There is opposition to it, but to me the crucial thing about KERS is that it's inconceivable that, in 50 years' time, when you put the brakes on in your car, the energy will just burn off in heat. That won't happen. But the first thing we need is a system that's capable of absorbing all the energy when you put the brakes on. The next generation of Formula 1 cars will be like that.'

Eventually, BMW found what had caused the Jerez problem.

'The mechanic suffered an electric shock after touching the sidepod and steering wheel of the car,' said its head of powertrain development, Markus Duesmann.

'There was a high frequency AC voltage between these contact points, the cause of which has been traced back to the KERS control unit and a sporadic capacitive coupling from the high-voltage network to the 12-volt network. The voltage ran through the wiring of the 12-volt network to the steering wheel and through the carbon chassis back to the control unit.

'Only a small amount of energy can be transferred through this capacitive coupling effect. However, the energy is sufficient to cause an extremely painful reaction.

'The driver was insulated against the car by his racing overalls and gloves and therefore not in any danger.'

BMW-Sauber made the findings of its investigation available to the other teams at a meeting of the Technical Working Group and supplied a copy to the FIA.

'In addition to the measures required to tackle the issue at hand, the extremely far-reaching analysis we conducted also gave rise to other recommendations which are of great value for the development of electric KERS systems,' Duesmann added. 'Among the measures arrived at are changes in the design of the control unit to avoid capacitive coupling effects, extended monitoring functions for high frequencies and a conductive connection of the chassis components to avoid any electric potential.'

He further explained that the results of the investigation were such a long time coming because of the complicated nature of the new system.

'It was not possible initially to reproduce the capacitive coupling effect in the car, as the problem was caused by a sporadic error in the control unit,' he explained. 'Due to the extremely high frequency of the voltage in the steering wheel, the safety mechanisms and data recordings did not pick up on the error. In the absence of data, all the theoretical possibilities had to be systematically investigated and analysed in tests. Furthermore, the capacitive coupling effect only occurs under certain conditions. Without the option of driving the KERS test car used in Jerez again, we had to reconstruct these conditions.'

A Ferrari team member wears protective rubber gloves to guard against the risk of electric shock when working on the KERS-equipped F60 at the 2009 Malaysian Grand Prix. (sutton-images.com)

The other major criticism of KERS centred on cost, and there it was much harder to defend Mosley's stance. At a time when everyone was seeking means of slashing costs, KERS added as much as $60 million to some developmental budgets. And there was even talk of a standardised version being mandated for 2010, which made that expenditure seem ludicrous and completely unjustifiable in the straitened economic times. It was small wonder that a small outfit such as Brawn, the phoenix that rose winningly from the ashes of Honda F1 early in 2009, declared that it had no intention whatsoever of looking at KERS in its first season.

'Inevitably, a new technology of this kind requires significant resources in order to develop a safe and effective solution,' Luca Marmorini confirmed. 'Costs have been particularly significant with KERS because it is a major new technology for Formula 1 and there are a number of potential solutions which had to be looked at.'

Mosley said blithely: 'If you imagine you could have a super-efficient KERS system, five to ten years sooner than you would otherwise get it, then multiply it by the number of cars in the world, then Formula 1 costs will be a drop in the ocean.'

As he was uttering those very words, many manufacturers were wondering if they would still be in business in that timescale, such was the extent of the global recession. Nevertheless, BMW, Williams, Toyota, McLaren Mercedes and Ferrari remained committed to the cause and resistant to demands, from the likes of Renault's Flavio Briatore, to push the technology back to 2010 at a meeting in Maranello which led to the formation of the Formula 1 Teams' Association. Honda, too, was working on two systems, back-to-backing electrical and flywheel designs that would, ultimately, be stillborn when it announced its withdrawal from F1 on 4 December 2008.

'Our point of view is that it is good, not just for BMW but for the sport,' Theissen reiterated. 'And if it is good we should have it as soon as possible. No technical project has become cheaper by delaying its introduction.'

Sir Frank Williams said: 'It is an exciting challenge, that we are enjoying. There were two or three against the delay, but we want to carry on with what we are doing.'

Ron Dennis, while still team principal at McLaren Mercedes, said at Fuji in 2008: 'From a technology standpoint we totally embrace KERS. It is hugely challenging. It is technically very interesting, and it may give us the opportunity to produce more overtaking opportunities. Having said that, it is extremely costly technology, and that really doesn't sit well from the cost point of view in the climate in which we are currently operating.

'As you grow older you have a greater capacity for saying, "I was wrong". Do I think KERS is good for F1? Actually, I do. But, there are some real challenges to make it safe, to make it reliable, and it is most certainly an extremely expensive technology to pursue.'

Another insider, who did not wish to be identified, said: 'It is so wasteful. I mean, we are going to be dumping somewhere between £50,000 and £100,000 worth of batteries every Grand Prix. They won't be recyclable, they have very limited shelf-life, and you could be having an accident with a hell of a lot of energy stored up. The amount of work we have done to get through the safety gates is just phenomenal. Is it going to have any relevance to any production car? None at all.'

Not even design philosophies and methodology?

'We don't think so. I mean, yeah, we could be wrong, but this is so, so, so, so hybrid.'

Then there were the problems associated with deployment of the system, and the challenges to perceived knowledge of what a racing car really needs to be quick. Of course it needs good aerodynamic qualities and engine power, but the most critical thing is balance. Balancing a car in all the conditions in which it will run is extremely difficult. And one of the things about harvesting energy is that you are putting reverse torque into the back wheels which means that the potential impact for it to unbalance the car is quite extreme. So engineers are constantly trying to manage the influence of engine retardation which comes through the friction in the engine, when a driver decelerates into a corner. The ability to lock up the rear wheels is one thing, but at least that is a consistent situation. Harvesting horsepower under deceleration was a different matter, and left engineers unsure about the consistency from corner to corner. That was one of the big challenges, how to keep the car balanced. It was clear that you didn't need to be very out of balance to lose all the time you might have gained through deployment of KERS. All the mathematics showed there was the potential for three- to four-tenths of a second a lap with KERS, over the lap. What that didn't show was that you might get that in a very short period of time, as an energy boost that might allow you to overtake, and that you might be three- or four-tenths faster down one straight. But initially there was insufficient knowledge about the potential destabilisation of the car under deceleration, which could cost that time, and more. When engineers began to develop KERS, it was one challenge to harvest the energy and another to discharge it. How they dealt with the two would be a key to their success with the technology. The smarter found a useful way to offset the loss of engine braking management, which had gone out the window together with traction control with the advent of the standard ECU in 2008.

It didn't take anyone long, when KERS made its race debut in Australia on the McLaren, BMW and Ferrari cars, to recognise that the boost in acceleration it conferred was worth having. The Brawn, Williams and Toyota cars were the class of the field, with their two-tier diffusers (neither Williams nor Toyota chose to race KERS), but the early laps were enlivened by charges from McLaren's Lewis Hamilton and Ferrari's Felipe Massa as they used their KERS to the maximum. The effectiveness of the systems in getaways from the start-line was even more evident in Malaysia. In the post-race press conference, as final podium finisher Timo Glock told his tale, winner Jenson Button and Nick Heidfeld stared open-mouthed at a replay of the accelerative power of Fernando Alonso's KERS-equipped Renault and Kimi Räikkönen's Ferrari.

A fascinating bit of FOM technology made its debut in Bahrain. It was called Line Comparison and overlaid one driver's line over another's to highlight similarities or differences. One such comparison involved Button's winning Brawn and Hamilton's KERS McLaren going into and accelerating out of the left-handed Turn 10. The Brawn had greater grip and the smoother line, but it was noticeable how Hamilton could reel Button in when he activated KERS on the exit…

Despite Renault using KERS, team principal Flavio Briatore launched a salvo at it in Bahrain. 'FOTA wants a ban on it from 2010,' he claimed, which seemed unlikely. 'We understood immediately that KERS was a money-sucking genius, and that the FIA should have taken note of that. It should have been discussed before the start of the season, and the same goes for diffusers. Having failed to do that has forced upon us expenses that are crazy as much as useless.'

Mosley, of course, remained reluctant to scrap the technology, not least because it was so important in giving the sport a much-needed green image. Instead, it was felt likely that he would mandate one system for 2010. He was said to favour Williams's flywheel design as being the safest, and with more new cars required to cater for the ban on refuelling for 2010, some felt that the flywheel system might better be accommodated in longer wheelbase cars. At the same time, if the FIA were to up the capacity of energy storage, that would also suit the flywheel systems and give them impetus.

But had KERS given F1 the green image that Max Mosley so craved? Or was it a white elephant that would soon become extinct? Early in the season the jurors, the teams that invested so much in the technology, were still locked in their private room, arguing passionately.

Between the Turkish and British GPs the pro-brigade crumbled further, after Renault had already started having second thoughts. Ironically it was BMW-Sauber, one of KERS's greatest proponents, that followed suit in dumping it for good, believing that it would be easier to improve its recalcitrant F1.09's performance more without the hybrid technology.

Team principal Dr Mario Theissen said the team had spent a lot of time considering whether to continue with it, before finally opting not to. 'We evaluated different alleys, proceeding with KERS or proceeding on the aero side and what could we do with no KERS on board,' he said. 'We had made some significant progress on the aero side which does not allow us to fit KERS, and we have taken a decision just a few days ago to run KERS no more this year because we see a more promising alley in developing the aero.'

Theissen insisted, however, that it had been beneficial to road car development within BMW.

'I would not say the technology is a flop, just the opposite. Given the very short development time it has been a huge success to get it up and running reliably and our system really works fine. We didn't have any flaws, not even in Malaysia in the torrential rain. But it depends on the set of regulations you have.

'If you want to push an innovation then you have to fully focus on it. If it is not mandatory to have the system on board, then now KERS is basically out-performed on the aero side. And I have to say what we have achieved, at least within BMW, has been transferred already to the road car side. Our engineers are currently supporting the road car R&D department and that will continue for quite some time because we have learned an awful lot which is applicable to not just hybrid cars but also electric vehicles and conventional cars, because a battery is on any car.

'I would say if it isn't made mandatory it will disappear. That is just natural. It is a pity in my view because this has been a unique chance to really position F1 as a technology carrier, as a pioneer of innovative technology, and it would have been very good in the current economic climate for F1 as a whole.'

Ferrari and McLaren continued to use their systems, but even the latter showed signs of wavering at Silverstone. On a track where the benefits of using KERS were less pronounced, Heikki Kovalainen's engineers chose to continue running the system while Lewis Hamilton's decided to focus on developing the most effective balance on the MP4-24 without it.

As many were then moved to denigrate the experiment, McLaren team principal Martin Whitmarsh said it was more a matter of circumstances militating against KERS rather than the technology being a failure.

'The concept of KERS was probably the right thing to do for F1, but two years ago at Silverstone it seemed it was getting out of control in terms of the technical openness of it, and every team bar Williams agreed to abandon it,' he said. 'At the end of last year it was every team bar BMW, and we've always taken a flexible view on it. On those two occasions we were prepared to get rid of it.

'The regulations are incredibly wide, and they are challenging in that to develop a KERS system within the weight and packaging constraints of F1, with the power and energy limitations and still have performance, is difficult. And if you look back on it now with hindsight, this industry has undoubtedly wasted a lot of money in that area, particularly if we are not going to be running with KERS next year.

'McLaren and Mercedes's position is that we believe we have come this far and should continue with KERS, but the spirit of co-operation that exists within F1 now with FOTA, we accept not using vetoes to block these things.

'A majority of teams want to block it and it has been unfortunate for us because we have put in a tremendous amount of effort, with the added potential distraction in our engineering programme and concept of this car.

'Like all of these things, you get the perfect storm of issues. Putting it as kindly as possible, we were not as adventurous in our diffuser interpretation, and that gave us limitations in how you respond to it.

'We were behind on the development of the overall aero concept, and we have put a lot of effort into KERS because F1 was committing to it. Looking back we could have made some different decisions, but that is how hindsight works.'

There was talk for 2010 of allowing teams to develop KERS that could harvest twice the power – around 160bhp – possibly in conjunction with CVTs, but the issue remained clouded as this edition went to press. It is likely that the technology will still be optional in 2010, and equally likely that nobody will take it up.

Subsequently, even BMW-Sauber canned the technology mid-season, but it received a timely boost when Lewis Hamilton won the Hungarian Grand Prix for McLaren Mercedes. That made a little bit of history, marking the first victory for a KERS car, and perhaps threw energy recovery systems a timely lifeline, especially as two races later Ferrari also won, at Spa.

Keeping KERS safe

After the BMW-Sauber problem during the test in Jerez in August 2008, teams became ever more vigilant about safety as far as their KERS systems were concerned.

McLaren Mercedes, for example, developed this mission statement: 'In all expected conditions of deployment, a single point of failure of KERS may not cause an electric shock hazardous to life.'

McLaren Racing developed the operational framework for the team's KERS programme, and Mercedes-Benz High Performance Engines (HPE) refined, developed and manufactured the unit. In the summer of 2008, McLaren commissioned an independent assessment of its system and procedures, which was carried out by technical consultancy QinetiQ, in parallel with HPE. Later, QinetiQ proof-tested McLaren's mission statement.

The team's KERS system had been developed in conjunction with monthly meetings of the FIA Safety Working Group and the FIA KERS Safety Working Group, while QinetiQ assessed the measures built into the whole programme, from its design and manufacture, through its dyno and track testing and into its integration and eventual deployment in races.

McLaren's safety philosophy was simple: KERS should be no more dangerous to use than any other electrical appliance. A household toaster could give the user an electric shock, but under normal operating circumstances it should pose zero threat to their safety.

There were three primary concerns. The high-voltage shock risk when running the KERS eMotor. The burn risks associated with machinery running at very high temperatures. And the additional risk of fire arising from such extreme temperatures.

QinetiQ endorsed McLaren's existing measures and worked with it to educate team members who would operate the KERS-equipped cars at races. Not only was training deemed important, but so was accurate logging of all training activities, to ensure that everybody within the team was *au fait* with the information generated. This even spread beyond the drivers and operational engineers and mechanics, to marketing staff and team guests visiting the garage.

All of the McLaren equipment was double-insulated to ensure that the high-voltage circuit was completely isolated, and there were regular inspections. An HPE engineer was responsible for each MP4-24's KERS system, but the cars also had a sensor that continuously monitored the quality of the isolation between the high-voltage circuits and the chassis, ready to alert engineers if any degradation was detected. Furthermore, all of the external components on the car were electronically connected together in order to reduce the difference in voltages between parts, to offer the maximum possible protection against significant electric shocks.

All KERS-related components and cabling were colour-coded to ensure high visibility, and a green light illuminated on the bodywork to indicate when the system was fully shut down.

The operational team backed all this up in testing with additional precautions, such as rubber gloves and mats to provide additional insulation for team members working on the car. As the system developed, the team returned to a normal state of operation, no longer needing the gloves and boots. Once testing was completed, the final 'race-ready' KERS unit required additional sign-off at McLaren director level to ensure top-down compliance throughout the entire organisation.

In general, when the racing started in 2009 and McLaren Mercedes, BMW-Sauber, Ferrari and Renault ran their systems from the start in Australia, there were surprisingly few problems, though in practice in Malaysia Kimi Räikkönen was obliged to bail out of his Ferrari in the pits when a short circuit fried the lithium iron batteries under his seat… And had that rain-stopped race subsequently been restarted, pit-lane insiders suggested that none of the KERS cars could have run because their systems were drowned.

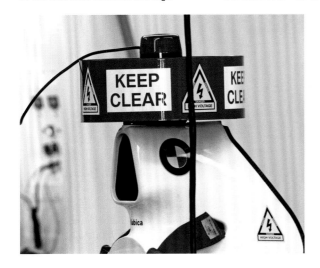

BMW-Sauber used this marker system to indicate the status of their KERS-equipped car during testing in 2008.
(sutton-images.com)

Chapter 14
Intellectual Property Rights
Spygate

The 'Spygate' scandal of 2007 sullied Formula One like nothing that had ever gone before, though FIA President Max Mosley had his own skirmish with disgrace the following season. It was made an even more extraordinary story because of the underlying acrimony not just between Ferrari and McLaren, but between McLaren and the FIA. And it was all down to that most vexatious 21st-century subject: intellectual property rights.

Ferrari's head of performance development, Nigel Stepney, and McLaren's chief designer, Mike Coughlan first worked together in the '80s at Team Lotus. Later they were colleagues at Benetton and then again at Ferrari. Coughlan then moved on to Arrows and from there joined McLaren in the summer of 2002. His McLaren contract ran out in the summer of 2006 and he signed a new three-year deal, just before he received an offer to move back to Ferrari.

In late 2006, Coughlan decided that he wanted to move on. He was unhappy with his level of remuneration at McLaren and aspired to join F1's elite group of millionaire engineers.

At the same time, Stepney had become deeply unhappy at Ferrari – Stwhere he had worked since January 1993. He had hoped to be promoted to a senior position after Ross Brawn left for his sabbatical in 2007, but team principal Jean Todt clearly did not agree with Stepney's assessment of his own worth. He was so unhappy that he gave a highly controversial interview over the course of the winter, which destroyed what was left of his relationship with Todt. Around the time of the Australian Grand Prix in March 2007, Coughlan received an e-mail from Stepney (although the latter later denied sending it) alerting him to questions about the legality of the Ferrari F2007's floor attachment mechanism. McLaren verified the claims and then went to the FIA, 'adopting the customary practice of asking the FIA Technical Department for their opinion'.

The McLaren questioning was so precise that other teams suspected from the paperwork – that was available to all of them – that McLaren had specific knowledge of the Ferrari.

The FIA replied that such devices would not be legal. McLaren said that: 'As far as we are aware, Ferrari ran its cars with this illegal device in the Australian GP, which it won', but decided not to protest.

After Melbourne the FIA confirmed that Ferrari's floor fixation system was illegal and the team changed its design. Others – Red Bull, Honda, Renault and BMW – also changed theirs.

McLaren argued subsequently that Stepney was not acting as a spy in this matter but rather as a 'whistle-blower'.

Opposite: McLaren was caught in the middle of a controversy over intellectual property rights to material belonging to Ferrari during the 2007 season. (LAT)

At the time, McLaren and Ferrari were discussing an agreement by which they would settle their differences out of the public eye, rather than via protests to the FIA. Team principal Ron Dennis did not, however, tell Ferrari about the whistle-blower. But McLaren Racing managing director Jonathan Neale told Coughlan to stop all communication with Stepney.

Stepney continued sending messages to Coughlan's personal e-mail address, and at the end of April Coughlan told Neale that the only way to stop this happening was for him to have a face-to-face meeting with Stepney.

On Saturday 28 April, Coughlan flew to Barcelona, where Stepney had a yacht moored in the nearby Marina Port Ginesta. The pair met for lunch and by an incredible stroke of fate, their meeting was witnessed by Mike Gascoyne, at that time Spyker's chief technology officer, who also had a yacht moored there.

In his subsequent affidavit, given to London's High Court, Coughlan stated that he took home with him a 780-page dossier from Stepney. This included details of Ferrari's F2007 car, the team's various technical systems, including its legendarily bulletproof preparation (which had been Stepney's true forte), and various practice, race and test strategies. Coughlan said he kept the documentation out of 'engineering curiosity'.

On Wednesday 2 May, Stepney made his first approach to Honda F1, saying that he had a group of engineers from different teams who wanted to work together there. Honda at that time was in deep technical trouble, and a meeting was arranged between Stepney and Honda Racing team principal Nick Fry at a hotel near Heathrow Airport on 9 May. There Stepney told Fry that Coughlan was one of the engineers involved in the plan.

Meanwhile, Ferrari suffered a disastrous failure of the rolling road in its wind tunnel at Maranello. It was out of action for nearly five weeks. Ferrari's on-track performance dropped off dramatically. It was also during this period that Stepney first told friends that he was under surveillance by agents of Ferrari.

Ferrari alleged that, on 21 May, Stepney put some 'white powder' into the fuel tanks of its cars as they were due to go to the Monaco Grand Prix on 27 May. Stepney vehemently denied this and later suggested that he was being framed in an attempt to discredit him.

The story made little sense. At Monaco there was practice on the Thursday (24 May), so any attempt to sabotage the Ferraris would have been discovered then and would have had little impact.

That same week Coughlan asked Neale for an early release from his McLaren contract, and they met for breakfast on Friday 25 May at a golf club near Woking.

Neale's view was that Coughlan would have to honour his contract. Coughlan later said that he then showed Neale one of the Ferrari documents. McLaren disagreed, saying that Neale refused to look at the document. He subsequently told the World Motor Sport Council that he told Coughlan not to bother showing him anything, assuming that it was a piece of equipment that Coughlan wanted Neale to invest in for the team. Others at McLaren suggested that Neale thought it might be a job offer from another team.

Coughlan also claimed that he showed a document to McLaren design engineer Rob Taylor, a diagram of the Ferrari brake balance system.

After the hearing at the World Motor Sport Council to which McLaren was summoned on 26 July,

Ron Dennis finally wrote a corrective letter to Luigi Macaluso, the president of Italy's national sporting authority, the CSAI, which represents Ferrari. Macaluso had requested, and was granted, an appeal hearing on Ferrari's behalf.

'Taylor had no idea whether this was an old or new diagram,' Dennis explained in his letter, 'and had no idea it came from Stepney. He was not given a copy and made no use of the diagram. He paid no attention to the incident'.

Neale reported back to Dennis that Coughlan now wanted promotion and a salary increase, something McLaren was not minded to grant.

On Friday 1 June, Stepney and Coughlan met again at Heathrow and this time they also met with Fry. Coughlan told him that he wanted to be technical director of Honda. It was also suggested during the World Motor Sport Council meeting on 26 July that at the same time, the two men had contacted Toyota for similar discussions. Only Fry at Honda came clean and admitted having had discussions.

At Indianapolis there were rumours that a new espionage scandal was about to break in Italy and Ferrari sources suggested that Stepney was involved. There were even (incorrect) stories that he had been arrested. The rumours suggested that a Ferrari team member was being accused of having sold designs to rival teams.

That may have been the trigger for Coughlan to call his wife Trudy to ask her to take the Ferrari documents to a print shop and have them scanned and copied on to two compact discs. She went to an establishment in Hersham, Surrey, where she paid with a personal cheque. The original documents were then destroyed, apparently having been shredded and then burned in the back garden of Coughlan's house in Bramley, also in Surrey.

On Thursday 21 June, Ferrari announced that it had made a complaint against Stepney and that he was under investigation. Stepney responded the following day saying that he was the victim of 'a dirty tricks campaign'.

The print shop proprietor contacted Ferrari to inform the team that a sizeable amount of its confidential data had been copied on to disc for one of its customers. The connection was made to Coughlan via the cheque used for payment, and on Monday 2 July Ferrari successfully applied to the High Court in London for a private (rather than police) warrant to search the Coughlans' home. Discs containing Ferrari's information were found.

By the end of that day McLaren had suspended Coughlan and instigated an internal investigation,

which was carried out by the security firm, Kroll.

From the very start, however, the case had been to a large extent a trial by media for the McLaren team. The most extraordinary stories thus appeared, especially in the Italian press but also in some UK dailies, which were not backed up by verifiable facts.

The FIA asked McLaren to attend an extraordinary meeting of the World Motor Sport Council to explain itself under Article 151(c) of the Sporting regulations, which deals with fraud or matters bringing the sport into disrepute. At this hearing, in Paris on Thursday, 26 July, the 26 Council members (many of them representatives of national sporting authorities all around the globe) ruled unanimously that while

McLaren team principal Ron Dennis emerges from the World Motorsport Council hearing in Paris on 26 July 2007. (LAT)

McLaren had by the letter of rule breached Article 151(c) insofar as it had collective responsibility for its employee's rogue actions, no action should be taken nor any penalty imposed.

Once the WMSC meeting was over, much more information was to come into the public domain. Three days later Macaluso requested Mosley to grant an appeal, on the grounds that Ferrari had been denied right to audience in the hearing. McLaren took a deep breath, considered for a few days and then

There was no love lost between Ferrari team principal Jean Todt and Ron Dennis during the 'Spygate' affair. (LAT)

sent out a devastating message via Dennis's five-page letter, which alleged that Ferrari had run an illegal car in Australia.

After a series of controversial events in the Hungarian GP in August, however, the situation reignited. Lewis Hamilton disobeyed team orders in qualifying to give way to team-mate Fernando Alonso, and when the Spaniard was subsequently penalised for blocking Hamilton in the pits, their spat triggered further revelations. Alonso, it was alleged, tried to blackmail Dennis on the morning of the race by threatening to reveal what he knew of the 'Spygate' affair, which was that he had been passed information by McLaren test driver Pedro de la Rosa who had in turn had it imparted to him by Coughlan. Dennis, aghast to learn that there was more to the situation than he had feared, did the honourable thing and immediately disclosed that to Mosley.

Now the FIA called another WMSC meeting to hear the fresh information. It was convened on the Thursday – appropriately enough the 13th of September – prior to the Belgian GP at Spa-Francorchamps. This time the WMSC found McLaren guilty.

It fined the team a Draconian $100m – by a factor of 20 the largest fine in motorsport history – and revoked all of its points in the 2007 World Championship for Constructors.

It emerged that the new evidence, which persuaded the FIA to reconvene the WMSC meeting of 26 July rather than hear the appeal against that hearing's findings on behalf of Ferrari, embraced a series of emails and SMS messages between the disgraced Coughlan and McLaren's two Spanish drivers. These disclosed information such as the Ferrari's weight distribution, details of its braking system, the gas used to inflate its tyres, its 'flexible' rear wing and the team's pit stop strategy from Australia.

Having effectively subpoenaed the McLaren drivers into revealing their email and SMS communications, the FIA learned that, unequivocally, de la Rosa and Alonso had received confidential Ferrari information via Coughlan; and that both knew its exact nature and that it had been received by Coughlan from Stepney.

Though they could not prove that such information had actually been used to improve the McLaren, the WMSC took the view that de la Rosa's evidence made it clear that there was no reluctance or hesitation about testing the Ferrari information for potential benefit.

The WMSC did not accept de la Rosa's claim that

he did not share the information and its source with other team members, but the evidence that he did remained purely circumstantial.

In his affidavit Coughlan said there were a number of contacts between him and Stepney and described incidents where specific Ferrari confidential information was transferred to him. New evidence strongly indicated that the transmission of confidential Ferrari information from Stepney to Coughlan was not limited to the 780 page dossier, and that a far greater level of communication existed between them than was originally appreciated at the 26 July WMSC meeting. This evidence was submitted by Ferrari and was deemed credible as it originated from the Italian police and was the result of an official analysis of records of telephone, SMS and email contacts between Coughlan and Stepney. The evidence suggested that at least 288 SMS messages and 35 telephone calls passed between them between 11 March 2007 and 3 July 2007. The WMSC suggested that the new evidence regarding the number and timing of the contacts made it far more likely that there was a systematic flow of Ferrari confidential information to Coughlan, leading to the conclusion that the illicit communication of information was very likely not limited to the transmission of the Ferrari

dossier discovered at Coughlan's home on 3 July. The WMSC also believed that Coughlan may have had a more active role in the design of the McLaren than it had previously appreciated, but this was not proved.

There was no evidence that any complete Ferrari design was copied and subsequently incorporated into the McLaren as a result of Coughlan passing confidential from Stepney to McLaren, but the FIA insisted: 'It is difficult to accept that the secret Ferrari information that was within Coughlan's knowledge never influenced his judgement in the performance of his duties. It is not necessary for McLaren to have copied a complete Ferrari design for it to have benefited from Coughlan's knowledge. For example, the secret Ferrari information cannot but have informed the views Coughlan expressed to others in the McLaren design department, for example regarding which design projects to prioritise or which research to pursue. The advantage gained may have been as subtle as Coughlan being in a position to suggest alternative ways of approaching different design challenges.'

The brutal and deliberately embarrassing staged attempt at public reconciliation between FIA President Max Mosley and Ron Dennis outside the McLaren Brand Centre at the 2007 Belgian Grand Prix. (LAT)

The WMSC also took into account the argument that there was little evidence of the information in question being disseminated to others at McLaren, and that Coughlan was a single rogue employee. However, it stressed that it was not necessary to demonstrate that any confidential Ferrari information was directly copied by McLaren or put to direct use in the McLaren to justify a finding that Article 151(c) was breached and/or that a penalty was merited. It felt entitled to treat possession of another team's information as an offence meriting a penalty on its own if it so chose.

In light of all the evidence placed before it, the WMSC did not accept that the only actions of McLaren deserving censure were those of Coughlan.

Back in 1994 the FIA had been happy to accept, when Benetton (now Renault) transgressed due to a junior employee erring, a defence that became known as the 'junior employee defence' and thus did not punish that team for removing a mandatory fuel filter to speed up its pit stops, but now the WMSC deemed that a number of McLaren employees or agents were in unauthorised possession of, or knew or should have known that other McLaren employees or agents were in unauthorised possession of, the confidential Ferrari information, and that there was an intention on the part of a number of McLaren personnel to use some of the Ferrari information in their own testing.

'The evidence leads the WMSC to conclude that some degree of sporting advantage was obtained, though it may forever be impossible to quantify that advantage in concrete terms,' it concluded.

The fact remained, however, that the WMSC was not able to prove conclusively that management at McLaren knew that the confidential information was being used, much less what specific benefit might have been derived.

Having effectively had to blow the whistle on his own team, Dennis then had to endure a grisly handshake with Mosley on the steps of McLaren's Brand Centre hospitality unit in the paddock at Spa. Most felt it was an unnecessary and vengeful piece of theatre.

Some believed that McLaren was merely the victim of a witchhunt, a point of view lent credence by the fact that a senior F1 figure told Dennis on the grid at Monza: 'If you resign, all of this will go away.'

There was a supreme irony hidden in all of this, which was that other teams were inadvertently violating McLaren's exclusive rights deal with Cambridge University when they began developing their own inerters for 2007. Dennis came to appreciate that there was no precedent for applying complex IP law from the real world to F1 design. If patent law were to be

enforced in F1, it would most likely bring the sport to a grinding halt. Discovering and interpreting each other's technology had, after all, always been a cornerstone of a highly competitive sport. In the end, Dennis decided the only fair course of action was to tear up the exclusive arrangement and see the big picture.

In Canada in 2008 there was a rapprochement between Ferrari and McLaren, which could only be brought about because Todt had been replaced as team principal by the urbane Stefano Domenicali. On 29 January 2009, the relationship and respect between the two teams deepened when Ferrari public relations guru Luca Colajanni was invited to visit the McLaren Technology Centre. McLaren's Matt Bishop subsequently visited Maranello. The mutual exchange was something that had not happened in living memory.

Later that year, on 23 February, the 'Spygate' story was finally wrapped up when Italian magistrates in Modena fined the disgraced Coughlan $200,000, and McLaren's Rob Taylor, Jonathan Neale and Paddy Lowe similar amounts for their alleged roles in the affair. Neither Ron Dennis nor Martin Whitmarsh received any penalty.

In 2007, however, there remained one more dramatic scene in the spying scandal. This time it was McLaren that brought a legal action against Renault, and it appeared to have a far more clear-cut case than that which Ferrari had brought against it.

Renault was obliged to confirm the suspension of one of its engineers, Phil Mackereth, following the FIA's order for it to appear before the World Motor Sport Council in Monaco on 6 December, to answer a charge in relation to a breach of article 151(c) of the International Sporting Code.

Mackereth had joined Renault from McLaren in September 2006, and brought with him some information that was considered proprietary to McLaren on old-style floppy disks. The information included drawings covered four basic systems as used by McLaren: the internal layout of the fuel tank, the basic layout of the gear clusters, a tuned mass damper and a suspension damper. Some Renault engineers said that having been shown the drawings briefly, none of the information was used.

This was extraordinary, given that the information relating to the suspension contained details of McLaren inerter (see Chapter 8).

Renault claimed to have cleansed its computer systems after initiating a formal investigation, and to have returned the disks to McLaren. Up to 15 Renault engineers were said to have seen 10 disks. According to McLaren they included chief designer

Tim Densham; deputy chief designer Martin Tolliday; deputy technical director James Allison; head of research and development Robin Tuluie; head of vehicle performance Nicholas Chester; head of mechanical design Peter Duffy; and head of transmission design Tony Osgood.

While it was never proved that anyone within the McLaren organisation saw the Ferrari data (Coughlan had it at home and showed it to de la Rosa, who told Alonso about it), McLaren's legal dossier, based on three independent forensic computer reports commissioned from Kroll Ontrack, alleged that 18 people within Renault admit having viewed 33 files of McLaren data on 11 separate Renault F1-owned computers. These files were said to contain more than 780 individual drawings outlining the entire technical blueprint of the 2006 and 2007 McLarens.

There was general incredulity when, having admitted to the same crime of receiving stolen intellectual

The strained relationship between Ferrari and McLaren was only exacerbated by their intense on-track battle for the 2007 World Championship. (LAT)

property for which McLaren had been fined $100m only months earlier and had its Constructors' World Championship points wiped out, Renault was let off by the WMSC even though it was proved that the McLaren data was so embedded in Renault's computer system that it could not actually be deleted.

In the past a Lotus employee had been caught measuring up the suspension and aerodynamic tunnels on a Williams; Tyrrell had been caught copying the Lotus 79 as the basis for its 1979 challenger; and the late Harvey Postlethwaite openly admitted that while he was a Ferrari designer he had broken into the Williams garage one year at Hockenheim to discover the true secrets of ground effect.

None of these transgressions was punished.

Chapter 15

The Application of Technology
F1 in the real world

On the surface, motor racing is purely about speed and intense competition. But beyond the insular world of the racing itself there is another kind of thrill which is shared by the scientists who operate in the background, the boffins who dream up radical new applications for F1 technology.

In January 2009 London's Science Museum opened a fascinating exhibition which put a wholly different complexion on the value of the sport, and showcased how some of this innovative technology impacts on the lives of everyday people, and in some surprising environments.

Ron Dennis, at that time still the CEO of McLaren Racing, addressed the media as he opened the exhibition with some inspirational comments.

'I think what makes the Science Museum such a compelling and engaging place to visit, is its ability to tell stories through everyday applications of science, technology and engineering. From steam engines to space travel, the exhibits that surround us here stand as testimony to dedicated scientific and creative minds, to those before us who have solved problems and overcome challenges for the betterment of man and the betterment of society.

'Which, in many ways, reflects the world in which I've spent my entire professional career – the world of Formula 1 motor racing.

'Because, contrary to popular belief, Formula 1 is not about glitz and glamour, or parties and celebrities. Of course it attracts more than its fair share of all of these; but, intrinsically, at its heart, it is about technological and scientific innovation, carried out under extremes of time pressure, with a relentless fortnightly assessment of progress and performance.

'We undertake this assessment under the glare and scrutiny of hundreds of millions of TV viewers – and we measure our successes or failures in fractions of seconds of lap time.

'The world of Formula 1 is no place for the faint-hearted. It is tough – ruthless, in fact – and, to paraphrase the great Charles Darwin in his anniversary year, it is all about the survival of the fittest. It is the pinnacle of not only motor racing, I would argue, but of innovation under pressure as well.

'Indeed, since I started in Formula 1 some 43 years ago, an incredible 79 Formula 1 teams have come and gone, carrying with them the hopes, dreams and fortunes of some incredibly bright, incredibly hard-working individuals – who, despite their best efforts, were simply not competitive enough to survive.

Opposite: In January 2009, Ron Dennis opened the Science Museum's exhibition highlighting how technology developed in Formula One has benefited the wider world. (LAT)

'And so it is no great surprise that successful teams in this high-stakes sport innovate at an incredible rate – by way of example we make a change to our cars on average every 20 minutes throughout the entire F1 season. And we do that every season.

'We innovate at such a rate, in fact, that technologies whose applications are far broader than racing are created as a matter of course. Such technologies often have their genesis in racing cars, but then find suitability to products or situations never foreseen by their creators.

'Countless otherwise unrelated industries have been beneficiaries of Formula 1 innovation – and just a few of these are represented here today in this fabulous showcase of scientific application. I am proud to say that a significant number of the innovations celebrated by this exhibition are the work of McLaren engineers and scientists – unsung heroes whose work continues to live well beyond our Technology Centre in Woking, Surrey.

'Industries as diverse as leisure and entertainment,

'You only need look around you in this great institution to be reminded of the amazing track record we have in this country for working our way out of crisis; for stimulating growth through innovation. The German philosopher Friedrich Nietzsche famously said: 'That which doesn't kill us, makes us stronger'. I, for one, have every confidence that the great British tradition of engineering and scientific excellence will again drive us forward to an era of prosperity and sustained competitiveness.'

The US military has become increasingly interested in F1's enviable safety record in the years since 1994. They saw that drivers had become cocooned inside safety cells that could absorb extraordinary impacts. That the cars were designed to deform in a certain way in such situations. That more often than not drivers were able to walk away virtually unscathed no matter how spectacular the incident. Think Robert Kubica, in Montreal in 2007...

F1's lightweight materials, and the design of the chassis, had created something that the US military really liked, and designers within the sport were quick to appreciate the interest from the defence sector.

The US military had suffered a large number of casualties from roadside bombs and mines in Afghanistan and engineers sought new ways to reduce the vulnerability of the soldiers riding in Humvee-style scouting vehicles. F1-style composites, particularly the chassis-manufacturing mix of carbon-fibre and Kevlar, offered the strength to absorb the energy of a bullet or shrapnel from an explosion, but were generally too expensive to be used on a large scale. But the aluminium honeycomb that is also used in certain applications within chassis offered a cheaper alternative. F1 engineers set about creating structures that could be placed on the floorpan of vehicles to contain explosions from land mines. Tests showed that such structures could reduce the blast acceleration from 50g to around 20, something which would significantly enhance the occupants' chances of survival.

It was John Barnard who was in the vanguard of carbon-fibre chassis design, via his unique McLaren MP4/1 of 1981. One of the outstanding innovators of the '80s and '90s, Barnard retired from his own B3 Technologies business in 2006. Today the 62-year-old is still exploring new ideas and recently joined forces with designer Terence Woodgate to transform the design of furniture. In 2008 they released an

healthcare, defence and even space exploration are featured here today, and they are just the tip of the iceberg.

'But this exhibition is not merely a chance to reflect on the past role of Formula 1, or even McLaren, in innovating. To me the most powerful role to be played by this exhibition is to inspire the next generation of Britons to embrace science, technology and engineering to provide answers to the problems of tomorrow.

'The challenges in the world today, and the challenges for Great Britain, are well documented.

'However, together we will overcome these challenges, as we have done before. We will overcome them by being a nation that embraces science, a nation that utilises engineering, a nation that encourages creativity in problem-solving – in much the same way as we in Formula 1 are required to do exactly that every day of our lives.

F1-inspired carbon-composite dining table; though it is 4m long it is just 2mm thick…

Similarly, architects have now started to look at the potential of the new materials to create elegant structures that have extraordinary strength. The unique structural properties of carbon-fibre means that they can produce curved stairs that are only 4mm thick yet can withstand more than 100 times their own weight. Staircases are just the beginning. The industry sees composite materials developed in F1 as a means of opening up the restrictions on structural elements in buildings that have long frustrated architects.

Artists, too, are looking at composites. South African Alastair Gibson was chief mechanic at Honda F1 until the end of 2007, working with Jenson Button and Rubens Barrichello. His latest creation is a shark sculpture called Racing Mako, which was unveiled at the Chelsea Art Fair in London in April 2009. The carbon-fibre sculpture was 2.5m long, and used actual parts from F1 cars in its detailing. Gibson is now branching out and developing his work and hopes to be the first artist to sculpt a human hand from composite materials.

Composite technology came to F1 from the rocket and aviation industries and it is interesting to note that

The BMW-Sauber's safety cell absorbed a series of extraordinary impacts during Robert Kubica's accident at the Canadian Grand Prix in 2007, allowing him to escape relatively unscathed. This safety-cell technology has potentially life-saving applications in the military field. (LAT)

in recent years the lessons learned by F1 engineers on Earth have been fed back into the aerospace industry to help to develop new machinery for space exploration.

In 2006 the Hinode satellite was launched in order to monitor how 'solar weather' affects the Earth. Aboard the craft was a 3m-long telescope designed to measure the small-scale changes that occur during the critical build-up of a solar flare. Scientists needed a telescope that was as light as possible but also immensely strong so that it would not to crack or deform during the blast-off process and durable enough to withstand exposure to the extreme atmospheric conditions of space. F1 materials were used to create a housing for the onboard instrumentation.

There are many other surfaces and treatments that have been developed in F1 that have applications in aerospace, notably on the Beagle 2 space probe that was launched in 2003. Its mission was to travel to Mars to ascertain if there was any form of life on the planet.

The lander was packed with sensitive equipment that needed to be protected during the moment of impact with the planet's rocky surface. Scientists turned to F1 again to use a special plastic coating that had been developed for the exhaust systems of F1 cars; since the exhausts operated at very high temperatures the coating was deemed to be perfect to meet the extreme rigours of space exploration.

Protecting delicate things is another area in which F1 has been able to apply its thinking, via technology for the medical profession. The heart of the modern race car is the survival cell monocoque which not only protects the driver but also provides the structure on to which all the car's other elements are attached. A British engineering company has used its experience manufacturing F1 parts to create the world's first commercially available 'monocoque' wheelchair, which is sculpted to fit the occupant's body. It accommodates them in comfort and protects them while at the same time creating a robust yet lightweight unit that can operate in places where conventional wheelchairs would simply be unable to work.

A similar application is the BabyPod, an F1-inspired unit designed to transport seriously ill babies to and from hospitals with a great deal more ease and safety than was possible with traditional heavy metal incubators. The infant is secured and insulated within the self-contained unit, which is similar in concept to an F1 cockpit. This is much lighter, making it easier for ambulance and emergency helicopter crews to handle. The unit can even be transported in a doctor's car if the case is really urgent.

Hospitals are increasingly adopting F1 techniques, where the process of moving patients from operating theatres to intensive care units is complex and time-critical. Doctors at the Great Ormond Street Hospital in London reckoned that they could learn a thing or two from F1 pit stop techniques and studied the way in which teams of mechanics work together and communicate to pull off the perfect pit stop. From this they formulated ways to streamline the handover process and reduce the possibility of errors being made as doctors perform complicated tasks under pressure. This helps to ensure that a patient is left unprotected for an absolute minimum period of time, thus improving their chances of recovery. Other hospitals are now following Great Ormond Street's initiative and looking to devise their own F1-derived systems.

Another area where F1 technology can help speed up recovery or even to avoid injury is a knee brace that has been developed by an F1 team, working with the US Marine Corps. Marines in the Green Berets regularly suffered knee injuries from standing in fast-moving inflatable boats skipping across broken seas. The sort of strains experienced were equivalent to jumping off a 2.5m-high wall every few seconds. An F1 car's contact with the road is optimised by hydraulic dampers which absorb the energy of bumps and rebounds, and similar systems have now been used to create a special lightweight support to help reduce damage and injuries to the knee. This helps to control the way in which the knee bends and realigns the joint before the next impact, thus making sure that there is less jarring and therefore less chance of the joint being injured.

The brace can also be used to make sure that patients recovering from knee injuries keep the joint correctly aligned at all times, thus increasing their mobility without the risk of the injury being aggravated.

Another area in which F1 is helping to revolutionise medical thinking is in the use of sensors. An F1 car is being monitored every millisecond it is running. Over 200 sensors in the average machine make around 150,000 measurements per second. Engineers then analyse this information in order to understand what needs to be done to improve its efficiency and performance. Using trackside experience of such

remote monitoring, F1 technicians have developed a human telemetry system that can help doctors monitor patients taking part in clinical trials.

Wireless sensors record patient data such as heart rate or motion. This information is transmitted in real time to the clinic, where doctors can assess how a patient is responding to treatment, giving them the opportunity to call the patient in for a 'pit stop' if they see problems developing. There are even opportunities for a remote change in the doses of drugs being administered, if necessary.

The technological developments are not all about safety, however. There is also much that can be done to use F1 ideas and technologies to improve human performance in other areas of life. The Beru F1 Systems company has used F1 technology and materials to produce the world's most advanced bicycle. This weighs in under 7kg and was designed with the same modelling and analysis software used to build F1 cars. The bicycle has an onboard computer and performance monitoring system, incorporating various sensors, a GPS and a radio transmitter that produce laboratory-quality data. As the cyclist rides, information about wheel speed, heart rate, humidity and bike angle is collected and stored ready for subsequent detailed examination. The rider can

Above left: John Barnard designed the first carbon monocoque to appear in Formula One for the 1981 McLaren MP4/1. He is seen here examining the prototype monocoque with Cosworth DFV engine designer Keith Duckworth.
(sutton-images.com)

The Beru F1 Systems company has used F1 technology and materials to produce the world's most advanced cycle, weighing under 7kg and incorporating various data logging functions. (LAT)

select the type of information to be collected from a touch-screen built into the handlebars.

The sensors used in F1 have many other potential uses outside the sport, notably in the realm of tyre safety. An incorrectly inflated tyre can mean the difference between winning and losing a Grand Prix and teams use special monitoring equipment to warn them if there are incipient problems with the tyres. This technology has been adapted for use in road cars and is now helping to reduce the risk of road accidents caused by tyre failure. Modern tyres have relatively stiff sidewalls which are designed to support the weight of a car for a short period after a puncture, and thus give little visual clue of a potential problem. F1-derived tyre pressure monitors fitted to road cars can detect a puncture as soon as the car is switched on, and thus alert the driver to the danger before the vehicle even moves. In an increasingly ecologically-aware society such sensors can also play a key role in ensuring that tyre inflation pressures are optimised to maximise fuel economy and tyre life. This is valuable in both the private and commercial sectors of world economies.

Tyre technology is another area in which F1 can help produce better consumer products. Racing tyres are made from soft rubber compounds that offer the best possible grip. They also feature specific tread patterns to sipe water away in the most efficient way when the track is wet. Using some of these concepts, the US firm Shoes for Crews has developed special slip-resistant footwear, which uses a special rubber material and tread pattern for people working in areas with wet and greasy floors. In a seven-month trial organised by the Health and Safety Executive's laboratory it was reported that there had been zero 'slip accidents' while personnel were wearing the footwear at a pet food company in Doncaster.

Workplace falls are a problem in many industries. It is estimated that in the UK, one person is injured in a slip or a fall every 25 seconds. This is particularly dangerous in the world of construction where a slip can result in fatal falls from elevated work areas.

Another area in which Formula 1 has had an impact is in the refuelling of armoured vehicles on active service in harsh environments, particularly in dusty desert conditions such as Iraq. Tank crews were encountering myriad problems such as dust ingestion, fuel spillage and long refuelling times. The British Army responded by looking at F1 refuelling systems for its 380 Challenger 2 Main Battle Tanks – which are expected to remain in service until 2035 – in order to reduce the time needed for refuelling and also to help to avoid fuel pump and engine failures that can occur because of contaminants in the system.

Essex firm Newton Equipment developed a 'Clean Fill' system for the tanks using the same ideas as F1 with a fuel nozzle that connects to the fuel filler hole of the tank. Seals render the parts gastight and leak-proof when they are pushed together, while a small nozzle allows air out of the tank.

F1 cars also have to deal with contaminants such as small metallic particles transported in oil, which can damage engine and gearbox components. Conventional filtering systems trapped the contaminants by size, but did not capture the smallest particles, so F1 engineers came up with the idea of using magnetic filters.

The Warwick-based firm Magnom realised that this would be useful in household boiler systems and produced the 'Boiler Buddy', which applies the same technology to filter out rust particles in central heating systems and thus reduce the risk of blockages. 'As a result,' said Katie Maggs of the Science Museum, 'your radiator is far more efficient and helps you reduce energy consumption. It just goes to show that this technology transfer really does affect the common man or woman.'

The technology can also be scaled up for commercial applications and even used in large-scale installations such as power stations. Other versions of the device have been used in nuclear power stations, earth-moving equipment and wind farms.

Dennis's presence at the Science Museum that day in January 2009 was particularly apposite, since the success of Nicola Minichiello and Gillian Cooke, who had recently won the Women's World Bobsleigh Championships in Lake Placid in the USA, had also marked a victory for the McLaren Group. The world title, which topped a superb top-three finish for Minichiello and her two brakewomen in the 2008–9 World Cup series, was achieved with the assistance of McLaren Applied Technologies – the innovations arm of McLaren Group – which had helped the impecunious team to identify several key areas that could be improved on its existing sled since the cost of a new one was prohibitive.

In his closing remarks, Dennis said: 'It is my fervent hope that the rate at which we, as a sport, innovate and change can provide inspiration to other industries, and act as an engine of growth for our nation.

'And it is also my fervent hope that this exhibition will help inspire a new generation of engineers, scientists and problem-solvers. Who knows, in years to come we may marvel at their work in this great institution.'

As a means of attracting, inspiring and motivating young engineers, motorsport has no peer.

Glossary

AIRBOX The opening at the front of the engine cover to encourage admission of ram air into the engine.

AUTOCLAVE An oven in which carbon-fibre composites are baked to cure them into their intended operational condition.

BARGE BOARD A vertical panel situated within the front suspension to influence airflow aft of the front wing. Also called a turning vane.

BUCK A wooden structure that duplicates the intended final shape of a component, such as a monocoque chassis, from which the chassis moulds are taken.

CAD Computer-aided design.

CAM Computer-aided manufacture.

CARBON-FIBRE A carbon-impregnated cloth used in chassis manufacture.

CDG Centreline downwash generating.

CENTRE OF GRAVITY The point on the car through which the forces generated by its weight are said to act.

CENTRE OF PRESSURE The point on the car through which all of the aerodynamic forces may be said to act.

CFD Computational fluid dynamics – a branch of mathematics used to create predictive models for aerodynamic study.

CLOSED LOOP A computer circuit in which the system operates automatically.

CVT Continuously variable transmission.

DIFFUSER The section of the undertray that sweeps up to release the air that has been speeded up during its journey beneath the car.

DOWNFORCE The pressure generated by the car's motion through the air, which tends either to push it (in the case of high-pressure flow over the body) or suck it (in the case of low-pressure flow beneath the car) on to the track.

DRAG Air resistance to the car's forward motion. Something that all aerodynamic research aims to reduce to a minimum.

ECU Electronic control unit.

ENDPLATE A vertical surface on the end of a wing, to influence airflow.

FEA Finite element analysis.

FIA Fédération Internationale de l'Automobile – the governing body of world motorsport.

FIVE AXIS MACHINE A cutting or milling machine capable of operating through a wide variety of angles.

FLY BY WIRE A system wherein there is no mechanical link between components, just electronic, as in a Formula 1 car's throttle system.

FOCA Formula 1 Constructors' Association – the association of Formula 1 teams.

FOTA Formula One Teams' Association.

FOUR-POSTER RIG A test rig comprising four posts, which can input forces to areas of a car on test. Used for static assessment of a car's behaviour.

GCU Gearbox control unit – the electronics system which controls the gearbox's shifting action.

G FORCE The force of gravity acting upon a car or driver.

GPMA Grand Prix Manufacturers' Association.

GRENADE ENGINE The name given in the past to special racing engines created purely to have a short life, and to produce maximum power, for qualifying. They were so close to the edge of mechanical reliability that they frequently self-destructed.

K&C Kinetics and Compliance.

KEVLAR A woven material used in race car chassis and component manufacture.

KERS Kinetic energy recovery systems.

LIFT The pressure of air flowing over or under the car when it is in motion that tends to try and lift it off the road.

LIFT OVER DRAG The ratio of downforce (negative lift) to drag. High figures are the best.

MONOCOQUE The name given to a racing car chassis structure in which the body and the chassis are integrated as one component.

OPEN LOOP A computer circuit in which the system must be operated manually.

OVERSTEER The tendency of the rear of a car to slide wide of the intended line through a corner, due to the rear tyre slip angles being greater than those of the front tyres.

OWG Overtaking Working Group, a sub-committee of the FIA's Technical Working Group.

PITCH The tendency of the front or rear of a car to move up and down, independently of each other, in reaction to changes in the road surface or aerodynamic loadings acting upon the car.

PITCH SENSIVITY Pitch sensitivity is a key to good handling. On a car that has low pitch sensitivity the aerodynamic balance doesn't shift around as the car pitches up and down over bumps, or tends to shift its centre of gravity under acceleration or deceleration.

PLANK The rubbing strip of wood – usually Jabroc – fitted longitudinally beneath the floor of a racing car.

PULLROD A suspension component that operates a bottom-mounted spring/damper unit by pulling in response to movement of the suspension wishbone.

PUSHROD A suspension component that operates a top-mounted spring/damper unit by pushing in response to movement of the suspension wishbone.

RAM Random access memory.

RIDE HEIGHT The height of a car's chassis above the ground reference plane. It can be set to different measurements at the front and the rear. The front is usually set slightly lower to give the car a degree of rake which helps its dynamic performance.

ROLL The lateral rolling motion of a car, especially during cornering.

ROLLBAR A metal bar, usually steel because of its strength properties, which acts like a spring in the suspension system to resist a car's tendency to roll during cornering.

ROLLOVER BAR A hoop incorporated into the chassis structure – immediately behind the driver's seat and also by his legs – to offer protection in the event of the car becoming inverted.

SCALLOP A shaped section of extra bodywork designed to influence airflow.

SEVEN-POSTER RIG A test rig comprising seven posts, which can input forces to areas of a car on test. Used for static assessment of a car's behaviour.

SIDEPOD Panel on the side of the car housing the water radiators, and an area of deformable structure.

SLIP ANGLE The actual angle at which a car corners, compared to the intended angle selected by the driver's positioning of the steering wheel. The angle may differ if the tyre is sliding across the road surface due to speed reducing its level of grip.

SLIPSTREAM The suction effect generated by airflow around the back of a car travelling at high speed.

SPLITTER A horizontal plate designed to separate – or split – airflow, thus directing it to different points of the car.

STRAKES Horizontal or vertical plates designed, like endplates, to control airflow over a car body.

TELEMETRY A system mounted on a car which gathers data electronically during power running, either storing it or transmitting it to the driver's pit.

TRACTION CONTROL A system of electronically monitoring road wheel speed and, at the onset of wheelspin, reducing engine power to control or obviate it.

TREAD The area of the tyre that interfaces with the road. On slicks it is full width; on grooved tyres the area is significantly less.

TWG Technical Working Group.

UNDERSTEER The tendency of the front end of a car to slide wide of the intended line through a corner, due to the front tyre slip angles being greater than the rears.

UNDERTRAY The detachable floor of the car.

WIND TUNNEL A structure, usually with belt-driven moving ground to simulate a car's motion over ground, in which scale models are tested in fast-flowing air to calculate a car's likely aerodynamic behaviour in full size.

WING An aerofoil-section horizontal surface designed to create downforce.

WINGLET A small extra wing, usually mounted on the bodywork just ahead of the rear wheel.

YAW The tendency of a car to move laterally away from its intended direction of travel.

Index

Jaafar, Jazeman, 157
Jaguar, 24, 32, 83, 142
  C-type, 137
  R3, 32, 121
  R4, 32
  XJ series, 162
Japanese GP, 2006, 131
Jenkins, Alan, 108
Jerez, 32, 34, 99, 169, 171, 174, 175
JOBS machine, 65–6
Jordan, 53, 66, 69, 142, 145, 150–1
Jordan, Eddie, 53
Judd engines, 105–6

Karthikeyan, Narain, 151
Knight, Jack, 103
Kolles, Colin, 92
Kovalainen, Heikki, 177
Kroll, 183
Kroll Ontrack, 187
Kubica, Robert, 90, 172, 174, 190, 191
Kyalami, 122

Lamborghini, 73
Lauterwasser, Dr Christoph, 164
Le Mans 24 Hours race, 1953, 137, 171
Lear removable seat, 65
Lectra cutting machines, 61–4
Life (née First), 69
Link, Edwin, 155–6
Liuzzi, Vitantonio, 91
Liverpool Data Research Associates Ltd (LDRA), 118–19
Lola, 53
Lotus, 17, 19, 53, 73, 116
  49, 7, 103
  49B, 18
  72, 7, 125
  76, 106
  79, 19, 106, 187
  86T, 24
Lowe, Paddy, 45, 46–8, 50, 186
Lucky Strike, 146

Macaluso, Luigi, 182, 183
Mackereth, Phil, 186
McLaren, 7–9, 12–15, 31, 41, 45, 46, 48, 49, 53, 97–9, 104–5, 110, 114, 115, 151
  FM engines, 7
  inerters, 131–4, 186
  kinetic energy recovery systems (KERS), 171, 176, 177–9
  M23, 7
  MP4/1, 193
  MP4/4, 104–5
  MP4/8, 115
  MP4-17, 7, 33
    MP4-17D, 7–8, 129
  MP4-18, 7–8, 13, 26, 31, 109
  MP4-19, 7–8, 12, 26, 109
  MP4-20, 131
  MP4-21, 31
  MP4-22, 26, 132, 134
  MP4-23, 98, 111, 155
  MP4-24, 28, 36, 38, 42, 43, 132, 165, 177, 179
  simulators, 47–8, 155, 158
  and Stepneygate spy scandal, 181–7
McLaren Applied Technologies, 194
McLaren Electronic Systems, 92, 95, 97, 99
McLaren Group, 98, 194
McLaren Mercedes, 91, 98, 143, 145
McLaren Racing, 178, 181, 189
McLaren Technology Centre, 186, 189
Maggs, Katie, 194
Magnom, 194
Magny-Cours, 117, 143
Malaysian GP
  1999, 24
  2007, 134
  2008, 57
  2009, 153, 175, 177, 179
Mansell, Nigel, 107–8
March, 103–4
  721X, 103–4
Mardle, John, 56
Marmorini, Luca, 172, 176
Martinelli, Paolo, 86–8, 89

Maserati V12 engines, 75
Massa, Felipe, 37, 50, 134, 159, 177
Mateschitz, Dietrich, 88–9, 92
Matra V12 engines, 75
Melbourne, 9, 99, 161, 181
Mercedes, kinetic energy recovery systems (KERS), 171, 176, 178–9
Mercedes-Benz, 8, 75, 78, 83, 88, 91, 92, 117
  High Performance Engines (HPE), 178–9
  Ilmor FO108T, 90
  V8 engines, 14–15
  V10 engines, 78
MES, 96–9
Mexican GP, 1986, 24
Michael, Sam, 114, 129, 147
Michelin, 113, 130, 145, 146, 148, 150–2
Michelin, Edouard, 152
Microsoft Corporation, 95
Midland Racing, 53, 92
Migeot, Jean-Claude, 31, 45
Minardi, 88–9, 91, 97, 107, 108, 117, 151
Minichiello, Nicola, 194
Mobil, 93
Monaco, 45, 91, 186
Monaco GP
  1969, 18
  2002, 114, 115
  2003, 81
  2007, 34, 182
  2009, 30, 49
Monte Carlo, 38, 93, 115, 129, 137, 140–2
  Beau Rivage, 140
  Portier corner, 140
  tunnel, 142
Monteiro, Tiago, 151
Montoya, Juan Pablo, 114
Montreal, 190
Monza, 8, 18, 47, 78–80, 91, 130, 134, 149, 186
Moog, 159
  valves, 102
Mosley, Max, 45, 47–8, 83–6, 88, 95, 119, 139, 145, 150, 152, 155, 164, 171, 175, 176–7, 181, 183–4, 185, 186
Moss, Stirling, 145
Moto GP, 88
MTS Systems Corp., 20
  `Flat-Trac' rolling road, 20
Mugen-Honda, 53
Murray, Gordon, 104–5, 137–8

Namco, 155
NCAP crash testing, 164
Neale, Jonathan, 181, 182, 186
Newey, Adrian, 8–9
Newton Equipment, 194
Nietzsche, Friedrich, 190
Nintendo Wii, 159
Northrop, 157
Nürburgring, 25, 41, 92

O'Rourke, Brian, 161
Osgood, Tony, 187
OWG, 38

Pearce, Ian, 57–61
Penske Cars, 53
Peterson, Ronnie, 19, 106
Peugeot, 53
  V10 engines, 78
Piquet Jnr, Nelson, 169
Plasse, Axel, 80, 81
Pole Position, 155
Portimao, 155
Postlethwaite, Harvey, 31, 105–6, 107, 187
Prodrive, 45
Prost, 114
Purnell, Tony, 47–8

QinetiQ, 178–9
Queen's Award for Enterprise in Innovation, 99

Räikkönen, Kimi, 7, 17, 83, 134, 143, 152, 177, 179

Rampf, Willy, 20, 21–2, 23
Ratzenberger, Roland, 76
Red Bull Racing, 24, 37, 51, 66, 88–9, 134, 153, 181
  kinetic energy recovery systems (KERS), 171
  RB2, 24
  RB5, 32, 38, 50, 122, 148
  simulators, 159
Renault, 35, 45, 46, 51, 57, 61, 65, 66, 73, 76–8, 81–2, 88, 89, 114, 130–1, 134, 151, 181, 186–7
  Enstone HQ, 54
  kinetic energy recovery systems (KERS), 171, 174, 176, 177
  R24, 35, 54
  R25, 54, 129–30
  R26, 24, 39, 54, 89, 130, 132, 163
  R27, 38
  R28, 57
  R29, 32, 36, 39, 103
  simulators, 159
  V6 engines, 77–8
  V10 engines, 75
  RS24, 81
Renault Sport, 81, 82
Repco V8 engines, 75
Revson, Peter, 122
RHS Harntec, 20
Rinland, Sergio, 32, 123
Rio de Jacarepaguá, 107–8
Rodriguez, Stéphane, 81–2
Rosberg, Nico, 98, 109, 169
Rossi, Valentino, 88
Rudd, Tony, 17
Russell, Kirk, 53

Sachs, 103
San Marino GP
  2004, 88
  2005, 131
  2006, 24, 41
Sauber, 20–3, 110, 151
  C20, 32, 123
  Hinwil wind tunnel, 18, 20
Sauber, Peter, 18–19, 20, 23, 110, 117
Sauber Petronas, 33, 116, 119
  C21, 117
Schnaider, Alex, 53
Schumacher, Michael, 14, 24, 34, 41, 45, 78, 81, 88, 131, 147, 151, 161
Schumacher, Ralf, 114, 150, 151
Science Museum, 189–90, 194
Senna, Ayrton, 24, 76, 151
Shanghai GP, 153
Shell, 93
Shoes for Crews, 194
Siffert, Jo, 137
Silverstone, 69, 138, 145
  Club Corner, 145
Simtek, 45, 159
SLEC Holdings, 88
Smith, Malcolm, 131–4
South African GP, 18
Spa-Francorchamps, 91, 148, 178, 184, 186
  La Source hairpin, 121
  Les Combes, 45
Spanish GP
  1969, 18
  1994, 152
  2001, 113
  2009, 29, 40
Spyker, 181
Stepney, Nigel, 181–2
Stepneygate spy scandal, 97, 180–7
Stewart, 108, 142
Stewart, Paul, 106, 108
Super Aguri F1, 45
Sutil, Adrian, 142
Sutton, John, 109
Suzuka, 81
Symonds, Pat, 45–8, 51

Taylor, Rob, 182, 186
Team Lotus, 181
Thales, 157
Theissen, Mario, 86, 92, 95–6, 153, 171–2, 176, 177
Tilly, Andy, 117

Todt, Jean, 93, 134, 181, 184, 186
Tolliday, Martin, 187
Toro Rosso, 88–9, 92
  STR04 Ferrari, 95
  V10 engines, 91
Toyota, 48, 50–1, 82, 83, 91, 110, 113, 118, 150, 159, 168, 182
  kinetic energy recovery systems (KERS), 171, 172, 174, 176, 177
  RVX-09, 92
  simulators, 159
  TF106, 41, 95
  TF107, 38, 140
  TF109, 30
Triumph Herald, 122
Trulli, Jarno, 114, 159
Tuluie, Robin, 187
Turbo Lufttechnik GmbH, 20
Turkish GP
  2007, 134
  2009, 40, 42, 177
Tyrrell, 31, 45, 187

United States GP, 2005, 150–2
Unser, Bobby, 43
US Army Air Force, 156
US Marine Corps, 193

Valencia, 45, 159
van Manen, Peter, 95, 96–9
Vasselon, Pascal, 172, 175
Vettel, Sebastian, 148, 153, 159
Viking horns, 48
Villeneuve, Jacques, 106, 129
VSEC, 159

Watkins, Prof Sid, 67
Watts, Colin, 50, 54, 66
Webber, Mark, 153
Weismann, Pete, 103–5
Weslake V12 engines, 75
White, Rob, 89, 109
Whiting, Charlie, 24–5, 45, 46, 47, 51, 67, 150
Whitmarsh, Martin, 7–9, 134, 178, 186
Williams, 14, 18–19, 23, 37, 50–1, 66, 69, 73, 86, 109–11, 114, 138, 143, 147, 148–9, 150, 151, 161, 165, 187
  FW12, 105–6
  FW22, 53
  FW24, 69, 126, 127, 132, 138
  FW25, 34, 128, 165
  FW26, 31, 39, 86
  Grove wind tunnel, 22
  inerters, 134
  kinetic energy recovery systems (KERS), 171, 172, 174, 176, 177, 178
  simulators, 157, 158, 159
Williams Cosworth FW28, 109, 110
Williams, Frank, 176
Williams Hybrid Power (WHP), 172
Willis, Geoffrey, 24–5, 159
Wirth, Nick, 45, 47, 48, 159
Wirth Research, 159
Women's World Bobsleigh Championships, 194
Woodgate, Terence, 190–1
World Championship, 15, 78, 89
  1967, 103
  2002, 145
  2003, 7, 81, 161
  2004, 7
  2005, 129–30
  2007, 184, 187
  2008, 14
  2009, 14–15
World Motor Sport Council (WMSC), 182, 183–7
Wright, Peter, 24, 47–8
Wurz, Alex, 37, 66

Yamaha, 73
YouTube, 171

Zandvoort, 19, 151
ZF transmission, 103
Zonta, Ricardo, 45

Acknowledgments

No book writes itself, especially a technical one. But in a world where secrets are guarded as closely as they are in Formula 1, the writer appreciates even more the help he is given by those who are prepared to 'break the code' and divulge meaningful information.

I'd thus like to thank the following for their assistance, and their insights into the elite club that is Formula 1 engineering these days:

Allianz: Martin Bendrich for his informative media information on all manner of technical matters; *BMW Sauber*: Dr Mario Theissen, Peter Sauber, Willy Rampf, Dirk de Beer, Markus Duesmann; *Brawn GP*: Ross Brawn, Jenson Button; *Cosworth Racing*: Nick Hayes; *Scuderia Ferrari*: Luca di Montezemolo, Jean Todt, Rory Byrne, Paulo Martinelli, Enrico Lombaro; *McLaren Mercedes*: Ron Dennis, Martin Whitmarsh, Mario Illien, Paddy Lowe, Peter van Manen; *Penske Cars*: Don Berrisford; *Renault*: Flavio Briatore, Bob Bell, Rob White, Bradley Lord for his excellent media information on dyno testing and chassis manufacture, John Mardle, Ian Pearce, Colin Watts; *Toyota*: Pascal Vasselon, Luca Marmorini, Frank Dernie; *Williams*: Patrick Head, Gavin Fisher, Sam Michael, Ian Foley. Special thanks too to Mike Gascoyne, for his always welcome views on engineering, and Jonathan Williams for his hospitality, waspish humour and the chance to photograph modern F1 cars in peace at Williams's excellent museum.

And to writer Mark Hughes for his assistance with inerters; and Joe Saward, my esteemed partner in our emagazine *Grand Prix +*, for permission to lean heavily on his work in Chapters 11 and 14.

Finally, but certainly not least, my thanks to the incomparable Giorgio Piola for his artistic skill within his unique technical illustrations, which brought the text alive.

David Tremayne
Darlington 2009